Lecture Notes in Artificial Intelligence   1020

Subseries of Lecture Notes in Computer Science
Edited by J. G. Carbonell and J. Siekmann

Lecture Notes in Computer Science

Edited by G. Goos, J. Hartmanis and J. van Leeuwen

W0245795

Springer
Berlin
Heidelberg
New York
Barcelona
Budapest
Hong Kong
London
Milan
Paris
Santa Clara
Singapore
Tokyo

Ian D. Watson (Ed.)

Progress in
Case-Based Reasoning

First United Kingdom Workshop
Salford, UK, January 12, 1995
Proceedings

 Springer

Series Editors

Jaime G. Carbonell
School of Computer Science, Carnegie Mellon University
Pittsburgh, PA 15213-3891, USA

Jörg Siekmann
University of Saarland
German Research Center for Artificial Intelligence (DFKI)
Stuhlsatzenhausweg 3, D-66123 Saarbrücken, Germany

Volume Editor

Ian D. Watson
University of Salford
Bridgewater Building, Salford, M5 4WT, United Kingdom

Cataloging-in-Publication Data applied for

Die Deutsche Bibliothek - CIP-Einheitsaufnahme

Progress in case based reasoning : first United Kingdom
workshop, Salford, UK, January 12, 1995 ; proceedings / Ian D.
Watson (ed.). - Berlin ; Heidelberg ; New York ; Barcelona ;
Budapest ; Hong Kong ; London ; Milan ; Paris ; Tokyo :
Springer, 1995
  (Lecture notes in computer science ; Vol. 1020 : Lecture notes in
  artificial intelligence)
  ISBN 3-540-60654-8
NE: Watson, Ian D. [Hrsg.]; GT

CR Subject Classification (1991): I.2

ISBN 3-540-60654-8 Springer-Verlag Berlin Heidelberg New York

© Springer-Verlag Berlin Heidelberg 1995
Printed in Germany

Typesetting: Camera ready by author
SPIN 10512300   06/3142 – 5 4 3 2 1 0   Printed on acid-free paper

Preface

These proceedings are of the 1st UK Workshop on Case-Based Reasoning, organised by AI-CBR and the British Computer Society Specialist Group on Expert Systems. AI-CBR, an Internet forum for discussion and dissemination of Case-Based Reasoning (CBR) research, was founded in February 1994. In less than a year it has grown to have several hundred members from many parts of the world and has become a focus for researchers in CBR. This workshop was organised to help the UK CBR community meet each other. Some of us know each other from other conferences and professional relationships, but for many this workshop was an opportunity to meet people who had previously only been e-mail names.

A decision was taken early in the planning of the workshop that it should be of a general nature, i.e., of both theoretical and practical value and of interest to academics and practitioners. To this end the event was divided into three broad areas:

1. papers on theoretical aspects of CBR,
2. presentations by CBR software tool vendors, and
3. papers on CBR applications.

It was hoped that this mix would be of interest to everyone. In particular, the event was the first opportunity for many people to see comparative demonstrations of the following leading CBR software tools:

- Inference demonstrated *CBR Express*, their successful help-desk tool. Some researchers criticise tools like CBR Express for being too simple (i.e., just case retrieval systems). However, many of us can learn from Inference's philosophy. Their tools provide complete *business solutions*, not just technology. It is thus no surprise that this US company is currently a market leader in the provision of case-based support to customer help desks with thousands of licences sold world-wide.

- Rob Milne of Intelligent Applications showed an undoubtedly more powerful tool from the US called *ReMind*. In contrast to Inference's product ReMind is packed with CBR technology and Rob did well to show most of its functionality in just 40 minutes. ReMind is a powerful and flexible tool that has been used successfully in a variety of applications, which were also briefly illustrated.

- ISoft is a French company with a relatively new tool called *ReCall*. As usual the Europeans at the event shamed us with their excellent command of a foreign language. ReCall in contrast to the US products is *object-oriented*. ReCall represents cases in an object hierarchy rather than the flat-file representation of the US products. ReCall's objects have feature slots and slot monitors or deamons. However, although OOPS has proven itself to be a powerful representational and programming paradigm in both AI and conventional systems it is yet to be proven whether case-bases benefit from the application of OOPS.

- Finally, Acknosoft demonstrated *KATE*, a mature and powerful toolkit that has evolved out of collaborative European research. This is another product that represents data as structured objects. KATE-INDUCTION can build decision trees from training cases whilst KATE-CBR dynamically builds paths to similar cases respecting the wishes of the user. A large complex aircraft engine diagnosis application incorporating multimedia was demonstrated.

In 1991, Ian Graham, chair of the British Computer Society Expert Systems conference, wrote that "*CBR promises to become one of the major new methods for developing expert systems*". Many of us would agree with this comment. Three years later, Derek Sleemen in his keynote address to the same conference commented that CBR appeared to be the *hot topic* at the conference. Whilst it is gratifying for one's own research area to be in the spotlight such attention carries with it a danger. Few of the older amongst us need reminding of the AI winter, which many believe was partially caused by the hype surrounding expert systems in the late 1970s and early 1980s.

We have a dilemma. We have to hype CBR in order to attract research funds and to interest companies and their managers in the technology. Yet by hyping CBR we may be raising expectations that could return to haunt us. For example, Fari Marir in his paper points out that CBR does not remove the knowledge elicitation bottleneck, as claimed by some, but merely eases it.

I would like to suggest that in the UK we co-ordinate a careful strategy. We need more good business solutions, like the ones Inference offer and the tools described by Chris Price or Jeremy Ellman, to show to industry that here is a low-risk technology that can really deliver solutions. At the same time we need research that pushes the limits of CBR within the laboratory and that explores potential solutions. We must try not to make our mistakes in public. For example, we should learn from the lessons of the expert system RI/XCON. It was a ground breaking rule-based system that really worked and saved DEC money. However, as its rule-base grew to 7000 rules and more it became nearly impossible to maintain. Therefore, issues of size and complexity of case-bases should be explored in the laboratory and not in the field.

To sum up, I believe that CBR is, for better or worse, a *hot topic*. It is up to the UK research community in collaboration with our European and international colleagues to ensure that we live up to the hype. This workshop has shown that we have mature software tools and inventive and articulate researchers to use them. There is also no shortage of researchers investigating novel CBR techniques for the next generation of tools. I therefore hope that this is the first in a regular series of CBR Workshops that help all in the community produce better work.

I would like to thank all those who helped in the preparation for and organisation of the event. In particular Farhi Marir and Srinath Perera who dealt with much of the administration, the Research & Graduate College of Salford University for providing such a good venue, the British Computer Society Specialist Group on Expert Systems for supporting the event, and EPSRC whose funding (research project no. GR/J42496) helped give me the time to organise it. Finally I would like to thank Jaime Carbonell, the series editor, for his help in publishing these proceedings.

Ian Watson
University of Salford, UK
October 1995

Contents

Part One

Case-Based Reasoning Theory

An Introduction to Case-Based Reasoning

Ian Watson

University of Salford
Bridgewater Building
SALFORD, M5 4WT
i.d.watson@surveying.salford.ac.uk

1. Introduction

Expert or knowledge-based systems (KBS) are one of the success stories of Artificial Intelligence (AI) research. In a recent survey the UK Department of Trade & Industry found over 2000 KBS in commercial operation many of them in manufacturing industries [DTI, 92]. It has been around twenty years since the first documented KBS (the trinity of classic systems: DENDRAL, MYCIN and PROSPECTOR) were reported, yet in that time the basic architecture of KBS has changed little. However, despite the undoubted success of knowledge-based decision support systems in many sectors, developers of these systems have met several problems:

- knowledge elicitation is a difficult process, often being referred to as the knowledge elicitation bottleneck;
- implementing KBS is a difficult process requiring special skills and often taking many years;
- once implemented model-based KBS are often slow and are unable to access or manage large volumes of information; and
- once implemented they are difficult to maintain

A not untypical story of implementing and deploying KBS was told by Richard Perkins of British Coal's IT division [Perkins, 92]. They found that the cost of developing large complex engineering decision support system was so great that they were not having any significant impact on the business. This was despite the fact that the individual systems were judged a success. (British Coal has recently disbanded its IT division and out-sourced its IT requirements).

Over the last few years a reasoning paradigm and computational problem solving method that seems to address the problems identified above has increasingly attracted more and more attention. Case-based reasoning (CBR) solves new problems by adapting previously successful solutions to similar problems.

- CBR does not require an explicit domain model and so elicitation becomes a task of gathering case histories,
- implementation is reduced to identifying significant features that describe a case, an easier task than creating an explicit model,
- by applying database techniques largely volumes of information can be managed, and

- CBR systems can learn by acquiring new knowledge as cases making maintenance easier.

This paper therefore has two objectives: first to outline the techniques and application of CBR to a new audience, and secondly, to demonstrate that the benefits of CBR can be commercially realised. A full review of CBR is available in Watson & Marir [94] and Marir & Watson [94], Aamodt & Plaza [94], and in more depth in Kolodner [93].

2. What is Case-Based Reasoning?

> *A case-based reasoner solves new problems by adapting solutions that were used to solve old problems* [Riesbeck & Schank, 89]

At its most simple case-based reasoning is based on the observation that when we solve a problem we often base our solution on one that worked for a similar problem in the past. An example would be driving to work. When you get in your car in the morning you don't explicitly plan your route, you take the route you usually take. If you meet a traffic jam you may remember how you avoided a similar jam in the past. If however you take an new route to avoid a jam and it's a success, you will remember it and perhaps use it again in similar circumstances in the future.

CBR is thus a deceptively simple problem solving paradigm that involves matching your current problem against problems that you have solved successfully in the past. The process can be augmented by adapting solutions so they more closely match the requirements of your current problem.

3. The Origins of Case-Based Reasoning

The work of Schank and Abelson in 1977 is widely held to be the origin of CBR. They proposed that our general knowledge about situations is recorded as scripts that allow us to set up expectations and perform inferences. Scripts were proposed as a structure for conceptual memory describing information about stereotypical events such as, going to a restaurant or visiting a doctor. However, experiments on scripts showed that they were not a complete theory of memory representation - people often confused events that had similar scripts. For example, a person might mix up room scenes from a visit to a doctor's office with a visit to a dentist's office. Such observations fell in line with the theories of concept formation, problem solving and experiential learning within philosophy and psychology [Tulving, 77, Smith et al., 78].

Roger Schank continued to explored the role that the memory of previous situations (i.e., cases) and situation patterns or memory organisation packets (MOPs) play in both problem solving and learning [Schank, 82]. At a similar time and of relevance to CBR, Gentner [83] was developing a theoretical framework for analogy whilst Carbonell [83] was investigating the role of analogy in learning and plan generalisation. Perhaps with the benefit of hindsight it is also possible to find references of significance to CBR in Wittgenstein's observation that natural concepts such as tables and chairs are in fact polymorphic and can not be classified by a single set of necessary and sufficient features but instead can be defined by a set of instances (i.e., cases) with family resemblances [Wittgenstein, 53]. This work has been cited by Aamodt and Plaza [94] as a philosophical basis for CBR.

4. The CBR Cycle

The processes involved in CBR can be represented by a schematic cycle (see Figure 1). Aamodt and Plaza [94] have described CBR typically as a cyclical process comprising the four REs:

1. RETRIEVE the most similar case(s);
2. REUSE the case(s) to attempt to solve the problem;
3. REVISE the proposed solution if necessary, and
4. RETAIN the new solution as a part of a new case.

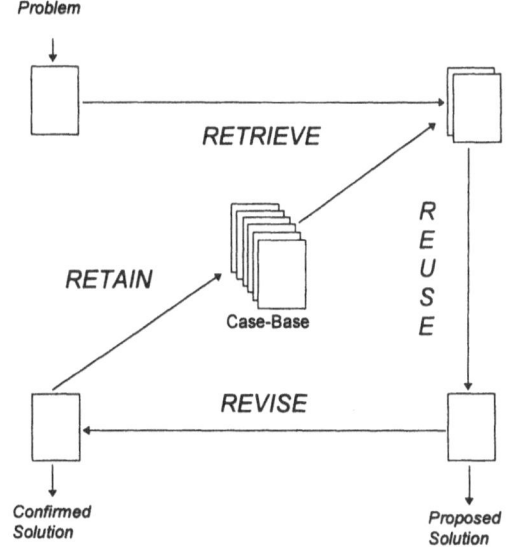

Figure 1 The CBR Cycle [adapted from Aamodt & Plaza, 1994]

A new problem is matched against cases in the case base and one or more similar cases are retrieved. A solution suggested by the matching cases is then reused and tested for success. Unless the retrieved case is a close match the solution will probably have to be revised producing a new case that can be retained.

This cycle currently rarely occurs without human intervention. For example many CBR tools act primarily as case retrieval and reuse systems. Case revision (i.e., adaptation) often being undertaken by managers of the case base. However, it should not be viewed as a weakness of CBR that it encourages human collaboration in decision support.

4.1 Case Representation

For the CBR cycle to be applied, cases must be represented in a structured manner. A case is a contextualised piece of knowledge representing an experience. It contains the past lesson that is the content of the case and the context in which the lesson can be used [Alterman, 89, David, 91; Kolodner, 93]. Typically a case comprises:

- the problem that describes the state of the world when the case occurred,
- the solution which states the derived solution to that problem, and/or
- the outcome which describes the state of the world after the case occurred.

Cases can be represented in a variety of forms using the full range of AI representational formalisms including frames, objects, predicates, semantic nets and rules - the frame/object representation currently being used by the majority of CBR software.

There is a lack of consensus within the CBR community as to exactly what information should be in a case. However, two pragmatic measures can be taken into account in deciding what should be represented in cases: the functionality and the ease of acquisition of the information represented in the case [Kolodner, 93].

4.2 Indexing

Case indexing involves assigning indices to cases to facilitate their retrieval. Several guidelines on indexing have been proposed by CBR researchers [Birnbaum & Collins, 89; Hammond, 89]. Indices should:

- be predictive,
- address the purposes the case will be used for,
- be abstract enough to allow for widening the future use of the case-base, and
- be concrete enough to be recognised in future

Both manual and automated methods have been used to select indices. Choosing indices manually involves deciding a case's purpose with respect to the aims of the reasoner and deciding under what circumstances the case will be useful.

4.3 Retrieval

Given a description of a problem, a retrieval algorithm, using the indices in the case-memory, should retrieve the most similar cases to the current problem or situation. The retrieval algorithm relies on the indices and the organisation of the memory to direct the search to potentially useful cases. Among well known methods for case retrieval are: nearest neighbour, induction, knowledge guided induction and template retrieval. These methods can be used alone or combined into hybrid retrieval strategies.

4.3.1 Nearest Neighbour

This approach involves the assessment of similarity between stored cases and the new input case, based on matching a weighted sum of features. The biggest problem here is to determine the weights of the features. The limitation of this approach include problems in converging on the correct solution and retrieval times. In general the use of this method leads to the retrieval time increasing linearly with the number of cases. Therefore this approach is more effective when the case base is relatively small.

A typical algorithm for calculating nearest neighbour matching is the one used by Cognitive Systems ReMind software reported in Kolodner [93] in which w is the importance weighting of a feature (or slot), *sim* is the similarity function, and f_i^I and f_i^R are the values for feature i in the input and retrieved cases respectively.

$$\frac{\sum_{i=1}^{n} w_i \times sim\left(f_i^I, f_i^R\right)}{\sum_{i=1}^{n} w_i}$$

Figure 2 A Nearest Neighbour Algorithm [Kolodner, 93 p.355]

4.3.2 Induction
Induction algorithms (e.g., ID3 [Quinlan, 79]) determine which features do the best job in discriminating cases, and generate a decision tree type structure to organise the cases in memory. This approach is useful when a single case feature is required as a solution, and when that case feature is dependent upon others.

4.3.3 Knowledge Guided Induction
This method applies knowledge to the induction process by manually identifying case features that are known or thought to affect the primary case feature. This approach is frequently used with other techniques because the explanatory knowledge is not always readily available for large case bases.

4.3.4 Template Retrieval
Similar to SQL-like queries, template retrieval returns all cases that fit within certain parameters. This technique is often used before other techniques, such as nearest neighbour to limit the search space to a relevant section of the case-base.

4.4 Adaptation
Once a matching case is retrieved, a CBR system should adapt the solution stored in the retrieved case to the needs of the current case. Adaptation looks for prominent differences between the retrieved case and the current case and then applies formulae or rules that take those differences into account when suggesting a solution. In general, there are two kinds of adaptation in CBR:

- *Structural adaptation*, in which adaptation rules are applied directly to the solution stored in a retrieved case. The most common technique is to *substitute* a component of the retrieved solution with an alternative value that may be provided by an auxiliary knowledge source. Thus for example the CHEF system would replace broccoli with snow peas in a Chinese recipe since they are both types of crispy green vegetables [Hammond, 86].

- *Derivational adaptation*, that reuses the algorithms, methods or rules that generated the original solution to produce a new solution to the current problem. This was first implemented in a program called ARIES [Carbonell, 86] that replayed the entire reasoning process from a previous case to solve new problems. In this method the planning sequence that constructed that original solution must be stored in memory along with the solution. This technique can only be used for cases that are well understood. However, the PRODIGY/ANALOGY program [Veloso & Carbonell, 93] has demonstrated, in a variety of complex domains, that the technique does scale up well and can be used to integrate general purpose problem solving with CBR.

5. CBR Applications

This section describes two commercially fielded CBR applications and discusses why CBR contributed to the success of the systems. Both applications are from US defence companies, a reflection that the Pentagon, through the DARPA program, was largely responsible for the research and development of CBR.

5.1 Lockheed

The first commercially fielded CBR application was by Lockheed in Palo Alto [Hennessy & Hinkle, 92]. Modern aircraft contain many elements that are made up from composite materials. These materials require curing in large autoclaves. Lockheed, the US aerospace company, produce many such parts. Each part has its own heating characteristics and must be cured correctly. If curing is not correct the part will have to be discarded. Unfortunately, the autoclave's heating characteristics are not fully understood (i.e., there is no model that operators can draw upon). This is complicated by the fact that many parts are fired together in a single large autoclave and the parts interact to alter the heating and cooling characteristics of the autoclave.

Operators of Lockheed's autoclaves relied upon drawings of previous successful parts layouts to inform how to layout the autoclave. However, this was complicated by the fact that layouts were never identical because parts were required at different times and because the design of the parts was constantly changing. Consequently operators had to select a successful layout that they thought closely matched and adapted it to the current situation.

This closely resembled the CBR paradigm and when Lockheed decided to implement a KBS to assist the autoclave operators they decided upon CBR. Their objectives were as follows:

- to reuse previously successful loadings,
- to reduce the pressure of work on one or two experts,
- to secure the expertise of the experts as a corporate asset, and
- help to train new personnel.

The development of CLAVIER started in 1987, and it has been in regular use since the Autumn of 1990. CLAVIER searches a library of previously successful autoclave layouts. Each layout is described in terms of:

- parts and their relative positions on a table
- tables, and their relative positions in the autoclave, and
- production statistics such as start and finish times, pressure and temperature.

CLAVIER finds substitutes for parts in a layout that do not match, and it recommends new layouts to operators. In adapting new layouts from previous ones CLAVIER:

- creates new layouts by adapting pieces of previous layouts
- minimises the number of required parts not included in the layout,
- maximises the number of high-priority parts included in the layout, and
- maximises the total number of parts in a layout.

CLAVIER acts as a collective memory for Lockheed and as such provides a uniquely useful way of transferring expertise between autoclave operatives. In particular the use of CBR made the initial knowledge acquisition for the system easier. Indeed, it is doubtful if it would have been possible to develop a model-based system since operatives could not say why a particular autoclave layout was successful. CLAVIER also demonstrates the ability of CBR systems to learn. The system has grown from 20 to over 150 successful layouts and its performance has improved such that it now retrieves or adapts a successful autoclave layout 90% of the time.

5.2 General Dynamics

In their Electric Boat Division the US company General Dynamics builds warships. They had a problem of how to select appropriate mechanical equipment (e.g., valves, heat exchangers, etc.) during ship design. Most of the problems were standard (i.e., they repeated regularly from ship to ship). However, non-conforming problems took a considerable amount of time to resolve. The company was particularly frustrated because the non-conforming problems repeated occasionally. They realised that they were wasting time and scarce expertise repeating decisions that had already been made because they had no facility to manage their knowledge.

General Dynamics' problem seemed like a classic knowledge-based system problem:

- expertise was scarce,
- solutions to problems were known, and
- methods for solving problems were known.

On advice, they implemented a rule-based system for the selection and adjustment of valves for on-board pipeline systems. The system was deployed in the late 1980's. The rule-based system worked but was brittle. That is, it could solve the standard problems well, but was not reliable at solving the non-conformers. Every time a non-conforming problem was encountered, an expert would solve the problem, and knowledge engineers would subsequently have to elicit new rules from the experts (taking up their valuable time) and add them to the KBS, possibly having to modify existing rules and then validate the system and release an update.

The company found that this continual maintenance was insupportable, and in 1991 a CBR version of the same system was developed. General Dynamics noted several findings:

1. The CBR system was developed in less than half the time of the rule-based system; however, this could partially be explained by the knowledge elicitation that had already taken place to develop the rule-based system.
2. The CBR system was less brittle since new problems frequently were solved by adapting old solutions. These new solutions, once validated, could be added as new cases and thus the system's performance was constantly improving.
3. Consequently maintaining the CBR system was not a problem.

In its first year of deployment the CBR system handled 20,000 non-conformities and made an estimated saving of $240,000 more than recouping the development costs. The system is now being extended to cover a wider range of mechanical devices.

6. The Case for Case-Based Reasoning

This section discusses the problems associated with developing knowledge-based decision support systems. It posits that CBR appears to offer solutions to many of these problems and presents evidence from the literature to support these claims.

During the last thirty years many KBS have been developed that have an explicit model of the problem domain in which they operate. In many such systems the model is implemented by rules, and perhaps more recently by objects. In second generation systems [Clancey, 85] a deep underlying causal model exists that enables the system to reason from first principles in its application domain. There is little doubt that such MBR systems (whether they be deep or shallow) can be very successful. However, there are five major problems with this approach:

1. knowledge elicitation is difficult,
2. knowledge-based decision support systems can be very complex and can take many man years to develop,
3. such systems are frequently slow or require expensive specialised hardware,
4. such systems are often poor at managing large volumes of information, and
5. once developed they are difficult to maintain.

The first problem was recognised as soon as KBS were built and was often attributed to the knowledge elicitation bottleneck [Hayes-Roth et al., 83]. The second problem is familiar to any KBS developer and has partially been responsible for the increasing interest in the last few years in KBS development methodologies and of knowledge modelling languages and ontologies. The third problem has partially been overcome by the ever decreasing cost of processing power, whilst solutions to the fourth have been sought through the integration of AI techniques with database technology. However, for many years practitioners believed that KBS were easy to maintain - almost all books on KBS development written during the eighties will contain a quote similar to "maintaining a rule-base is easy, being simply a matter of adding or subtracting rules from the knowledge-base" Easier than maintaining procedural C or FORTRAN code true, but not easy. Unfortunately, the experience of XCON/R1 [Bachant & McDermot, 84] and others [Coenen, & Bench-Capon, 92; Vargas & Raj, 93] has shown that maintaining KBS is not as simple as adding or subtracted rules or objects. As a knowledge-base grows it becomes a complex debugging task.

However, there is a more fundamental problem that has been overlooked. KBS practitioners did not consider how to build a KBS when there was no model available. Overlooking this problem reflects the heritage of KBS in academic research laboratories. The early KBS (e.g., DENDRAL, MYCIN, PROSPECTOR) all operated in domains in which there were good underlying models (either from first principles or statistical) - scientists are comfortable with working with models; they build them for a living. Unfortunately, in a commercial environment and outside of Universities many people make decisions without reference to first principles and underlying causal or statistical models.

These people solve problems by using their experience. It is no surprise that expert and experience derive from the same root. We posit that the KBS community was seduced by rules and neglected the truism that experts solve problems by applying their experience, whilst only novices attempt to solve problems by applying rules they have recently acquired. The application of experience to problem solving is the hallmark of CBR. Thus, CBR is proposed by some as a psychological theory of human cognition [Slade, 91] and one that provides a cognitive model of how people solve problems [Kolodner, 93]. It offers a paradigm that is claimed to be close to the way people solve problems and one that overcomes the brittleness of MBR systems [Barletta, 91; Helton, 91]

Hence, there is a strong case for CBR since it has several potential advantages over model-based reasoning:

- CBR systems can be built without passing through the knowledge elicitation bottleneck since elicitation becomes a simpler task of acquiring past cases. This was demonstrated by the CLAVIER system and by General Dynamics.
- CBR systems can be built where a model does not exist; this is also well demonstrated by the CLAVIER system.
- Implementation becomes a simpler task of identifying relevant case features, and moreover a system can be rolled out with only a partial case-base as happened with CLAVIER. Indeed, in CBR a system is never complete since it will be continually growing. This removes one of the bug-bears of KBS - how to tell when a knowledge-base is complete.
- CBR systems can propose a solution quickly by avoiding the need to infer an answer from first principles each time - this is important when a decision is required quickly.
- Individual or generalised cases can be used to provide explanation that are perhaps more satisfactory than explanations generated by chains of rules, important in many domains with legal implications.

- CBR systems can learn by acquiring new cases making maintenance easier as demonstrated by CLAVIER and General Dynamics.
- Finally, by acquiring new episodic cases CBR systems can grow to reflect their organisation's experience. If a rule-based KBS was delivered to six companies and used for six months, after that time each system would be identical, assuming no maintenance had taken place. If six identical CBR systems were used in a similar way after six months there could be six different systems as each could have acquired different episodic cases.

The claim that CBR systems can be implemented faster than model-based systems was supported by a study conducted by Cognitive Systems which stated that it took two weeks to develop a case-based version of a system that took four months to build in rule-based form [Goodman 89]. Also, and more recently, developers at Digital Equipment Corporation confirmed that a rule-based system called CANASTA took more than eight times longer to develop than CASCADE a case-based system with the same functionality [Simoudis, 92; Simoudis et al., 93]. They also claim that the maintenance of CANASTA is continual whereas CASCADE needs almost no maintenance. Related claims are provided by Hennessy and Hinkle [92] concerning CLAVIER and Vargas & Raj [93]. However, claims such as these should be treated with caution lest CBR is hyped in the same way the knowledge-based systems were a decade or more ago. We should also not overlook the fact that for well understood domains model-based systems can be very effective and are a relatively mature and well understood technology.

7. Conclusion

Although CBR as a decision support technology is only about ten years old, it has already delivered commercially successful engineering decision support systems. As a comparison neural computing was first proposed in the 1950's and has only recently delivered commercial applications. CBR seems to offer solutions to many of the problems that have beset knowledge engineering since the discipline was founded. Namely, the difficulty of eliciting reliable knowledge, encoding that knowledge and subsequently maintaining systems as knowledge changes. At recent meetings the author has attended many companies using CBR have made the following observations:

- They view CBR as a low risk technology, as opposed to more traditional AI techniques such as rule-based systems, neural computing or exotica such as fuzzy logics and genetic algorithms - in effect it is easy to sell CBR to senior management.
- They report that their experts are more comfortable recounting cases rather than attempting to distil rules that explain occurrences or behaviour.
- In many instances experts and even end users author cases themselves thus giving them a sense of ownership of the system and assisting the system's acceptance. That is the system is not viewed as being developed by boffins who speak predicate calculus and do not really know what the users' problems are.

- They welcome the ability that CBR systems have of acting as knowledge repositories that can easily grow and can be used as an archive of best or even worst practise, thus preventing people from reinventing wheels or repeating mistakes.

Thus, in conclusion if you are considering implementing an engineering decision support system you would be well advised to at least consider CBR. Mature reliable software tools are available, and the paradigm addresses many of the problems often associated with knowledge-based systems.

8. References

Aamodt, A. & Plaza, E. (1994). Case Based Reasoning: Foundational Issues, Methodological Variations, and System Approaches. AI Communications, 7(i): pp 39 59.

Alterman, R. (1989). Panel discussion on case representation.In, Proceedings of the Second Workshop on Case Based Reasoning, Pensacola Beach. FL, US.

Bachant, J., & McDermott, J., (1984). R1 Revisited: Four years in the Trenches. The AI Magazine, 5(iii).

Barletta, R., (1991). An introduction to case-based reasoning. AI Expert, August 1991, pp.42-49.

Birnbaum, L. & Collings, G. (1989). Remindings and Engineering Design Themes: A Case Study in Indexing Vocabulary. In, Proceedings of the Second Workshop on Base Based Reasoning, Pensacola Beach, FL.

Carbonell, J.G. (1983). Learning by analogy: Formulating and generalising plans from past experience. Machine Learning Vol. 1.

Carbonell, J.G. (1986). Derivational analogy: A theory of reconstructive problem solving and expertise acquisition. Machine Learning Vol. 2.

Clancey, W.J., (1985). Heurestic Classification. Artificial Intelligence, 27: pp289-350.

Coenen, F. & Bench Capon, T.J.M. (1992). Maintenance and Maintainability in Regulation Based Systems. ICL Technical Journal, May 1992, pp.76 84.

David B.S. (1991). Principles for case representation in a case-based aiding system for lesson planning. In, Proceedings of the Workshop on Case Based Reasoning, Madison Hotel, Washington, 8-10 May, 1991.

DTI (1992). Knowledge Based Systems Survey of UK Applications. Department of Trade & Industry, UK.

Gentner, D. (1983). Structure mapping - a theoretical framework for analogy. Cognitive Science, 7: pp.155-70.

Goodman, M. (1989). CBR in battle planning. In Proceedings of the Second Workshop on Case Based Reasoning, Pensacola Beach, FL, US.

Hammond, K.J. (1989). On Functionally Motivated Vocabularies: An Apologia. In, Proceedings of the Second Workshop on Case Based Reasoning, Pensacola Beach, FL, US.

Harmon, P. (1992). Case-based reasoning III. Intelligent Software Strategies, 8(i).

Hayes-Roth, F., Waterman, D. & Lenat D., eds. (1983). Building expert systems. Addison Wesley, Reading, MA, US.

Helton, T., (1991). The Hottest New AI Technology- Case-Based Reasoning. The Spang Robinson Report on Artificial Intelligence, Vol. 7, No. 8.

Hennessy, D. & Hinkle D., (1992). Applying Case Based Reasoning to Autoclave Loading. IEEE Expert, 7(v): pp.21 6.

Kolodner, J. L. (1993). Case Based Reasoning. Morgan Kaufmann.

Marir, F., & Watson, I.D. (1994). Case-Based Reasoning: A Categorised Bibliography. The Knowledge Engineering Review, Vol. 9 No. 4.

Perkins, R. (1992). Diagnostic System Designer. Manufacturing Intelligence, No. 10 pp.16-19.

Quinlan, J.R. (1979). Induction over large databases. Rep. No. HPP-79-14, Heuristic Programming Project, Computer Science Dept., Stanford University, US.

Reisbeck, C.K, & Schank, R.C. (1989). Inside Case Based Reasoning. Lawrence Erlbaum Associates, Hillsdale, NJ, US.

Schank, R.C. & Abelson, R.P. (1977). Scripts, Plans, Goals and Understanding. Erlbaum, Hillsdale, New Jersey, US.

Simoudis, E. (1992). Using Case-Based Retrieval for Customer Technical Support. IEEE Expert, 7(v): pp.7 13.

Simoudis, E., Mendall, A. & Miller, P. (1993). Automated support for developing retrieve-and-propose systems. In Proceedings of Artificial Intelligence XI Conference, Orlando, Florida.

Slade. S. (1991): Case-based reasoning: A research paradigm. AI Magazine 42-55.

Smith, E.E. Adams, N. & Schorr, D. (1978). Fact retrieval and the paradox of interference. Cognitive Psychology, 10: pp.438-64.

Tulving, E. (1977). Episodic and semantic memory. In, Organisation of Memory (Tulving, E. & Donaldson, W. Eds.), pp.381-403. Academic Press.

Vargas, J.E., & Raj, S. (1993). Developing maintainable expert systems using case-based reasoning. Expert Systems, 10(iv): pp.219-25.

Veloso, M.M. & Carbonell, J.G. (1993) Derivational analogy in PRODIGY. Automating case acquisition, storage and utilization. Machine Learning, Vol. 10(iii): pp.249-78.

Watson, I. & Marir, F. (1994) Case-Based Reasoning: A Review. The Knowledge Enginering Review. Vol 9. No.4: 355-81.

Wittgentstein, L. (1953). Philosophical Investigations. Blackwell, UK.

9. Further Information

The following section contains sources that may be of use to people seeking further information about CBR.

9.1 CBR Software Tools
The following papers and reports provide comparative reviews of CBR software tools:

Harmon, P. (1992). Case based reasoning. *Intelligent Software Strategies*, 8(1).

Watson, I. & Marir, F. (1994) Case-Based Reasoning: A Review. The Knowledge Enginering Review. Vol 9. No.4 (in press).

Althoff, K-D, Auriol, E., Barletta, R. & Manago, M. (1995). *A Review of Industrial Case-Based Reasoning Tools*. AI Intelligence, Oxford, UK. ISBN 1 898804 01 X

9.2 CBR Tool Vendors

At the time of going to press (Summer 1995) the following software tools with a CBR component are commercially available and supported.

AknoSoft, **KATE**
58a, Rue du Dessous des Berger 75013
Paris, France
Tel: (33-1) 44 24 88 00
Fax:(33-1) 44 24 88 66

Cognitive System Inc., **ReMind**
220-230 Commercial Street, Boston, MA
02 109, USA.
Tel: (617) 742-7227
Fax: (617) 742-1139.

Esteem Software Inc,. **ESTEEM**
302E. Main street Cambridge City, IN
47327, USA
Tel: (317) 478-3955
Fax:(317) 478-35550

Inductive Solution Inc., **CasePower**
380 Rector Place, Suit 4A,
New York, NY 10280, USA
Tel: (212) 945-0630
Fax:(212) 945-0367

Inference Corporation,
ART*Enterprise,CBR 2.
101 Rowland Way, Suite 310, Novato,
California, CA 94104, USA
http://www.inference.com/

Isoft, **ReCall**
Chemin de Moulon
F-91190 Gif sur Yvette France
Tel: (33-1) 69 41 27 77
Fax: (33-1) 69 41 25 32

The Haley Enterprise Inc, **Eclipse**
413 Orchard Street
Sewickley, PA USA 15143
Tel: (412) 741-6420
Fax: (412) 741-6457

tecInno GmbH, **S₃-CASE**
Sauerwiesen 267661
KAISERSLAUTERN Germany
Tel: +49 6301-60-60
Fax: +49 6301-60-666

Astea International, CASE-1
55 Middlesex Turnpike
Dedford, MA 01730, USA
Tel: (617) 275-5440
Fax: (617) 275-1910

9.3 Internet CBR Sources

The following section presents sources that provide information via the Internet on CBR.

AI-CBR an Internet email forum for the discussion of all aspects of CBR research and practice. Membership is free and members include academics, industrialists, and most of the CBR software vendors. In addition to an electronic conference AI-CBR contains papers and articles on CBR that may be downloaded along with a bibliography of CBR research. Information on how to join can be obtained from i.d.watson@surveying.salford.ac.uk

The European CBR Newsletter is an electronic newsletter on case-based reasoning and is delivered to the members of the German AK-CBR and to the participants of the EWCBR-workshops Thus, the CBR Newsletter addresses mainly a continental European readership. Its objective is to support an exchange of information, news, and opinions on CBR that relate to both scientific and application-oriented issues. People who want to receive the CBR Newsletter should contact:: Dietmar Janetzko at: dietmar@cognition.iig.uni-freiburg.

CBR-MED is an Internet forum for the discussion of case-based reasoning applied to medicine. This site also contains information on people, publications and demonstrations of CBR applied to medicine. URL:
> *http://cs-www.uchicago.edu:80/discussions/cbr-med/*

The CBR Site maintains links to CBR sites of interest and to AI-CBR at:
> *http://www.salford.ac.uk/docs/depts/survey/staff/IWatson/cbr01.htm*

CBR in the Web maintains a comprehensive listing of CBR people, research and papers and pointers to other Web sites at:
> *http://bern.informatik.uni-kl.de/~wess/cbrWeb.html*

CBR Home Page also provides information and links to CBR WWW sites at:
> *http://mnemosyne.itc.it:1024/avesani/html/cbr.html*

The Case Based Reasoning Server is maintained by Edwina Rissland's research group at the University of Massachuesetts and provides information on their projects and links to other sites. at:
> *http://cbr-www.cs.umass.edu/*

Inference Corporation maintain a Web site that provides details on their product range and an interactive demonstration of CasePoint operating over the Internet at:
> *http://www.inference.com/*

The source code for CASPIAN a CBR tool in the public domain can be obtained by ftp from: *ftp.dcs.aber.ac.uk/pub/casp*

The source code for PROTOS a CBR tool in the public domain can be obtained by ftp from: *ftp.cs.utexas.edu/pub/porter*

10. Acknowledgements

This work was partially funded by EPSRC project number GR/J42496.

Evolutionary Case Based Design

John Hunt
Centre for Intelligent Systems,
Department of Computer Science,
University of Wales, Aberystwyth,
Penglias Campus, Aberystwyth,
Dyfed, SY23 3DB.
United Kingdom,
Email: jjh@uk.ac.aber
Tel: [+44] (0)1970 622537
Fax: [+44] (0)1970 622455

22 June, 1995

Abstract
This paper extends the basic framework of case based reasoning (CBR) to include
an evolutionary approach to adaptation. Such an extension allows the CBR system
to consider a number of alternatives in parallel rather than forcing it to make a
choice about the most appropriate case to process or the best way to modify that
case. This results in a system which integrates the efficiency benefits of a CBR
system with the flexibility of an evolutionary system, to provide an evolutionary
CBR system. The paper illustrates how such a system can be used to solve design
problems in a simple civil engineering application.

1. Introduction

Case based reasoning (CBR) [Kolodner, 1993] has been successfully applied in a wide
variety of domains for a range of applications. In this paper we concentrate on the use
of case based reasoning for design. Many Case Based Design (CBD) systems have
employed some form of reasoning system which can act in conjunction with the main
CBR system to perform some subtask of the design process. These "hybrid" CBR
systems often employ systems such as a constraint satisfaction system [Maher and
Zhang, 1993] or a simulation system [Navinchandra, Sycara and Narasimhan, 1991] to
actually perform legal adaptation of the design case which has been retrieved. These
"associated" systems have been termed "Co-reasoners" [Hunt and Miles, 1994].

This paper describes a CBD system which employs an evolutionary component
to aid in the adaptation process. However, this evolutionary component is integrated
into the CBD system rather than being a separate "co-reasoner". The justification for
this is that a CBD system is inherently evolutionary. For example, over time new
cases are generated through adaptation and are saved into the system's case database;
the abilities of the system therefore evolve. In this paper, the evolutionary analogy is
carried further, by introducing an evolutionary structure to the adaptation phase. This
structure allows domain knowledge to be applied as part of a set of "genetic"

operators, which are used to generate a set of "competing" solutions. These competing solutions are then evaluated and the best are either selected as solutions to the current problem or evolved until a suitable solution(s) is found.

The remainder of this paper is structured in the following manner: Section two discusses the CBR process. In section three we consider how the Genetic Algorithm (GA) uses genetic operators and natural selection to evolve "optimal" solutions. In section four we consider how an evolutionary adaptation algorithm can be incorporated in a CBD system, while in section five we present an example application which exploits this approach. In section six we consider the behaviour of the evolutionary CBR system.

2. Case based reasoning for design

2.1 Case based reasoning

CBR has been applied to a variety of applications from device diagnosis, and design through interpretation and classification to legal argumentation [Goel, 1992; Hammond, 1986; Hua and Faltings 1993; Rissland and Skalak, 1991]. Figure 1 illustrates the basic structure of many CBR systems. The most important element in a case based system is the case database itself. This is a repository of past problem solutions and is the basis for the whole reasoning process. As such, the way in which a case is represented is critically important. For example, a good case representation will allow the important features of the problem to be identified and reasoned about. It will also promote the effective and efficient search of the case database.

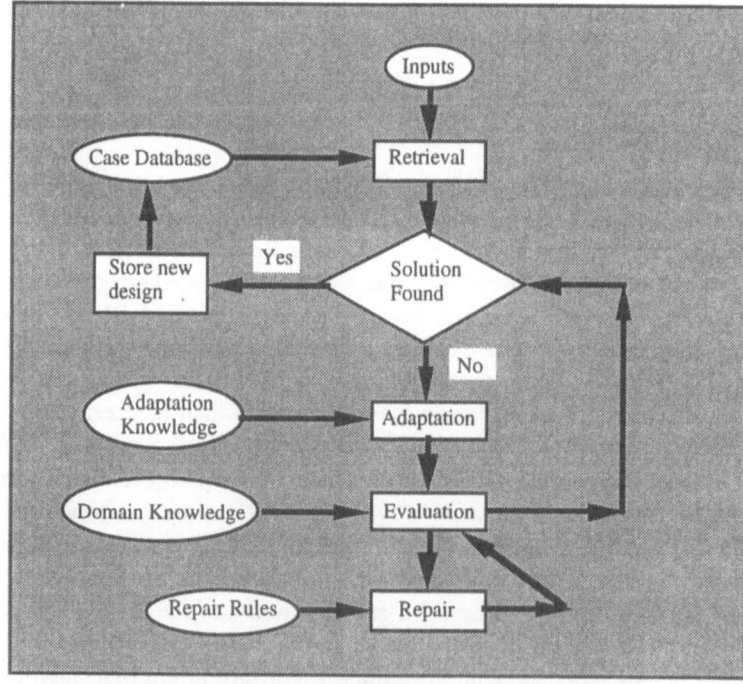

Figure 1 An example CBR system architecture

Once a case database has been obtained, the first step performed by a CBR systems is to analyse the inputs to the system in order to determine the important features to use in selecting past cases from the case database. These features are then passed to the retrieval step along with the initial inputs. The retrieval step then uses the information provided to it to obtain a list of past cases which match the current situation. This matching process can be performed in a number of ways including using indices to direct the search, decision trees generated using induction algorithms, nearest neighbour formulas etc. From this list the best case can be selected.

Once the best match has been retrieved, it is often the case that it must be altered to match the current situation. (this is called adaptation). A variety of methods have been used to perform adaptation, these can include heuristic rules, interaction with the user, first principles analysis and formulas. The actual method chosen depends on the application and the domain.

Once the case has been adapted, it must be evaluated to determine whether it does provide a solution to the current problem. Again a variety of techniques can be used to perform this evaluation. For example, interaction with the user may be employed, or a proposed solution can be simulated or a set of constraints may be tested. Again, the actual method chosen depends on the task and the domain. If the case is accepted by the evaluation step, then it is presented as the solution to the problem and stored in the case database for future use.

If some aspect of the current problem is not solved by the case, then the case must be repaired such that all aspects of the problem are addressed. This is done by first identifying why the case failed to solve the problem (e.g. some constraint on the problem was not met) and then using this information to guide the repair process. The repair process is most often guided by a set of heuristic repair rules. These rules can capture general knowledge about how to "repair" cases in the current domain.

In some situations it may be possible to abandon the current case and to select a new case from the case database. The explanations for why the previous case was inappropriate can then be crucial in helping to select a new (more suitable) case from the case database.

2.2 Case-based design

The use of case-based reasoning techniques for design has been growing during the last few years [Goel and Chandrasekaran, 1992; Hunt and Lee, 1992; Maher and Zhang, 1993]. One of the features of case-based design (CBD) is that both modified designs and completely new designs can be incorporated in the case database in exactly the same way. This leads to the development of corporate databases of good designs.

[Hua and Faltings, 1993] provide a number of justifications why CBD is desirable, including:

1. A CBD system does not require a complete domain model, but can produce complete and complex designs even with a small knowledge base. However, as Hua and Faltings point out, a great deal of information is still required.

2. Designs start from complete cases, implicitly achieving trade-offs among several functions and avoiding the problem of multi-criteria optimisation.

3. Using the complete design reduces the complexity and thus can make the problem solving process more efficient.

4. Using cases as the source of knowledge allows learning by storing new cases.

In many CBD systems, adaptation is either performed by heuristic knowledge [Roderman and Tsatsoulis, 1993] or by a separate "co-reasoner" [Hua and Faltings, 1993; Navinchandra, Sycara and Narasimhan, 1991]. This is because, the process of adaptation in design can be additionally complex. For example, if a design is modified in some way, care must be taken to ensure that any physical, legal or other constraints have not been violated.

3. The Genetic Algorithm (GA)

There are a number of techniques which have been developed under the title of evolutionary algorithms, however the most suitable for the type of application required in a CBR system is the Genetic Algorithm. Genetic Algorithms (GAs) were invented by John Holland in the early 1970's [Holland, 1976] and were inspired by the findings of evolutionary biologists. GAs effectively carry out a simulated form of evolution on populations of genes. In "classical" GAs, genes are formed of strings of bits (while in "hybrid" GAs the strings can be formed of any suitable representation).

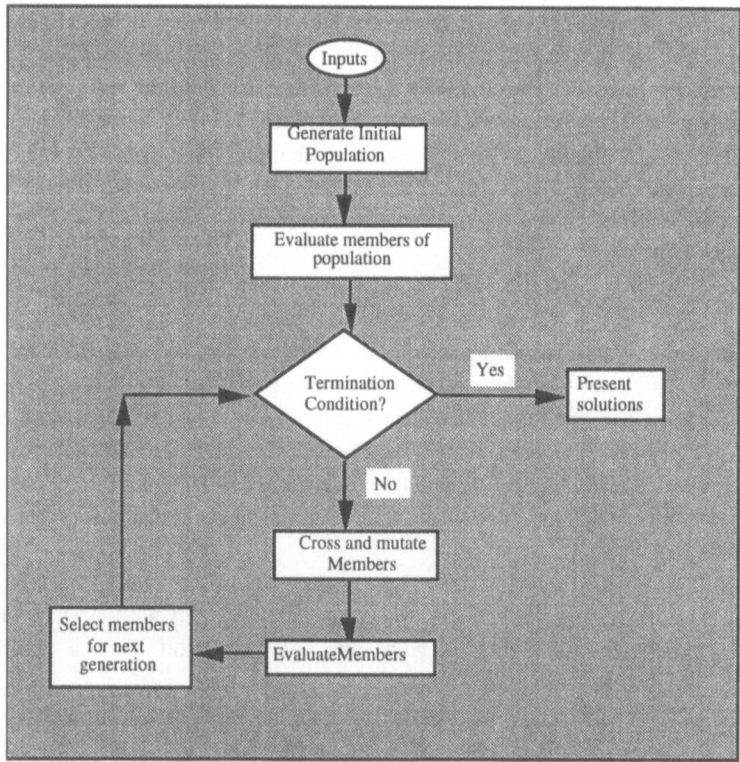

Figure 2 The Genetic Algorithm

The GA manipulates these strings by means of simple mutation and crossover operators. This is done without reference to the type of problem being solved and without knowledge of the application domain. The only way in which the GA can ascertain what forms a good solution is through a fitness function. This function evaluates how good a particular gene is as a solution to the problem (hence it is in the fitness function that any domain knowledge may be found). See [Davis, 1991; Goldberg, 1989] and [Holland, 1976] for further discussions on GAs and the issues associated with GAs.

The basis of all GAs is the algorithm illustrated in figure 2. Essentially a population of genes is generated, each of which represents a potential solution to the problem in hand. In many GA systems the initial population is randomly generated (although there is no reason why it should be).

Each member of the population is then evaluated using a fitness function, which provides a measure of how well it solves the problem. Then, until a predetermined number of generations have been produced, the population is mated (also known as crossover), and mutated. The first of these steps (crossover) results in two genes being selected as parents and then crossed to produce two offspring. This results in some of the features of one parent being combined with those of another. For example:

a f c b g d	parent 1
D E C A F B	parent 2
a f c A F B	offspring 1
D E C b g d	offspring 2

In the above case, the two parents have been split exactly in half, with each child receiving half the parent. Genes with higher fitness values are more frequently selected for crossover (thus enhancing their chances of passing on their traits to the next generation). This is an example of the survival of the fittest.

The other evolutionary operator is mutation. Mutation is used to alter one or more elements in the gene. For example, given the gene: a b d f a g, mutation might select the element at position 4 and change it to a Z thus resulting in a new gene: a b d Z a g

The new gene generated by either crossover or mutation can then be introduced to the population and evaluated. This can be done immediately (incremental GAs) or on mass when a certain number of new genes have been generated (generational GAs). Whichever approach is used, it is normally the case that an equivalent number of genes are deleted from the population.

Crossover acts as an accelerator of the search process performed by the GA. That is, crossover allows a GA to quickly combine beneficial new traits in the population. This means that crossover makes it possible to merge good solutions to generate potentially better ones. Mutation on the other hand helps to ensure diversity in the population. In terms of the search space, it helps the GA to jump to other parts of the space. Biologically speaking, it introduces features which may prove to be useful, but which were not previously present.

4. Evolving design cases

Evolutionary computing methods offer a framework for applying complex adaptation rules, and analysing various trade offs, which need to be considered if innovative applications of designs or innovative modifications of designs are to be constructed. One of the main application areas at which evolutionary computing is aimed is the design of products. [Rechenberg, 1989] has used evolutionary strategies for the design of wings in a wind tunnel, pipe couplings and load bearing frameworks, while [Goldberg, 1989] has used genetic algorithms for the design of gas pipelines and control systems. By combining GAs and CBR we aim to exploit features of both approaches to design.

4.1 Using evolution within CBD

If we first consider what requirements an evolutionary algorithm has, if it is to be used in a design system, the following list can be identified:
1. a representation of the set of possible designs,
2. a way of evaluating each possible design,
3. methods for combining different designs,
4. processes which allow existing designs to be altered to make new designs.
   CBD provides a framework for providing solutions to these issues.

Although evolutionary computing has been applied mainly to the generation of complete designs from scratch, we believe that it can also be used to adapt existing designs to meet changed user constraints. The design cases retrieved from the case database can act as seed designs for the evolutionary adaption stage. Once generated the completing designs could be presented to the user for further analysis, selection etc. Equally, such designs could be fed back into the evaluation stage and processed as normal by the CBD system.

If we consider the four points listed above, then the design cases provide a representation for the individual cases and the case database provides a set of possible designs to draw upon. In turn the evaluation phase of a CBR system provides a way of evaluating competing designs. In situations where designs can be decomposed, the recomposition elements of a design oriented CBR system can be used to combine different designs in different ways as part of a design recombination process or as part of a design crossover process. Finally, the adaptation steps of a CBR system inherently provide a way to alter a design to make a new deisgn.

4.2 Integrating CBR and evolution

Figure 3 illustrates how an evolutionary adaptation approach can be introduced into the framework of a CBR system. The flowchart illustrates that a set of past cases will be retrieved from the case database. These past cases will be treated as the basis of the evolutionary adaptation phase. Note that more than one case will be used. This is because in many situations it can be difficult to select the single most appropriate case. That is, if a nearest neighbour selection method is used, it may be that the top 3 or 4 cases are all close matches and that in "traditional" CBR one of these would be selected (normally the top case).

In our implementation of this system we have used a nearest neighbour matching strategy for case retrieval. The value of the match can then be used as the "fitness" of the case for the current problem. This allows an existing CBR technique to be used to *evaluate* the cases which are being generated via adaptation.

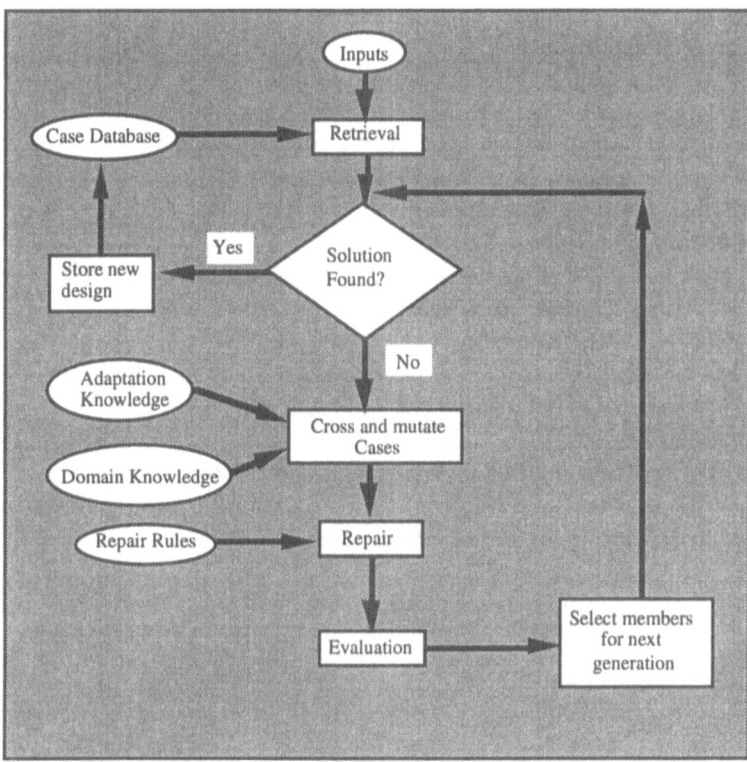

Figure 3 Evolutionary CBR Framework

The evolutionary adaptation phases then goes into a loop in which the cases are evolved and, if necessary, are repaired, before being *evaluated*. In the beam example in section 5, this evaluation is performed using a set of equations which calculate the bending stress, shear stress and deflection of the beam. These numbers are combined together to generate an overall fitness measuremeant for the beam.

The first evolutionary operator which may be applied is crossover. This represents the situation in which part of the description for one case is joined to part of the description for another case. However, depending on the application such an operator may or may not be appropriate. It is therefore necessary to consider the domain, what each case represents and whether the cases represent different version of a single solution or completely different solutions. In the latter case it is unlikely that crossover will be of much use. However, in those domains where it may be applied, it may be extremely useful. This is because, in GAs, it is crossover which is the main search operator. That is, it is the crossover operator which is mainly responsible for the improvement in the population as a whole.

The mutation evolutionary operator modifies selected cases in a similar manner to an adaptation module in a "conventional" CBR system. That is, it uses domain knowledge to determine how the case can be modified, such that it may provide a better solution to the problem. One way in which it does differ is that it is not necessary to make a decision about the single most effective way to modify a case.

Instead multiple new cases can be constructed by modifying the original case in a number of different ways.

The main loop of figure 3 is repeated until either a prespecified number of iterations have been completed, or one of the cases being evolved achieves a match value above a certain (user specified) threshold. This indicates that an acceptable case has been generated and that no more analysis need be performed. Once the main loop terminates, the newly generated case can be presented to the user and if appropriate saved into the case database for future use.

Note that in the evolutionary CBR framework, the basic CBR steps are still present, i.e. the first step performed is the retrieval of a set of appropriate cases and that once the cases have been *evolved*, a repair step is present to ensure that no "illegal" modifications, generalisations or specialisations have been introduced. Once a suitable solution has been generated, the newly created case is then saved back into the case database for future use. This is important as the basic genetic algorithm has no concept of selecting an initial population from previous solutions, nor does it consider issues such as repairing members of the population and it certainly does not include the concept of saving solutions for future use.

5. A civil engineering example

We have implemented the system described in section 4 in POP11 [Barrett, Ramsey and Sloman, 1985] using the Flavours object oriented language extension within the POPLOG environment. This system has been applied to the optimisation of materials in structural elements, either as an element of a larger structure or as a single structure. In this paper a single rectangular, simply supported timber beam, carrying a distributed load will be analysed.

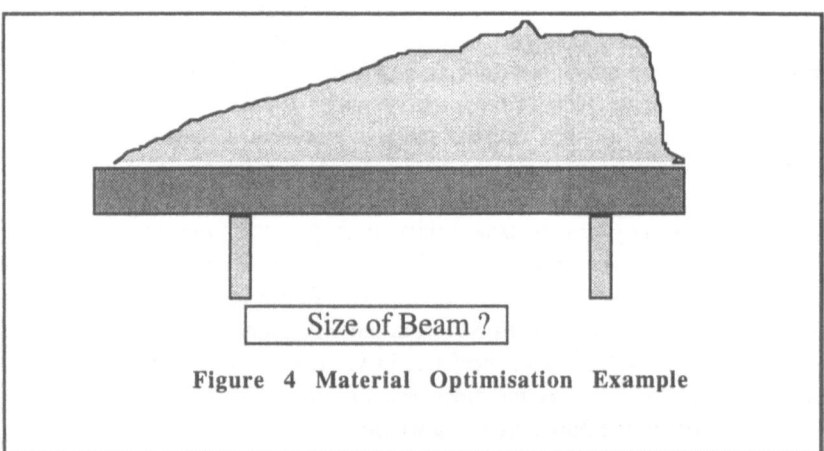

Figure 4 Material Optimisation Example

Given the design situation illustrated in figure 4, the aim of the CBR system is to optimise the amount of material used in the beam, while still ensuring that the beam is robust, reliable and accurate.

5.1 Case representation

The cases in this system represent the span (length), the depth and the width of various beams of a variety of materials and the situations in which they were used (see figure 5). The actual representation used is a decimal one, in which the numeric values are represented in real numbers (e.g. 23.45) and the materials are also binary coded (e.g. 001 = Wood). This facilitates simple crossover and mutation operators.

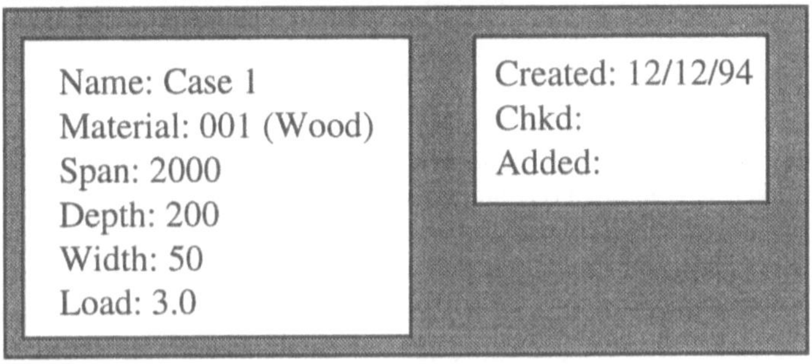

```
Name: Case 1                    Created: 12/12/94
Material: 001 (Wood)            Chkd:
Span: 2000                      Added:
Depth: 200
Width: 50
Load: 3.0
```

Figure 5 An example case

5.2 User input

The user of this system provides a basic set of parameters, which describe the current problem. The information requested by the system is:

SPAN	Horizontal distance between centres of supports (in metres).
LOAD	Expected maximum load (in KN/m).
PBC	Permissible bending stress (in N/mm2).
PQ	Permissible shear stress (in N/mm2).
Pδ	Permissible deflection (either 3mm or SPAN/360).

5.3 Case retrieval

Once the user has provided the appropriate inputs, the system then calculates the size of the structural member, taking into account not only the strength of the material, but also the structural stiffness and amount of material. It does this by first selecting up to 4 cases from the case database using a nearest neighbour matching strategy. These cases are then checked to see if any of them is sufficiently close to the specified problem, that it provides an acceptable solution. If none provide such a solution, the evolutionary adaptation steps begin.

5.4 Evolutionary adaptation

First the four cases are crossed to generate 4 new cases. The cases to cross are chosen at random. This results in two cases acting as *parents* for a new case. The new case is created by taking each of the three real numbers representing the span, depth and width in both *parents* and dividing them by half. Each number is added to its corresponding number in the other case. This provides a single new case which has been constructed by adding elements of the two *parent* cases together. For example, if case1 is 23.5, 12, 6 and case2 is 15, 7, 2, then the new offspring case would be $(11.75 + 7.5, 6 + 3.5, 3 + 1) \Rightarrow 19.25, 9.5, 4$. Note that, a single offspring is generated, rather than two offspring as in many GA systems. Of course this is just one way in which the cases could be crossed, for example another way might have been to take one number from one case and the others from another case.

Next the set of 8 cases (the original 4 plus the 4 offspring) are mutated. This is done by selecting each case in turn and randomly selecting the *mutation rule* to apply. The mutation rules currently defined are:

- Apply any appropriate Adaptation Rules (as in traditional CBR systems). However, if more than one adaptation rule could be applied, then do so. This can generate more than one new case and represents a "keeping our options open" approach. That is, if there are two adaptations which may be useful, but we are not sure what their effect on the later design process will be, why not try both?
- Real number creep. One of the three real numbers representing the span, depth and width is chosen at random. It is then randomly increased or decreased by a small amount.
- Multiple Point mutation. Each of the three real numbers representing the beam is considered in turn. Each number is converted into a binary format. Each bit is considered in turn. If a mutation threshold is reached, then the bit is randomly set to 1 or 0. Once this process is completed, the binary number is converted back into decimal (note that 5.3 would be converted into two numbers 101 and 011 and rejoined after mutation).
- Material mutation. This operation mutates the material identifier by using a binary bit mutation operator.

Each mutated case is added to the set of cases being considered. This can result in a maximum of 16 cases. These cases are then considered for repair.

5.5 Case repair

Three constraints are used for the structural assessment of the beam, these are:
- Bending stress,
- Shear stress,
- Deflection.

Normally the load capacity of a beam is limited by at least one of these constraints. These constraints have therefore been encoded as simple rules which are applied during the *Repair* phase. For example, if the equations associated with any of the above three become negative, then the whole case is flagged as being undesirable. This will ensure that the evaluation phase will assign it a large negative number for its fitness. In addition another rule has been developed by experimentation. It states that there is a minimum width beyond which a beam design will not be considered. That is, a beam must not be too thin no matter what. This is a safety feature which aims to ensure a minimum safety level.

The use of these constraints is important as the system has not only to maximise load potential and minimise member weight, the system must also attempt to vary the aspect ratio of the rectangular section in an attempt to balance the three constraints. This allows at least two to be near their limit (by intuition, this should give a more efficient design, as resistance to both bending and deflection is affected exponentially by the depth of the section, subject to the limitations of buckling).

The remaining cases are then evaluated.

5.6 Case evaluation

The evaluation process is performed using a set of equations derived from those used in the civil engineering industry. These equations give values for the actual bending stress, shear stress and deflection. This is illustrated below (note **b** represents breadth, **d** represents depth, **FBC** represent the actual bending stress, **FQ** represents the actual stress and δ represents the actual deflection):

$$fbc = \frac{LOAD * span^2 * 6}{8 * b * d^2}$$

$$fq = \frac{span * LOAD}{2(b * d)}$$

$$\delta = \frac{5 * LOAD * span^4 * 12}{384ei} \qquad \text{where } e \text{ represents the material property}$$

obtained from look up tables, e.g. wood (8000) and $i = b * d^3$

These values are the then subtracted from the permissible bending stress, shear stress and deflection and their results are added together to give the stress fitness. This is illustrated below:

$$stress\ fitness = |(pbc - fbc)| + |(pq - fq)| + |(p\delta - \delta)|$$

The *area fitness* is also calculated as $b * d$.

The *stress fitness* and the *area fitness* are then combined together to provide the overall fitness. To allow a maximising fitness value for what is essentially a minimising function, the following function is used:

$$(100 - stress\_fitness) + \frac{(1,000,000 - area\_fitness)}{10,000}$$

This equation provides the total *fitness* value for each individual case.

This process continues until the termination condition on the main loop has been met.

5.7 Case output and update

The output is generated in the form of a report sheet which includes sufficient detail to permit full appraisal by the user, or by a checking authority (e.g. structural engineer, government department etc.). If the solution is accepted by the user it can be saved back into the case database for later use.

5.8 Solution explanation

A final requirement which is worth noting is that the system should be able to "explain" how it arrived at the specified design. As the design originates from a specific case the original justification can be provided, along with the steps taken during the evolutionary adaptation phase. This provides both the context and the analysis of the design for the end user. Such an explanation would not be possible from a GA design system.

6. Worked example

In this example, the information provided by the user is:

SPAN	2000 mm	**LOAD** 3.0 kN/m.	
PBC	6.0 N/mm².	**PQ**	1.0 N/mm².
Pδ	3 mm.		

The retrieval step retrieves the following cases from the case database. These cases are chosen as they are the four cases which ranked highest using the nearest neighbour algorithm:

[[Material: Wood Span: 2000 Depth: 200 Width: 50 Load: 2.5]
[Material: Wood Span: 2500 Depth: 250 Width: 60 Load: 3.2]
[Material: Wood Span: 2200 Depth: 210 Width: 40 Load: 2.0]
[Material: Wood Span: 1500 Depth: 150 Width: 30 Load: 1.8]]

Each of these cases is close to, but not exactly the same as, the situation described by the user. The system therefore applies the crossover and mutation evolutionary operators. This results in the following (additional) four cases:

[[Material: Wood Span: 1750 Depth: 175 Width: 40 Load: 2.15]
[Material: Wood Span: 2250 Depth: 225 Width: 55 Load: 2.85]
[Material: Wood Span: 1850 Depth: 180 Width: 35 Load: 1.9]
[Material: Wood Span: 2350 Depth: 230 Width: 50 Load: 2.6]]

To these eight cases the mutation operator is applied (generating 8 new cases) resulting in a total of 16 cases. These cases are the processed by the repair step. As none of the cases breaks any of the constraints they are all passed onto the evaluation step. This applies the equations described in section 5 to each case in order to obtain a ranking for the cases (note that the desired load is used, rather than the load defined in the case). For example, case 1 results in the following:

$$fbc = \frac{3.0 * 2000^2 * 6}{8 * 50 * 200^2} = 4N/mm^2$$

$$fq = \frac{2000 * 3.0}{2(50 * 200)} = 0.3N/mm^2$$

$$\delta = \frac{5 * 3.0 * 2000^4 * 12}{384 * 8000 * 50 * 200^3} = 2.34mm$$

These values are the then subtracted from the permissible bending stress, shear stress and deflection and their results are added together to give the stress fitness. This is illustrated below:

stress fitness = $|(6.0 - 4.0)| + |(1.0 - 0.3)| + |(3.0 - 2.34)| = 3.36$

The *area fitness* is also calculated as *50* 200=10,000*

The *stress fitness* and the *area fitness* are then combined together to provide the overall fitness for case 1:

$$(100 - 3.36) + \frac{(1,000,000 - 10,000)}{10,000} = 195.64$$

This is repeated for each case, and from the (ordered) list of cases, the best 4 are selected to go forward to the next generation.

The whole process is then repeated until either a maximum number of iterations has been completed or a termination threshold has been reached.

A comparison worth making is with the performance of a Genetic Algorithm designed for the same task. To generate an optimum result using the evolutionary CBR method took between 4 and 6 iterations. This compares very favourably with the pure genetic algorithm which took in the order of 50 iterations for the same task.

7. Discussion

Although the case study presented in section 5 and 6 is very simple, it can be seen that the evolutionary adaptation phase and the case library act together to provide a system which has the strengths of the two different techniques, without some of the limitations. For example, the cases which are present in the case library act as seeds to the evolutionary adaptation phase. This results in a far more efficient search than could be performed using a GA with a random set of initial cases. In addition the design cases provide the basis for a (rudimentory) level of explanation. For example, the case(s) from which the final case is derived, plus a list of the modification steps applied, provide some of the justification behind the values within the case. Of course, the longer the evolutionary process continues, the less reference there will be between the original case(s) and the final case. Therefore, this facility is limited.

In turn, the evolutionary aspect enables the designs to be explicitly optimised given the current set of constraints. A similar process has often been performed within other CBR systems, however in these systems the mutation and modification operators have been encoded in the form of rules. In this system, the effect of these rules has been made explicit and placed within an appropriate framework.

Finally, the CBR framework is made more flexible and can inherently search a number of possibilities at a time. For example, it no longer needs to select a single case, instead it can select a number of cases which are then processed in parallel. In a similar manner the system does not need to select a single adaptation, it can apply a number of them, generating multiple (new) cases. In addition, features of these cases can be crossed allowing useful elements of one case to be joined with useful elements of another case (a potentially very powerful capability).

8. Conclusions

This paper illustrates that a hybrid evolutionary CBR system can be useful in design. The cases which are present in the case library act as seeds to the evolutionary adaption phase. This evolutionary aspect, in turn, enables the designs to be optimised given the current set of constraints. The resulting system overcomes some of the computational expense of a "traditional" evolutionary system (it does not start from scratch, instead it starts from a previous solution), whilst providing additional flexibility to the CBR system.

Acknowledgements

I would like to acknowledge the help of Richard Fletcher, of the University of Wales, Aberystwyth for providing the civil engineering knowledge essential for the case study used in this paper. I would also like to thank Dr. Terrance Fogarty of the University of the West of England, for some useful discussion during early consideration of this work.

References

[Baldwin 1896] Baldwin, J. M. 1896. A new factor in evolution, *American Naturalist*, 30, pp 441-451.

[Barrett, Ramsey and Sloman, 1985] Barrett, R. Ramsey, A. and Sloman, A. 1985. *POP11: A Practical Language for Artificial Intelligence*, Pub. Ellis Horwood.

[Davis, 1991] Davis, L. (ed). 1991. *Handbook of Genetic Algorithms*, Pub VanNostrand Reinhold.

[Goel, 1991] Goel, A. 1991. A model-based approach to case adaptation, in Proc. of the *13th Annual Conf. of the Cognitive Science Society*. Northvale, NJ: Erlbaum.

[Goel, 1992] Goel, A. 1992. Representation of design functions in experience-based design. In *Intelligent Computer Aided Design*, D. Brown, M. Waldron and H. Yoshikawa (eds), Amsterdam:North-Holland.

[Goel and Chandrasekaran, 1992] Goel, A. and Chandrasekaran, B. 1992. Case-based design: A task analysis, in *AI approaches to engineering design, Vol 2: Innovative design*, Ed. C. Tong and D. Sriram, Pub Academic Press.

[Goldberg, 1989] Goldberg, D. E. 1989. *Genetic Algorithms in Search, Optimization and Machine Learning*, Pub. Addison Wesley.

[Hammond, 1986] Hammond, K. 1986. CHEF: A model of case-based planning. In *Proc. of AAAI-86*, Cambridge MA: AAAI Press/MIT Press.

[Holland, 1975] Holland, J. H. 1975. *Adaptation in Natural and Artificial Systems*, MIT Press, Cambridge, Mass.

[Hua and Faltings, 1993] Hua, K. and Faltings, B. 1993. Exploring case-based building design - CADRE, *AIEDAM* 7(2), pp 135-143.

[Hunt and Lee, 1992] Hunt, J. E. and Lee, M. H. 1992, Towards a Knowledge-Based Design Assistant, *Engineering Applications of Artificial Intelligence*, Vol 5, No. 4, pp 275-288.

[Hunt and Miles, 1994] Hunt, J. E. and Miles, R. G. 1994. Hybrid Case-Based Reasoning, in *Knowledge Engineering Review*, Vol 9, No. 4, pp 383-397.

[Kolodner, 1993] Kolodner, J. 1993. *Case-Based Reasoning*, Pub. Morgan Kaufmann CA.

[Maher and Zhang, 1993] Maher, M. L. and Zhang, D. M. 1993. CADSYN: A case-based design process model, in *AIEDAM*, 7(2), pp 97-110.

[Navinchandra, Sycara and Narasimhan, 1991] Navinchandra, D. Sycara, K. P. and Narasimhan, S. 1991. A Transformational Approach to Case-Based Synthesis, *AIEDAM*, Vol 5(1), pp 31-45.

[Rissland and Skalal, 1991] Rissland, E. L. and Skalak, D. B. 1991. CABARET: Rule Interpretation in a hybrid architecture, *IJMMS* Vol 34, pp 839-887.

[Roderman and Tsatsoulis, 1993] Roderman, S. and Tsatsoulis, C. 1993. PANDA: A case-based system to aid novice designers, *AIEDAM* 7(2), pp 125-134.

Formalising the knowledge content of case memory systems

A D Griffiths and D G Bridge

Department of Computer Science, University of York, YORK YO1 5DD, UK
Email: {tony|dgb}@minster.york.ac.uk

Abstract. Discussions of case-based reasoning often reflect an implicit assumption that a case memory system will become better informed, i.e. *will increase in knowledge,* as more cases are added to the case-base. This paper considers formalisations of this 'knowledge content' which are a necessary preliminary to more rigourous analysis of the performance of case-based reasoning systems. In particular we are interested in modelling the learning aspects of case-based reasoning in order to study how the performance of a case-based reasoning system changes as it accumulates problem-solving experience. The current paper presents a 'case-base semantics' which generalises recent formalisations of case-based classification. Within this framework, the paper explores various issues in assuring that these semantics are well-defined, and illustrates how the knowledge content of the case memory system can be seen to reside in both the chosen similarity measure and in the cases of the case-base.

1   Introduction

Responsible engineering of knowledge-based systems should involve setting error bounds on the performance of the system and, in the case of systems that are to 'learn from experience', guaranteeing that the accumulated experience will actually enhance the performance of the system. We believe that a necessary preliminary to these activities is to be able to state formally the *knowledge content* of a knowledge-based system. Given that a system has 'knowledge' to guide its operation and that it may 'gain knowledge' through problem-solving experience, of what does this knowledge consist and how may it be compared between systems? A formalisation suitable for some aspects of the operation of a case memory system is discussed here.

Some theoreticians [7] [8] have attempted to describe knowledge content from a *logical* point of view, i.e. in terms of the logical propositions that might be derived from a case memory system. These presentations necessarily use non-monotonic logics in order to capture the way in which the set of propositions entailed by a case-base changes as new cases are added. This approach has not however had much success, we believe, in explicating knowledge content and has no demonstrated application to the engineering issues which we believe must be addressed. In contrast the view adopted here is a *functional* one in that the knowledge content of a case memory is modelled as a mapping between input and output domains.

A functional viewpoint has been used in the work of Dearden [3] in the engineering of the user interface of case memory systems and, of more relevance to our own work, it has also been assumed in much of 'computational learning theory'. This theoretical study of learning systems models the current state of a learner as a function which is adjusted to accommodate the data presented to the system. We are currently making progress in the study of various case-based learning algorithms within this framework [4].

2 Generalised Case-Base Semantics

We consider the general case where the case memory system is intended to represent a mapping between an input domain X_1 and an output domain X_2. Additionally, X_1 and X_2 are both finite sets. Using Dearden's terminology [3] we refer to the elements of X_1 & X_2 as 'descriptions' and 'reports' respectively. In [3], the knowledge content of the case memory system is embodied in the 'retrieve' function, which maps from a domain of problem statements into the space of partial orders over the cases in the case-base. This gives a very general view of the operation of a case memory system and one that is clearly necessary for discussing the interface properties of such systems. We opt here for a simpler model; we assume that for each description $x_1 \in X_1$ there is a unique, 'correct' report $x_2 \in X_2$ which we would like the case-memory system to return, so that the ideal behaviour of the system is described by a functional mapping from the set $(X_1 \to X_2)$. This assumption is common in the non-Bayesian forms of learning theory, and in that context the mapping is often called a 'target function'. Here, the notion that a single output value is appropriate to describe the operation of the system is something of a restriction, but has the advantage that it allows a straightforward definition of the error in a system's output, and allows the role of the similarity measure in the system to be demonstrated more clearly.

Following the work of Jantke [5] a case memory system is modelled as a pair $\langle CB, \sigma \rangle$ consisting of a case-base CB and a similarity measure σ. The case-base is a set of description-report pairs. i.e. CB is an object of type:

$$CB : \mathcal{P}(X_1 \times X_2)$$

In the current paper, we assume that cases in the case-base are free from observational error, so that given some target function $f \in (X_1 \to X_2)$:

$$\forall x_1 \in X_1, x_2 \in X_2 \cdot (x_1, x_2) \in CB \to f(x_1) = x_2 \tag{1}$$

This is equivalent to the statement $CB \subseteq f$, and so CB can also be seen as a partial function between X_1 and X_2. The task of a case memory system is to interpolate the *partial* function represented by the case-base so that the system as a whole represents a *total* function which will return some report value for any description presented to the system. The two-place model $\langle CB, \sigma \rangle$ emphasises that the interpolation made by the system is *dependent on the choice of similarity measure*. For the purposes of the model we consider a similarity measure to be a function over pairs of descriptions returning a normalised real value indicating the degree of similarity between the two objects:

$$\sigma : (X_1 \times X_1) \to [0,1]$$

Given a problem description $x \in X_1$ we can therefore define the set of nearest neighbours of x with respect to CB and σ:

$$\forall x \in X_1 \cdot NN(x, CB, \sigma) \,\hat{=}\,$$
$$\{(x_1, x_2) | (x_1, x_2) \in CB \wedge \forall (x_1', x_2') \in CB \cdot \sigma(x, x_1) \geq \sigma(x, x_1')\} \qquad (2)$$

The essence of case-based reasoning is very simple. We wish the case memory system to return the report from the case whose description is most similar according to the similarity measure σ to the description of the current problem. In order to consider $\langle CB, \sigma \rangle$ as a functional mapping between X_1 and X_2 we need only resolve the question of 'ties'. That is, where the set of nearest neighbours defined in equation (2) contains more than one exemplar from the case-base, we must specify a way of choosing the case used to justify the system's output. Jantke [5] offers three suggestions for resolving such ties:

1. In the case of ties, the output of the system is undefined. That is, the case memory system is interpreted as a partial function.

2. Ties are resolved by a preference ordering over *descriptions*.

3. Ties are resolved by a preference ordering over *reports*.

Option 1 is an undesirable state of affairs in that we may often have perfectly good grounds for choosing one 'equally similar' case over another. In the latter two options the system is equipped with some additional domain knowledge which allows the nearest neighbour with the most preferred description or report to dictate the output. (This might be interpreted, for example as knowledge of the *a priori* plausibility of different descriptions or reports.) In what follows, we consider a general model of preference relations over the set of reports X_2. Option 2 is passed over for the moment principally because this knowledge is potentially subsumed in the similarity measure. Thus we define the function $f_{\langle CB, \sigma \rangle}$ represented by a case-memory system $\langle CB, \sigma \rangle$ as (c.f. [5, p.219]):

$$f_{\langle CB, \sigma \rangle}(x_1) = x_2 \text{ where } \max_{\sqsupseteq}\{x_2' | (x_1', x_2') \in NN(x_1, CB, \sigma)\} = \{x_2\} \qquad (3)$$
$$f_{\langle CB, \sigma \rangle}(x_1) = x_2 \text{ where } NN(x_1, CB, \sigma) = \{\} \wedge x_2 \in \max_{\sqsupseteq} X_2 \qquad (4)$$

$\sqsupseteq$ is a partial order defining preferences over X_2 so that for a pair of reports $x, x' \in X_2$, $x \sqsupseteq x'$ reads 'x is preferred to x'', and $\max_{\sqsupseteq}$ are the maxima with respect to that ordering defined as follows:

$$\max_{\sqsupseteq} X = \{x \in X | \forall x' \in X \cdot x' \sqsupseteq x \to x = x'\} \qquad (5)$$

The 'case-base semantics' given in equations (3) & (4) are a generalisation of interpretations given elsewhere for the special case of case-based systems for classification. This is illustrated below.

Example 1. **Case-base semantics for classification**

If we take the special case where the output domain $X_2 = \{0, 1\}$, then we are concerned with the task of classification. Given a problem description from X_1, we require that our system outputs a 'yes' or 'no' result classifying the problem description as an instance of some concept. Elsewhere in our work [4] we have used the following equation as semantics for a case-based classifier, related to the 'standard semantics' of Jantke and Lange [6, p.142] (see also [9, p.84]).

$$f_{\langle CB,\sigma \rangle}(x) = \begin{cases} 1 \; if & \exists (x_{pos}, 1) \in CB \cdot \forall (x_{neg}, 0) \in CB \cdot \sigma(x, x_{pos}) > \sigma(x, x_{neg}) \\ 0 \; otherwise \end{cases}$$

(6)

Informally, a point x from X_1 is positively classified by $h_{\langle CB,\sigma \rangle}$ if and only if there is a stored positive exemplar x_{pos} which is strictly more similar to x according to the chosen similarity measure σ than any of the stored negative exemplars x_{neg}. In other words this interpretation resolves 'ties' between equally similar near neighbours by preferring '0' reports to '1' reports; this might be called a conservative classification strategy. Formally, equation (6) is an instantiation of equations (3) & (4) given the preference order $\sqsupseteq = \{(0, 0), (0, 1), (1, 1)\}$. □

Clearly equations (3) & (4) require a little more discussion in the general case. $f_{\langle CB,\sigma \rangle}$ is defined as a functional mapping only if the preference relation is able to choose a single maximum in every case; not all partial orders will be sufficient for this. In Example 1, '0' is (trivially) preferred to every other report, and this value will therefore be returned by equation (6) on any description for an empty case-base. In general, the preference ordering $\sqsupseteq$ must define a unique maximum on the set of reports X_2 in order for equation (4) to be well defined. For a non-empty case-base however, the set of the reports of the nearest neighbours with respect to some point in the input domain X_1 will in general be a subset of X_2. We require in addition that any such set of reports has a single maximum defined by the preference ordering in order for (3) to be well defined; this condition depends on both the preference ordering and the similarity measure. Specifically, for any domain value $x \in X_1$, the set of nearest neighbours with respect to σ must have an upper universal bound, defined as an element which is maximal with respect to the preference ordering $\sqsupseteq$ and in addition is comparable to all other elements in the nearest set. These constraints are developed in the following statements:

Definition 1. Upper Universal Bound $x \in X$ is an upper universal bound for a poset $\langle X, \sqsupseteq \rangle$ iff x is a member of the maxima of $\langle X, \sqsupseteq \rangle$ and also x is comparable to every element $x' \in X$ $(x \in \max_{\sqsupseteq} X \land \forall x' \in X \cdot x \sqsupseteq x')$.

Lemma 2. *Given a poset $\langle X, \sqsupseteq \rangle$, $\sqsupseteq$ defines a single maximum x_{max} on X ($|\max_{\sqsupseteq} X| = 1$), iff x_{max} is an upper universal bound for X.*

36

Proof. **a) Only if.** Assume there is one value x_{max} in the maxima. It must be shown that $x_{max} \sqsupseteq x'$ for any $x' \in X$, hence x_{max} is an upper universal bound to X (Definition 1). From equation (5):

$$\forall x' \in X \cdot x' \sqsupseteq x_{max} \to x_{max} = x' \tag{7}$$

Additionally, there is only one value x_{max} satisfying this equation. Hence:

$$\forall x' \in X \cdot x' \neq x_{max} \to \exists x'' \in X \cdot x'' \neq x' \wedge x'' \sqsupseteq x' \tag{8}$$

For any $x' \in X$, by equation (8) either $x_{max} = x'$ and hence $x_{max} \sqsupseteq x'$ by reflexivity, or there is some x'' which is distinct from x' and which is preferred to x' in the preference ordering. Equally, equation (8) applies to x'', and either $x'' = x_{max}$ or there is some x''' preferred to x''. Since $\sqsupseteq$ is a partial order and defines an acyclic graph on X, then eventually the path through the graph of the preference ordering must reach x_{max} for finite sets X. Hence by transitivity $x_{max} \sqsupseteq x'$ for any $x' \in X$ and x_{max} is an upper universal bound for X.

b) If. Assume $\sqsupseteq$ defines an upper universal bound for X, i.e. for any $x_{max} \in \max_{\sqsupseteq} X$ then $x_{max} \sqsupseteq x'$ for any $x' \in X$. Since $\sqsupseteq$ is a partial order and anti-symmetric, there can only be one such x_{max}. $\qquad\square$

Definition 3. Admissible Preference Relation A preference relation $\sqsupseteq$ is admissible with respect to a similarity measure σ and a function space F, iff $\sqsupseteq$ defines an upper universal bound for the set X_2 and in addition, for every domain value $x \in X_1$ and for every non-empty case-base valid for some $f \in F$ (i.e. $CB \subseteq f$), $\sqsupseteq$ defines an upper universal bound for the set $\{x_2 | (x_1, x_2) \in NN(x, CB, \sigma)\}$.

Corollary 4. *The generalised case-base semantics expressed in equation (3) will be defined, i.e. the preference relation will choose only a single value from the set of nearest neighbours, iff $\sqsupseteq$ is an admissible preference relation with respect to σ and F.*

Since both the preference relation and the similarity measure share responsibility for discriminating between more and less applicable cases, we can picture a 'trade-off' between the information content of the similarity measure and the preference relation. That is, a less informed preference relation is compensated for by a more discriminating similarity measure and vice versa. In the light of this, the following proposition considers the case where $\sqsupseteq$ contains no extra information, and shows the minimum constraint on the similarity measure entailed by Definition 3 in this situation.

Proposition 5. $\sqsupseteq_I$, *the identity relation on X_2, is an admissible preference relation with respect to a similarity measure σ and a space of functions F iff for any function $f \in F$ and for any domain values $x, x', x'' \in X_1$ then f maps to a different value on x' and x'' only if the similarities $\sigma(x, x')$ and $\sigma(x, x'')$ return different values. i.e $\sqsupseteq_I$ is an admissible preference relation with respect to σ and F iff*

$$\forall f \in F \cdot \forall x, x', x'' \in X_1 \cdot f(x') \neq f(x'') \to \sigma(x, x') \neq \sigma(x, x'') \tag{9}$$

Proof. Note that $x \in X \rightarrow x \in \max_{\sqsupseteq_I} X$, hence $\max_{\sqsupseteq_I} X$ is a singleton iff $|X| = 1$ (and hence by Lemma 2, $\sqsupseteq_I$ defines an upper universal bound on X iff $|X| = 1$). **a) If.** Therefore it must be shown that if equation (9) holds for some σ and F then for any domain function $f \in F$ and a non-empty case-base $CB \subseteq f$, the nearest neighbours in CB w.r.t σ to a problem instance $x \in X_1$ share a a a common report x_2. For any such x & x_2, from equation (2):

$$\exists x_1 \in X_1 \cdot ((x_1, x_2) \in CB \wedge \forall(x_1', x_2') \in CB \cdot \sigma(x, x_1) \geq \sigma(x, x_1')) \qquad (10)$$

It must be shown that x_2 is unique. i.e.

$$\forall x_2' \in X_2 \cdot x_2' \neq x_2 \rightarrow$$
$$\forall x_1' \in X_1 \cdot ((x_1', x_2') \notin CB \vee \exists(x_1'', x_2'') \cdot CB \wedge \sigma(x, x_1') < \sigma(x, x_1'')) \qquad (11)$$

Take some $x_2' \in X_2$ distinct from x_2. For a given domain value $x_1' \in X_1$, either $(x_1', x_2') \in CB$ or not. If there is no such exemplar, then equation (11) is satisfied directly. Otherwise $(x_1', x_2') \in CB$ and it must be shown there is some other exemplar (x_1'', x_2'') in the case-base such that $\sigma(x, x_1') < \sigma(x, x_1'')$, which would prevent (x_1', x_2') being a nearest neighbour. Now from equation (10) it follows firstly:

$$\exists x_1 \in X_1 \cdot (x_1, x_2) \in CB \qquad (12)$$

and additionally for some such value of x_1 and for any other exemplar $(x_1'', x_2'') \in CB$ then $\sigma(x, x_1) \geq \sigma(x, x_1'')$. Therefore specifically:

$$\sigma(x, x_1) \geq \sigma(x, x_1') \qquad (13)$$

But from equation (9), then $f(x_1) \neq f(x_1') \rightarrow \sigma(x, x_1) \neq \sigma(x, x_1')$. Since in this case $x_2 \neq x_2'$ then clearly $f(x_1) \neq f(x_1')$ by equation (1). Hence in addition to equation (13) we have $\sigma(x, x_1) \neq \sigma(x, x_1')$ and:

$$\sigma(x, x_1') < \sigma(x, x_1) \qquad (14)$$

Hence by equations (12) & (14) (x_1, x_2) is an exemplar satisfying equation (11), and (11) is satisfied under all circumstances. **b) Only If.** Assume that equation (9) does not hold and therefore there is some $f' \in F$ and some x, x' & x'' s.t.:

$$f(x') \neq f(x'') \wedge \sigma(x, x') = \sigma(x, x'') \qquad (15)$$

Therefore consider the case-base $CB = \{(x', f(x')), (x'', f(x''))\}$. Since $f(x') \neq f(x'')$ we have two distinct reports satisfying equation (10) with respect to x. Hence $|\{x_2 | (x_1, x_2) \in NN(x, CB, \sigma)\}| > 1$, and equation (9) necessarily follows from the case where $\sqsupseteq_I$ is admissible with respect to σ and F. $\qquad \square$

3 Consistency of case-based learning algorithms

The similarity measure σ has been defined above only as a binary function from the space $(X_1 \times X_1 \rightarrow [0, 1])$; the property of *consistency* motivates some minimum constraints on a useful similarity measure. A consistent learner is one which, having seen some training sample, is able to correctly reproduce the examples it has seen in that sample. Although it is not optimal in domains where noise is expected, consistency is clearly a desirable property where it is assumed, as here, that the exemplars available to the system are error free. Since we also assume that the functions being represented are defined on a finite domain, consistency is sufficient to guarantee that as more training examples are seen the system will eventually converge to a good approximation of the target function [2, Chs 3 & 4]. This holds even in the worst case where the system is able to make little or no suitable generalisation of the seen examples. Since consistency is a property of learning *algorithms*, we must state explicitly the case-based learning algorithm we wish to consider. A family of the simplest such algorithms is defined below:

Definition 6. $CB1(\sigma)$ Algorithm for Case-Based Learning of Functions

```
set CB = ∅
for i = 1 to m do
    set CB = CB ∪ {(x_i, f(x_i))}
set CB1(σ)(s̄) = f_⟨CB,σ⟩
```

These simple algorithms learn by adding each and every member of the training sample $\bar{s}$ (a series of m examples of the target function $(x_i, f(x_i))$) to the case-base and 'hypothesise' an approximation to the target function defined in terms of the case-base and a single fixed similarity measure σ. One of the simplest ways of ensuring $CB1(\sigma)$ is a consistent learning algorithm is to constrain σ so that the system will always retrieve an exemplar from the training sample whenever that exemplar is presented as a query. The following definition is related to this intuition and is necessary and sufficient to ensure the consistency of $CB1(\sigma)$, a claim also proved below. The proof of Theorem 8 assumes that the case-base semantics of the previous section have been instantiated with an admissible preference relation.

Definition 7. Predictivity of a Similarity Measure with respect to a function space F and preference ordering $\sqsupseteq$. A similarity measure is predictive of a function space $F \subseteq (X_1 \rightarrow X_2)$, iff for a function $f \in F$:

1. For any pair of problem instances $x, x' \in X_1$, the similarity of x to x' will exceed the similarity of x to itself only where $f(x) = f(x')$:

$$\forall f \in F \cdot \forall x, x' \in X_1 \cdot \sigma(x, x') > \sigma(x, x) \rightarrow f(x) = f(x') \qquad (16)$$

2. For any pair of problem instances $x, x' \in X_1$, the similarity of x to x' will equal that of x to itself only if $f(x')$ is either equal to $f(x)$ or it does not precede $f(x)$ in the preference relation.

$$\forall f \in F \cdot \forall x, x' \in X_1 \cdot \sigma(x, x') = \sigma(x, x) \rightarrow f(x) = f(x') \vee f(x') \not\sqsupseteq f(x)) \qquad (17)$$

Theorem 8. Consistency of $CB1(\sigma)$. *For a space of functions $F \subseteq (X_1 \rightarrow X_2)$, $CB1(\sigma)$ is a consistent learning algorithm for F if and only if the chosen similarity measure σ is predictive of F.*

Proof. a) **Sufficiency.** Assume that a similarity measure σ is predictive of F, satisfying equations (16) & (17). For some example $(x, f(x))$ in the training sample, denote the members of $NN(x, CB, \sigma)$ by $(x_i^{NN}, f(x_i^{NN}))$. The definition of $CB1(\sigma)$ indicates that $(x, f(x))$ will be a member of CB and hence $\sigma(x, x_i^{NN}) \geq \sigma(x, x)$. Consider first the case where the inequality is strict. Hence $f(x) = f(x_i^{NN})$ for any of the nearest neighbours by equation (16) and immediately $h_{(CB,\sigma)}(x) = f(x)$. Hence in this case $CB1(\sigma)$ is a consistent learning algorithm. Assume instead that $\sigma(x, x_i^{NN}) = \sigma(x, x)$, and by equation (17):

$$f(x) = f(x_i^{NN}) \vee f(x_i^{NN}) \not\sqsupseteq f(x) \tag{18}$$

By definition 3, the set of reports of the nearest neighbours $(x_i^{NN}, f(x_i^{NN}))$ must have a maximally preferred value. Thus there is a nearest neighbour x_i^{NN} s.t. $f(x_i^{NN}) \sqsupseteq f(x)$, and by equation (18) then $f(x_i^{NN}) = f(x)$. Since this $f(x_i^{NN})$ is also preferred to the reports of all other nearest neighbours then $h_{(CB,\sigma)}(x) = f(x)$ and hence the algorithm is consistent. b) **Necessity.** Assume that equation (16) does not hold. Therefore there is some function $f \in F$ for which there are a pair of domain values x and x' s.t:

$$\sigma(x, x') > \sigma(x, x) \wedge f(x) \neq f(x')$$

Consider the training sample $\langle (x, f(x)), (x', f(x')) \rangle$. Clearly $CB1(\sigma)$ produces a hypothesis $\langle CB, \sigma \rangle$ s.t. $h_{(CB,\sigma)}(x) = f(x')$, which is an inconsistent hypothesis. Assume alternatively equation (17) does not hold. Hence there are some f, x, x' s.t.

$$\sigma(x, x') = \sigma(x, x) \wedge f(x) \neq f(x') \wedge f(x') \sqsupseteq f(x)$$

Again, consider the hypothesis $\langle CB, \sigma \rangle$ produced by $CB1(\sigma)$ on the training sample $\langle (x, f(x)), (x', f(x')) \rangle$. Since x is equally similar to itself and to x', and $f(x')$ is preferred to $f(x)$ in the preference ordering, then $h_{(CB,\sigma)}(x) = f(x')$; again this is an inconsistent hypothesis. $\square$

Example 2. **Simple Concept Learning.**

As above, we illustrate this result with reference to the special case of classification systems. In [4] we prove a version of Theorem 8 in terms of the following definition of 'special' predictivity for classification functions:

$$\forall f \in F \cdot \forall x, x' \in X_1 \cdot \sigma(x, x') \geq \sigma(x, x) \rightarrow f(x) = 1 \rightarrow f(x') = 1 \tag{19}$$
$$\forall f \in F \cdot \forall x, x' \in X_1 \cdot \sigma(x, x') > \sigma(x, x) \rightarrow f(x) = 0 \rightarrow f(x') = 0 \tag{20}$$

The following result re-expresses the special case [4, Thm 5] as a corollary of the general framework presented here:

Corollary 9. Consistency of Case-based classifiers $CB1(\sigma)$ *is a consistent learning algorithm for a space of classification functions* $F \subseteq (X_1 \rightarrow \{0,1\})$ *iff the similarity measure* σ *is predictive of* F *according to the 'special' definition of equations (19) & (20).*

Proof. Taking $X_2 = \{0,1\}$ and $\sqsupseteq = \{(0,0),(0,1),(1,1)\}$, then equations (16) & (17) become

$$\forall f \in F \cdot x, x' \in D_N \cdot \sigma(x,x') > \sigma(x,x) \rightarrow f(x) = f(x') \tag{21}$$
$$\forall f \in F \cdot x, x' \in D_N \cdot$$
$$\sigma(x,x') = \sigma(x,x) \rightarrow [f(x) = f(x') \vee (f(x') = 1 \wedge f(x) = 0)] \tag{22}$$

By Theorem 8, $CB1(\sigma)$ will be a consistent learning algorithm for F iff equations (21) & (22) are satisfied. Hence it must be shown that a similarity measure σ satisfies (21) & (22) iff equations (19) & (20) are satisfied. **a) Only if.** Assume f, x & x' s.t. $\sigma(x,x') \geq \sigma(x,x)$ and $f(x) = 1$. Either the inequality is strict or the similarities are equal. In the case of a strict inequality, then $f(x') = 1$ by equation (21). Where the similarities are equal, and also $f(x) = 1$, then clearly equation (22) allows only $f(x') = 1$. Hence (19). Assume f, x & x' s.t. $\sigma(x,x') > \sigma(x,x)$ and $f(x) = 0$. From equation (21), immediately $f(x') = 0$. Hence (20). **b) If.** Assume x & x' s.t. $\sigma(x,x') > \sigma(x,x)$. For a given $f \in F$, either $f(x) = 0$ or $f(x) = 1$. If $f(x) = 0$ then from (20) we have $f(x') = 0$ also. If $f(x) = 1$ then also $f(x') = 1$ by equation (19). Hence (21). Finally assume x & x' s.t. $\sigma(x,x') = \sigma(x,x)$ and some $f \in F$ s.t. $f(x) = 1$ and $f(x') = 0$. But from (19), $f(x') = 1$ giving a contradiction. Hence (22). $\square$

4 Conclusions

This paper has attempted to answer the question of how the knowledge content of a case memory system might be formalised. We have presented a view in which the case memory system is interpreted according to the semantics given as a function which approximates to some ideal mapping between input and output. The results presented explore a generalisation of the generally accepted decision function for a case-based classifier to a more general class of case-based systems which generate output from an arbitrary set of output values. The paper gives necessary and sufficient conditions for the well-definedness of our semantics and also for the consistency of case-based learning algorithms within this framework.

The functional view of knowledge content has a number of benefits, notably that it allows the error in the case memory's knowledge to be quantified straightforwardly in a way that is compatible with the assumptions of computational learning theory, allowing us to appeal to more general results in machine learning. We are finding that this allows some progress in understanding analytically the learning behaviour of various case-based reasoning systems [4]. The formalisation presented here might also be of use in emphasising the insight of Wess & Globig [9] that the knowledge content of a case memory system rests in the similarity measure as well as the stored cases.

Future work will attempt to make use of this framework in a model of case-based reasoning systems suitable for simple instances of the design task. We hope to make progress in understanding the nature and sources of error in the operation of a case memory system, and to develop these insights in a way that allows claims about the performance of case-based reasoning systems to be rigourously stated and proven.

Acknowledgements The first author is funded by an EPSRC grant and receives additional support under the CASE award scheme from Logica Cambridge Ltd.

References

1. D W Aha, D Kibler, and M K Albert. Instance-based learning algorithms. *Machine Learning*, 6:37–66, 1991.

2. M Anthony and N Biggs. *Computational Learning Theory*. Cambridge University Press, 1992.

3. A M Dearden. *The use of formal models in the design of interactive case memory systems*. PhD thesis, University of York, UK, 1995.

4. A D Griffiths and D G Bridge. On concept space and hypothesis space in case-based learning algorithms. In Nada Lavrac and Stefan Wrobel, editors, *Machine Learning: ECML-95 (Proc. 8th European Conf. on Machine Learning, 1995)*, Lecture Notes in Artificial Intelligence 914, pages 161 – 173, Berlin, Heidelberg, New York, 1995. Springer Verlag.

5. K P Jantke. Case-based learning in inductive inference. In *COLT92 Proceedings of the 5th ACM Workshop on Computational Learning Theory, July 92, Pittsburgh PA*, pages 218–223. ACM Press, 1992.

6. K P Jantke and S Lange. Case-based representation and learning of pattern languages. In *EWCBR-93 Working Notes of the first European Workshop on Case-Based Reasoning*, volume 1, pages 139–144. University of Kaiserslautern, 1993.

7. P Koton and M P Chase. Knowledge representation in a case-based reasoning system: Defaults and exceptions. In R J Brachman and H J Levesque, editors, *Proceedings of the First International Conference on Principles of Knowledge Representation and Reasoning*, pages 203–211. Morgan Kaufmann, 1989.

8. M Mehl. Retrieval in case-based reasoning using preferred subtheories. In G Brewka, K P Jantke, and P Schmitt, editors, *Nonmonotonic and inductive logic (2nd International Workshop)*, pages 284–297. Springer Verlag, 1993.

9. S Wess and C Globig. Case-based and symbolic classification algorithms - A case study using version space. In S Wess, K-D Althoff, and M M Richter, editors, *Topics in CBR: Selected papers from the First European Workshop on Case-Based Reasoning - EWCBR-93, Kaiserslautern, Germany, November '93*, Lecture Notes in Computer Science vol. 837, pages 77–91. Springer-Verlag, 1994.

Beauty vs. the Beast: The Case Against Massively Parallel Retrieval

Dr Mike Brown and Dr Nick Filer

Department. of Computer Science
University of Manchester
Oxford Road
Manchester M13 9PL
UK
(email:michaelb/nick@cs.man.ac.uk)

Abstract

One of the most researched areas of CBR is the task of case retrieval. Several, well-established techniques, such as indexing and similarity-based retrieval, have proven sufficient for relatively small-scale, single-purpose applications. In this paper, a comparative review of different retrieval techniques is given. Memory-driven retrieval is seen as being a new, more powerful and flexible approach though correspondingly the most difficult. Massively parallel marker passing is identified as an appealing implementation medium for memory-driven retrieval. However, this paper questions both the necessity and sufficiency of a brute-force solution alone. Rather, the combination of explicit use of "context" and statistical measures is shown, by example, to allow many retrieval problems to be potentially solved on serial architectures. The paper concludes with a proposal for a general-purpose, hybrid retrieval

Introduction

The research described in this paper focuses on the case retrieval problem. This stage in the CBR process is the most important and one of the most researched. All the following stages are dependent on the ability to retrieve the best (i.e. most appropriate) possible cases from memory. Retrieval from a large memory of cases is a difficult problem. Once retrieval has been achieved the rest of the CBR cycle can be completed via interaction with specialist knowledge based systems or with human experts [26]. The provision of a viable generic case retrieval shell is, therefore, a commercially interesting project and many such systems already exist on the market [10, 3].

CBR becomes particularly potent as a problem solving technique if indirect as well as direct memory retrievals are supported. Direct retrievals from memory can be indexed on many of the features of the case. This, for instance, might use the abilities of a database query language such as SQL [8] to encode complex questions relating diverse features of both the prompt case and multiple stored cases (c.f. [25]). Indirect retrievals inevitably complicate the retrieval problem. For example, figure 1.i shows an illustration of a simple direct (deterministic) retrieval and this can be compared to figure 1.ii which shows an example of an indirect (non-deterministic) retrieval (see also section 2.5). The distinguishing characteristic of non-deterministic retrievals is that they involve a search through memory for an intersection of features which relate to the query but are not made explicit in the query [5]. The area of memory searched can be very large, which has lead to the frequent claim that massively parallel architectures are required to implement this type of retrieval.

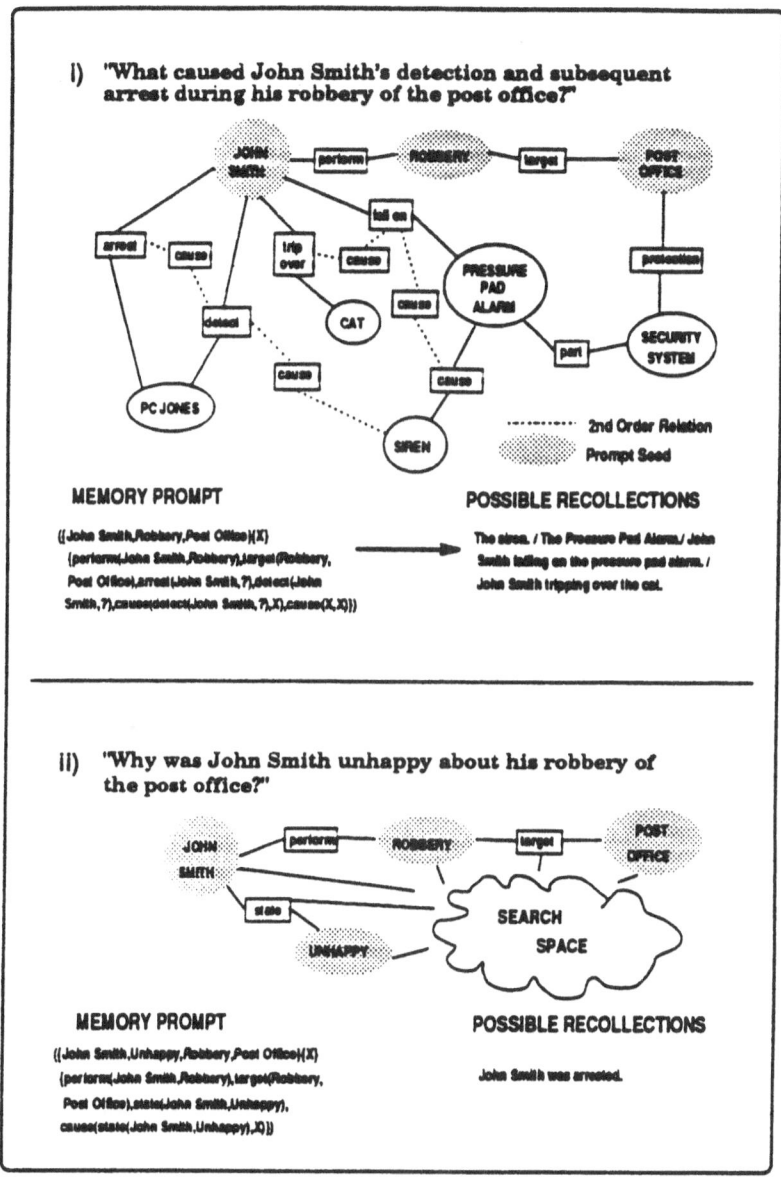

Figure 1: i) An Example of a Deterministic Memory Prompt
ii) An Example of a Non-Deterministic Memory Prompt

The remainder of this paper is structured as follows. In section 2, a comparative study is made of commonly used retrieval techniques. The most sophisticated retrieval technique is identified as memory-driven retrieval. Section 3 explains why the marker-passing paradigm is well suited to the implementation of memory-driven retrieval. Section 4 goes on to describe the appeal that massive parallelism has for implementing marker passing. However, this section also provides a number of examples of how the reliance on parallelism can be reduced by adopting a suitable memory structure. Section 5 concludes with a summary of the paper and outlines a research plan for the development of a powerful, hybrid case retrieval system.

Paradigms for Case Retrieval

In this section, several methods for case retrieval are examined. The purpose is to determine the situations in which each method can be efficiently utilised. Three main criteria are used:

- The nature of the questions the method can respond successfully to.

- How much work must be done in carrying out a retrieval.

- The architecture of the machine on which the method is ideally executed.

As a first step, what is meant by retrieval should be clearly defined. The view adopted is that a memory prompt initiates retrieval and establishes a set of constraints that should be satisfied in order that a returned case be *valid*. If each constraint is taken independently, it can be used to select a subset of the cases in memory. If n constraints are taken from the memory prompt then n corresponding subsets of cases can be retrieved as matches from memory. The intersection of these subsets equates to the set of valid retrievals from the whole prompt.

More formally, let a memory prompt be defined as a tuple $p = S, Q, R$ where; $S = s_1,...,s_k$ represents the initial known facts or "seeds", $Q = q_6$ $_1,...,q_m$ represents requests for additional information and $R = r20_1,...,r_n$ represents the constraints on the retrieval. A valid recollection is one that assigns values to all the elements of Q and for which all the constraints in R hold.

Pattern Matching
The most basic mechanism for retrieval involves selection of data based on a simple string matching function. The method is so important that many efficient algorithms for carrying out serial searches of very large quantities of data exist (e.g.[29]). Examples include the family of "grep" commands in the UNIX[TM] operating system and tree search methods for keyword lookup used in, for example, free text databases.

String search using regular expression grammars is very flexible. Almost every imaginable combination of characters can be matched at a reasonable speed. However, string search does not provide any guidance to the user. The method is susceptible to the choice of an appropriate prompt. Even when an appropriate prompt is used (e.g. exact match of a specified string), the method is not very robust. Many spurious retrievals will almost inevitably accompany the valid ones. Another problem is that string search has no way for semantically close but syntactically different descriptions to be linked in retrieval. Though techniques for solving this last problem do exist [20], they have a much higher matching cost per retrieval.

String search and matching is intrinsically sequential. For each data source, the algorithms proceeds from start to finish. However, coarse-grained parallel implementations are not hard to imagine where multiple data sources are searched at the same time in a distributed environment.

The biggest problem with simple string search is that, as noted above, typical retrievals involve the intersection of the results of several searches. The problem is that only one set per application of the method is retrieved. Also, this set typically contains many spurious retrievals and only a few relevant retrievals. Much wasted effort is therefore expended in finding the appropriate intersection. Even given all these negative points, string search is still a very important retrieval method for small case memories where only a small number of string prompts are used.

Indexing
A step up in sophistication from simple string search is the use of indexes to reduce the cost of searching for data. Indexing requires that the features of cases which are to be used as the basis for *useful* retrieval be predetermined. As indexes permit paths to data to be very efficiently searched, the cost of indexed retrieval is typically much less than the cost of simple string search.

Indexing is suited to applications where a set of features that describe a problem can be easily extracted [1]. The set of features should be capable of being used to describe the complete set of retrieval prompts required to access cases in memory. The definition and representation of indexes is a knowledge engineering problem. For this acquisition problem to be soluble at a reasonable cost, the type of problem to which the indexing technique is applied usually needs to have a fairly narrow scope.

A drawback with indexing is its inflexibility because the access paths to cases are rigidly defined [5, 6] and predetermined. This is sufficient, provided that the set of indexes is complete and will not evolve; if the set of indexes changes (e.g. addition or deletion), all the representations of cases in memory and all the retrieval paths in memory may need to be updated.

Some techniques do exist for widening the scope of data that an index accesses. For example, in [28], index transformation techniques, including; elaboration, mutation, abstraction and generation, are proposed as a general means of increasing the robustness of index-based retrieval by allowing "near-miss" cases to also be retrieved. However, near misses are still a long way from analogy or metaphor, which is required for a case retrieval system to exhibit "intelligent" behaviour [17], nor does index transformation help tackle non-deterministic retrievals.

Indexed retrieval, like string search, is mainly sequential in character. Searches on individual indexes normally involve tree traversal techniques. However, the branches of a tree could be traversed in parallel and hence, each index can be traversed simultaneously. This means that the intersections of multiple indexes can be found by parallel exhaustive traversal of all the cases linked to each index being used. Indexed retrieval also maps well on to database technology and this method is frequently used in case retrieval systems as the main retrieval methodology.

Similarity-Based Retrieval
Similarity-based retrieval can generally be thought of as an extension of indexing. The principle is to define a "similarity metric" to be applied to the cases in memory such that the cases that score most highly are selected. As described in [2], what constitutes a similarity metric varies from some quantitative measure over all case features through to the identification of particular indexes by which cases can be qualitatively compared.

Similarity-based retrieval permits some limited tolerance for noise in the prompt case or stored cases as it is possible to match a prompt case with only subset of the features of a stored case. In this way, the technique implements a form of partial matching retrieval which may appear to be fuzzy.

Clearly, this technique can support parallel access to cases because the similarity metric can be simultaneously applied to all the cases in memory. This has been advocated by many researchers as a means for rapid yet flexible case access (e.g., [9, 13]).

Database Querying
Databases provide the memory infrastructure for most CBR shells [10]. They provide a basis for the controlled storage of very large quantities of data. Modern databases permit complex queries to be matched with the contents of the database. Such queries can include alternative matches and wild cards. They have the capability to retrieve all the cases in memory which exactly match a prompt. However, databases lack robustness to noise and omissions from the initial memory prompt. Recent work [25] on implementation of similarity-based retrieval on top of a database may go some way to solving this problem. However, this method relies on a brute force application of many variants of a memory prompt and is therefore cumbersome. Index transformation, introduced in section 2.2, may be more acceptable in many situations as the secondary search is more localised.

The advance from index driven retrieval to databases is in the ability to construct much more complicated retrieval patterns. Hence, databases are capable of carrying out highly indirect retrievals which are not suited for indexed retrieval techniques alone. These retrieval patterns can, in addition to the directly relevant features of the prompt case, also make use of incidental features. This leads to much greater retrieval flexibility though the direct route to relevant cases provided by indexing is lost. If indexing is to be used to aid indirect retrieval, it may be possible to capture such indirect paths as "abstract case features" [23]. This means that the indirect path into memory is, in effect, hard coded and makes such retrievals more direct and hence efficient. The advantage of the indexing approach to indirect retrieval is that the burden of searching a complex path is removed. The disadvantage is, again, a severe loss of flexibility.

Because database queries often involve conjunctive and disjunctive expressions involving multiple indexes within a single memory retrieval access, it is clearly possible for each combination in the database query to be searched for in parallel [25]. A further parallel access capability is present when either indirect or similarity-based retrieval is required. This derives from the fact that each alternative query can be tried simultaneously in a parallel system.

Memory-Driven Retrieval
It is taken here that the term Memory-Driven Retrieval (MDR) refers to retrieval where the acting constraints are no longer fully determined in the initial prompt; part of the role of retrieval is to uncover further indexes and indirect retrieval paths [5, 14,16, 18, 19, 22]. This requires that the encoding of cases and the links between case features be explicitly represented in memory in a traversable manner. For this retrieval technique, the metaphor of the human brain is frequently adopted and an underlying assumption is that the structure of memory is made up of a large number of relatively simple processing elements [11, 27].

MDR is potentially very powerful and flexible, providing a possible platform for non-deterministic and analogical retrievals to be accomplished [5]. As an illustration, from the example of figure 1, there is no direct representation of why John Smith was unhappy in the case description. There are numerous reasons why he might be upset. Most people can however, make the inference that he was unhappy because he had triggered an alarm and that this could lead to his arrest which is, in turn, an upsetting occurrence. Indeed, there may be a path in memory equivalent to:

> *Being arrested can lead to prosecution. Prosecution can lead to punishment. Punishment is designed to make people feel unhappy.*

Finding this information in memory requires an indirect search through a network of world knowledge as the constraints in the initial prompt are not adequate to completely define the required retrieval path. In large-scale memories, the search space to be navigated is gigantic. Powerful heuristics may be required, both to make the search space more tractable and to filter the retrieved cases so that the relevant cases are not swamped by a large number of incidental cases.

The most famous attempt at constructing a very large knowledge base is the CYC [18] project. In CYC, a pragmatic approach to the memory search problem is adopted. The massive knowledge base is represented at two levels (with automated translation supported between them); the *epistemological* level where a single, generic representation language and reasoning technique are used, and a *heuristic* level where search is made tractable via an *ad hoc* collection of specialised inference rules, purpose-specific representations, meta-reasoners. The heuristic level can be thought of as an optimisation to deal with commonly occurring query types. In contrast, the techniques for efficient MDR proposed in section 4 are more generic, though the knowledge that they capture is of a similar pragmatic nature to that in CYC's heuristic level.

Clearly, MDR is ideal for parallel implementation. Each possible case feature that is explored provides paths to many other case features. The search of each path between case features can be carried out simultaneously. More coarse-grained parallelism may also be possible; for MDR, the construction of the set associated with each constraint in the initial memory prompt itself involves a search problem. Each of these individual searches can potentially be implemented simultaneously.

Summary
This section has compared a number of methods for implementing case retrieval from memory. The results are depicted in figure 2.

There has been a rough trend towards the provision of greater `retrieval power' through the sections, where retrieval power is some combination of the filtering power of the retrieval technique and its potential flexibility. This trend has been offset by an inverse trend towards greater complexity, space cost and reduced search efficiency. However, the possible exploitation of parallel implementation architecture's for case retrieval (especially massively parallel methods) has also been examined. Each of the techniques to some extent can be implemented in a parallel environment. However, the only method which is inherently based on a parallel architecture is MDR which also provides the most powerful retrieval capability. In the next section, marker passing is advocated as the ideal implementation technique for MDR. The presumption of the need for a massively parallel implementation for marker passing is, however, questioned in section 4.

Retrieval Methods	Parallel Applicability	Flexibility	Initial Filtering Ability
Pattern Matching	Weak Coarse grain	Fairly Good	Very weak
Indexing	Less weak Exaustive parallel tree search	Weak	Good
Similarity Based	Good	Fairly Good	Fairly Good
Data Base Query	Quite good Several possibilities	Good	Very good
Memory Driven	Very good	Very good	Needs help!

Figure 2: Comparing Different Retrieval Techniques

Retrieval by Marker Passing

Marker passing is a technique that performs search through a network-based knowledge representation using local rules contained within the nodes of the network[11]. Reasoning, such as the inferences required to complete a non-deterministic retrieval in MDR, is performed by passing markers from node to node; a process that, if properly controlled, can permit meaningful paths through the network to be extracted[7, 15]. Markers typically carry some rudimentary information ranging from a simple type tag through to a more complex description of the path so far taken by the marker. The control of the transportation of markers is governed by localised information, contained in the node possessing the marker, the immediate neighbours of that node and in the marker itself.

It is the localised control of marker passing that makes it an ideal candidate for parallelism. Each node in the network representation can be considered to be a single processing elements [11]. The data dependencies between the processing elements is confined to the immediate neighbourhood, hence, there is little communication overhead to cripple the parallelism. Recently, novel computing architectures, such as SNAP [21], have been created for precisely this type of application, bringing the goal of massively parallel MDR in large-scale knowledge bases one step closer to fruition. However, the need for such expensive computing resources is questioned below.

Serial vs. Massive Parallel Retrieval

The advantage of massive parallelism can be pin-pointed as the ability to perform the set intersection task, identified in section 2 as fundamental to case retrieval, in a single time step [11]. Consider the following example taken from the literature:

"John wanted to commit suicide. John got a rope.

Most people readily make the connecting inference that John intends to use the rope as a hang-noose. However, to make this inference in a network representation requires an indirect search. The advocates of massively parallel marker passing would claim that the only way to make this inference is as follows:

1.   Place a "1" marker on the "rope" node.
2.   Find all possible uses of "rope".
3.   Place a "2" marker on the "suicide node".
4.   Find all possible methods of "suicide".
5.   Extract any nodes (i.e. "hanging") that have received both "1" and "2" markers.

For a massively parallel implementation, steps 2 and 4 take a single time step, whereas for a serial implementation these two steps potentially take a time proportional to the size of the two sets of nodes accessed.

Appealing though the parallel implementation solution is, there are problems. The first problem is that, if the number of candidate solutions is high, or where the search for an intersection involves an indirect search (i.e. retrieval is non-deterministic), massively parallel marker passing alone is *insufficient* to select the best items of knowledge from memory. For example, consider again the non-deterministic retrieval of figure 1. Assuming that the knowledge base contains a comprehensive model of the world, many reasons may be represented as to why a person could be unhappy and hence, a plethora of answers as to why John Smith is unhappy will be retrieved; the system suffers from an "embarrassment of riches" [5, chp 3]. Precisely this type of problem plagued early marker-passing systems used for sentence comprehension tasks, such as Charniak's WIMP system [7]. The problem is that additional constraints and heuristics, must be used to prioritise the candidate recollections.

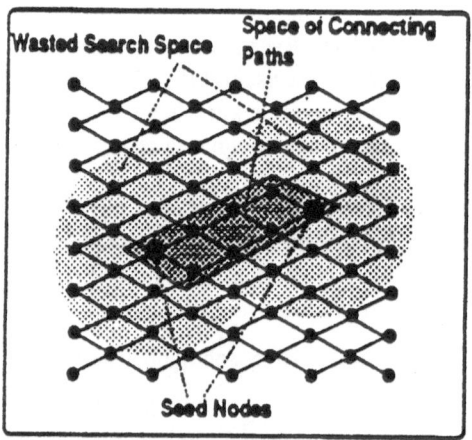

Figure 3: The Search Space for Set Intersection

The general combinatorial problem with searching any network data structure is that the search space grows exponential with distance travelled. This means that in performing the set intersection problem by exhaustive search, a large amount of the effort is wasted, as depicted in figure 3. If one assumes that the required additional knowledge is available for the selection of the best few candidates from the many possible, an intriguing possibility is that this knowledge can be used to constrain retrieval at an earlier stage. This could prune the explosive search space sufficiently to allow for a serial implementation of marker passing retrieval (see figure 4); that is to say, massively parallel marker passing may also be *unnecessary*. This was the inspiration for the development of the CRASH system [4, 5, 6]. Two types of constraining knowledge identified are "context" and statistical measures. How each of these may be used to solve the above "suicide" example is explained below.

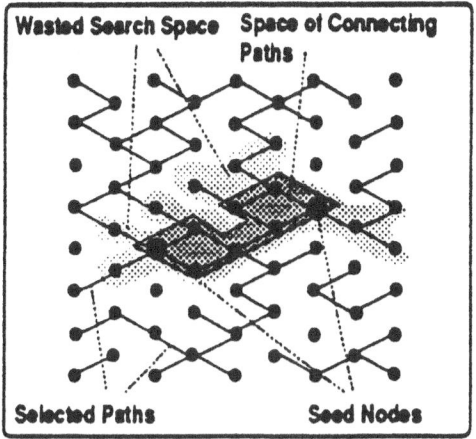

Figure 4: The General Effect of Pruning on the Set Intersection Search Space

Context

Context is taken to be a meta-level relationship that is orthogonal to the actual relationships that connect the knowledge items held within memory. Context is realised as an explicit link from a given knowledge item to all relationships in the network which are selected by that knowledge item [4]. An example is shown in figure 9. In this example, context links have been inserted from the "suicide" node to all appropriate relationships between it and "rope". With these context links in place, as soon as both "suicide" and "rope" receive a marker, the passage of markers from "rope" to "suicide" can become guided by context and no deviation from the desired path will then occur (assuming no other contexts are currently activated). It follows that, in this way, the search space can be sufficiently pruned to allow for a serial implementation.

In general, there is a trade-off between the number of context links used (space efficiency) and the directness of the search patterns they produce in memory (computation efficiency) [5, chp 3]. It follows that context links should only be used where they are most cost effective:

- For paths where there is potentially a high "fan-out" in the search space; i.e., the effect of a new context link is high.
- For paths which have been empirically determined as of high value (for example due to their repeated navigation during retrieval); i.e. a new context link has high benefit.

Context links are, therefore, a means for partially hard-coding successful paths through memory after repeated use, but do not necessarily aid in the discovery of such paths.

Statistical Measures

In a structured case memory, statistical measures can be derived, for example based on the frequency of occurrence of a particular case feature [6]. A statistical measure of particular importance for guiding retrieval is *typicality* [5]. Informally, this is a measure of the proportion of all cases in memory for which a particular relationship holds. In a serial implementation of marker passing, the set of relationships branching out from a given node will be searched one after another. Selecting to traverse the most typical relationships first is a powerful control heuristic for retrieval because it means that the inductive principle that "what held true most often in the past is most likely to be true in the future" is a bias on the search process.

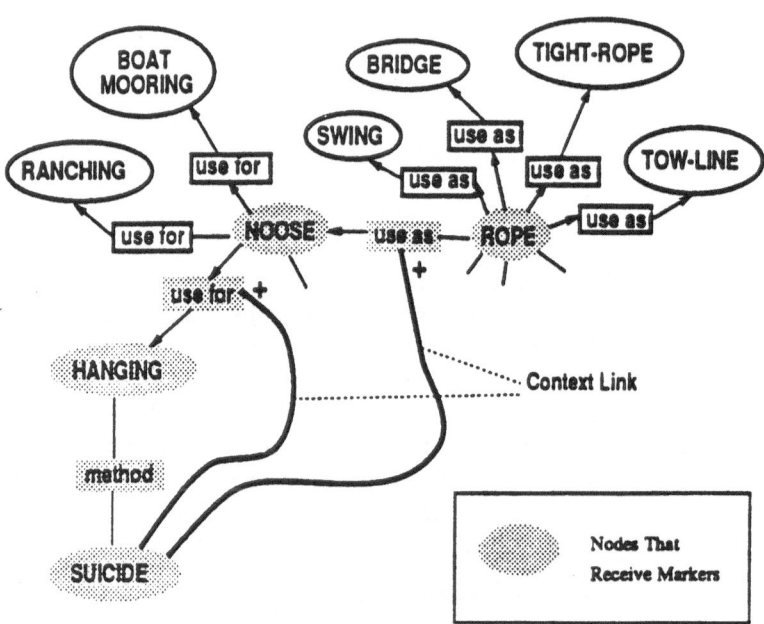

Figure 5: Contextual Strengthening of Intersecting Paths

As an example, reconsider the suicide example shown in figure 6. In this example, a set of plausible typicality values have been placed on the relationships associated with "suicide" and "rope". In this case, the search space is greatly reduced simply because "hanging" is a highly typical form of suicide; once this node is selected, the effort required to complete the path to "rope" is exponentially decreased. Although typicality cannot guarantee that some deviation from this path does not occur (such as considering "over-dose" as a method of "suicide"), in many circumstances, it may be a sufficient constraint to allow the search space to be navigated by a serial implementation of marker passing.

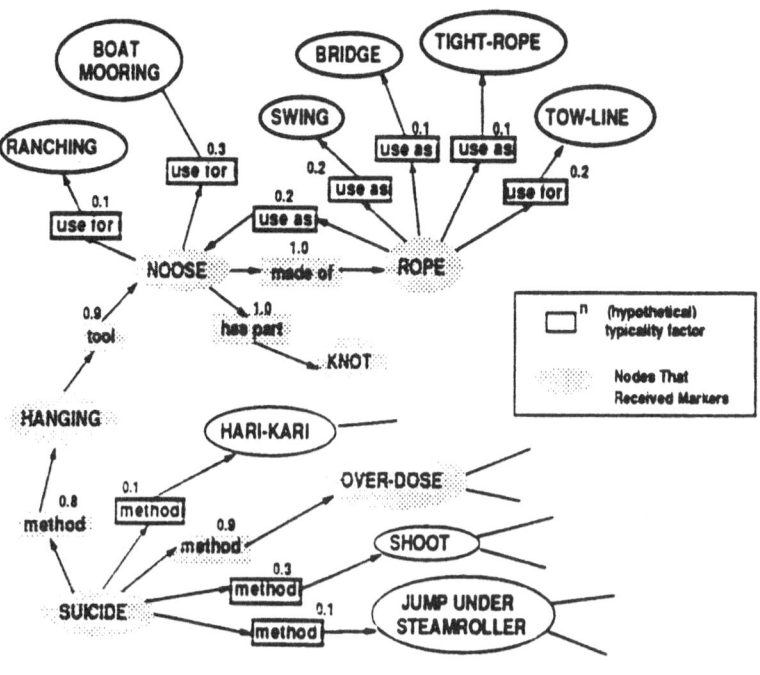

Figure 6: Typicality as a Heuristic Guide to Path Generation

In order not to effect the tractability of retrieval, statistical measures, such as typicality, must be determined prior to retrieval. This is a trade-off as it limits their discriminating power. For example, an approach is suggested in [22] whereby measurements are not determined statically, based on all cases in memory, but dynamically, based only on those selected candidate cases for a retrieval. In this way, the statistical measures are tailored to the conditions of the specific retrieval, but the computational expense of retrieval is greatly increased (i.e. massive parallelism is required).

In summary, context and statistics provide powerful constraints that allow for the tractable completion of many retrieval problems without resorting to the brute-force of massive parallelism. This is not intended as a complete negation of the need for parallel implementations in all circumstances, merely a recognition that, for many retrieval problems, the brute-force approach is not required nor desirable (due to the excess of irrelevant recollections it can produce). From the above, parallel marker passing is required if:

- Context links have not yet been placed on the retrieval path; either this is the first navigation of the path or the path has yet to gain sufficient importance to warrant the creation of context links along it.

- The information required from memory is out of the ordinary, hence its selection cannot be guided by statistical measures.
- The number of cases in memory that satisfy the prompt is low; much searching is required to find a valid recollection.

In other words, massive parallelism is reserved as a safety net technique to be used in the occasional circumstances when the in built constraints of a structured representation of memory fail to contain the explosive search or fail to find appropriate information.

Conclusions

This paper has provided an in-depth discussion of general issues concerning case retrieval. A range of qualitatively different retrieval techniques have been considered with respect to a number of practical issues. These issues include: the types of retrieval problem for which the technique is suited, the computational properties of the technique and its suitability for parallel implementation.

The most powerful retrieval technique identified is memory-driven reasoning which is seen to have sufficient flexibility to deal with non-deterministic and indirect retrievals but at the cost of navigating a potentially vast search space. Massively parallel marker passing has been seen as one potential solution to this problem, but a tacit reliance on a brute-force approach has been questioned. The use of additional knowledge constraints, such as the explicit representation of context and statistical weighting, has been put forward as an alternative that allows for a serial implementation of MDR.

Current Status and Future Work

This work has stemmed directly from the research surrounding the CRASH case retrieval tool [5], a serial implementation of activation passing for MDR. There are other relevant research projects also in a mature state at the University of Manchester. Noteworthy amongst these is current work concerning the development of a generic interface for database access [12]. This provides the basis for a number of extremely powerful data manipulation tools, including a generic mapping engine to support the automated translation from one data format to another (e.g. as for schema evolution), based on the work of [24].

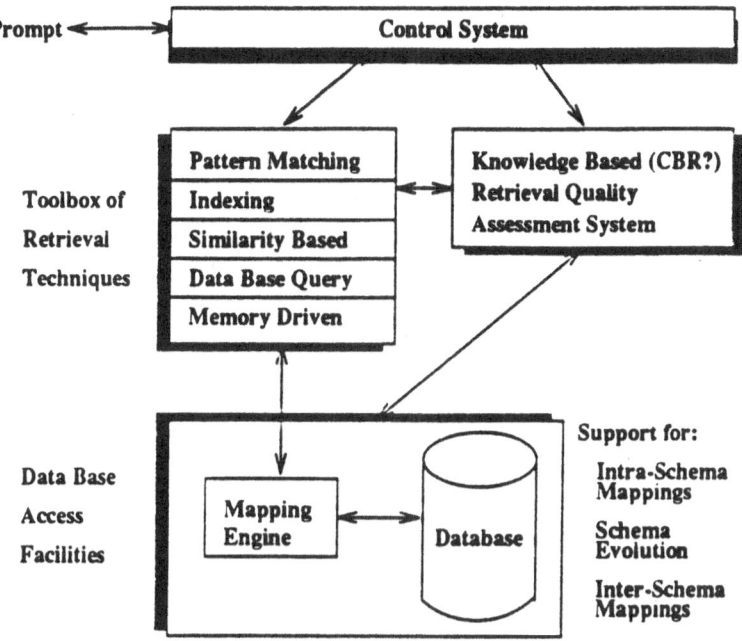

Figure 7: A Proposed Architecture for a Novel Case Retrieval Tool

The direction for future work is to amalgamate these research projects in the development of a general-purpose shell for case retrieval. A proposed architecture for such a shell is shown in figure 7. The architecture consists of a number of different functional modules:

- **Retrieval Technique Toolbox**: This will provide a range of basic retrieval techniques, such as discussed in section 2, including an MDR component based on CRASH. Each technique will involve an idiosyncratic representation of the case base tailored to the mechanics of the retrieval technique involved. Nevertheless, all retrieval techniques will be built upon the same set of underlying database access facilities.

- **Database Access Facilities**: This will exploit the flexibility of the existing, generic interface [12] to insulate the representation of the cases (as used by the various retrieval techniques) from the specifics of the actual database used for data storage. In addition, a number of important mapping facilities will be provided. Firstly, *intra-schema mappings* will be supported, for example, to connect the various components in a distributed case representation [9]. This is particularly useful where multiple views of a single case are possible, such as in support of multi-purpose case bases. Secondly, *schema evolution* facilities will allow the representation of a single case to be modified overtime, with the mapping relationships between each case schema version being maintained. This lends support for novel research into learning algorithms. These algorithms go beyond simple restructuring of memory and induction of general rules to changing the way a case is represented (e.g. trimming irrelevant features or allowing the case description to be extended with new feature types). Finally, *inter-schema mappings* will allow for the possibility of forging links between cases in separate case bases, perhaps in separate knowledge domains. This type of mapping is particularly pertinent to the notion of memory-driven retrieval, as discussed in this paper.

- **Retrieval Assessment Unit:** The aim of having a toolbox of retrieval techniques is to support their *co-operative* work. In order to support this aim, the retrieval assessment unit must monitor the progress of each retrieval technique and provide appropriate information to the control system. For example, through profiling of the search performed during retrieval, this unit may be able to heuristically determine if a given retrieval prompt is deterministic or non-deterministic which heavily inluences the selection of appropriate retrieval strategy). One task that needs to be performed prior to construction of this module is to more rigorously define the circumstances under which each retrieval technique functions best.

- **Control System**: This module has the task of assigning (and possibly reassigning) the retrieval technique(s) to best suit a given memory prompt. This will rely largely on a heuristic body of knowledge concerning characterisation of the complexity of a given memory prompt and characterisation of the search power of each retrieval technique. In addition, provision for a combined serial and parallel implementation is to be considered. In accordance with section 4, resorting to massively parallel retrieval should only be adopted in circumstances where serial retrieval is most likely to fail. Resolving this decision will be another duty of the control system.

References

[1] Kevin D Ashley. Indexing and Analytic Models. In Proceedings of the Case-Based Reasoning Workshop, pages 197--202.Morgan Kaufmann Publishers, 1989.

[2] R Bareiss, J King, K Ashley, J Kolodner, B Porter, and P Thagard. Panel Discussion on ``Similarity Metrics''. In Proceedings of the Case-Based Reasoning Workshop, Pensacola Beach, Florida, 1989. Morgan Kaufmann Publishers.

[3] Ralph Barletta. A Hybrid Indexing and Retrieval Strategy for Advisory CBR Systems Built With ReMind. In EWCBR-94, Proceedings of the Second European Workshop on Case-Based Reasoning, pages 49--58, Chantilly, France, November 1994.

[4] Mike G Brown. Incorporating Similarity Measures Into Case Retrieval Using Analogue Marker Passing. In Bernd Neumann, editor, ECAI-92, Proceedings of the Tenth European Conference on Artificial Intelligence., pages 590--592, Vienna, Austria, August 1992. John Wiley and Sons, Inc.

[5] Mike G Brown. A Memory Model for Case Retrieval by Activation Passing. PhD thesis, University of Manchester, 1993.

[6] Mike G Brown. An Under-Lying Memory Model to Support Case Retrieval. In Lecture Notes in Artificial Intelligence - Topics in Case-Based Reasoning, volume 837, pages 132--143, Kaiserslautern, Germany, 1994.Springer-Verlag. EWCBR-93: The First European Workshop, EWCBR - selected papers.

[7] Eugene Charniak. A Neat Theory of Marker Passing. In AAAI-86, Proceedings of the Fifth National Conference on Artificial Intelligence, pages 584--588, Philadelphia, 1986. Morgan Kaufmann Publishing.

[8] C.J.Date. A Guide to the SQL Standard. Addison Wesley, 2 edition, 1989.

[9] Diane J Cook. The Base Selection Task in Analogical Planning. In IJCAI 91, Proceedings of the Twelfth International Joint Conference On Artificial Intelligence, volume 2, pages 790--795, Sydney, Australia, 1991. Morgan Kaufmann Publishers, Inc.

[10] Paul Harmon (editor). Case-Based Reasoning: A Review of CBR Products. Intelligent Software Strategies, 8(1), January 1992.r

[11] Scott E Fahlman. NETL, A System for Representing and Using Real-World Knowledge. The MIT Press, 1979.

[12] Nick Filer, Mike Brown, and Zahir Moosa. Integrating CAD Tools into a Framework Environment Using a Flexible and Adaptable Procedural Interface. In Proceedings of EURO-DAC '94, Grenoble, 1994. IEEE-CS Press.

[13] Kenneth D Forbus and Dedre Gentner. MAC/FAC: A Model of Similarity-based Retrieval. In Proceedings of the Thirteenth Annual Conference of the Cognitive ScienceSociety., pages 504--509, Chicargo, Illinois, August 1991. Lawrence Erlbaum Associates.

[14] James A Hendler. Marker Passing over Microfeatures: Towards a Hybrid Symbolic/Connectionist Model. Cognitive Science, 13:pp79--106, 1989.

[15] Trent E. Lange and Michael G. Dyer. Frame Selection in a Connectionist Model of High-Level Inferencing. In Proceedings of the Eleventh Annual Conference ofthe Cognitive Science Society., pages 706--713, Ann Arbor, Michigan, August 1991. Lawrence Erlbaum Associates.

[16] Trent E Lange and Charles M Wharton. Analysis of an Integrated Comprehension and Episodic Memory Retrieval Model. In IJCAI-93: Proceedings of the Thirteenth International Joint Conference on Artificial Intelligence., pages 208--213, Chambry, France, 1993.

[17] Douglas B Lenat and Edward F Feigenbaum. On the Thresholds of Knowledge. In IJCAI 87: Proceedings of the Tenth International Joint Conference on Artificial Intelligence, pages 1172--1176, Milan, August 1987. Morgan Kaufmann Publishers.

[18] Douglas B Lenat, Ramanathan V Guha, Karen Pittman, Dexter Pratt, and Mary Shepherd. CYC: Towards Programs with Common Sense. Communications of the ACM, 33(8):30--49, August 1990.

[19] Charles Eugene Martin. Direct Memory Access Parsing. PhD thesis, Yale University, 1991.

[20] Salvador Mir. Heuristic Reasoning for an Automatic Commonsense Understanding of Logic Electronic Design Specifications. PhD thesis, The University of Manchester, 1993.

[21] Dan Moldovan, Wing Lee, Changhwa Lin, and Minhwa Chung. SNAP: Parallel Processing Applied to AI. Technical Report PKPL 91-3, University of Southern California,Dept. of Electrical Engineering Systems, University of Southern California, University Park, LA, August 1991.

[22] Christopher Owens. Domain-Independent Prototype Cases for Planning. In Janet Kolodner, editor, Proceedings of the Case-BasedReasoning Workshop, Florida, May 1988. Morgan Kaufmann Publishers.

[23] Christopher Owens. Plan Transformations as Abstract Indicies. In Proceedings of the Case-Based Reasoning Workshop, pages 62--65. Morgan Kaufmann Publishers, 1989.

[24] Paul K. C. Pun. Knowledge-Based Applications= Knowledge-Base + Mappings + Application. PhD thesis, The University of Manchester, 1991.

[25] Hideo Shimazu, Hiroaki Kitano, and Akihiro Shibata. Retrieving Cases from Relational Database s: Another Stride Towards Corporate-Wide Case Base Systems. In IJCAI-93, Proceedings of the 13th International Joint Conference On Artificial Intelligence, pages 909--914, Chabry, 1993. Morgan Kaufmann Publishers.

[26] Evangelos Simoudis and James Miller. The Application of CBR to Help Desk Applications. In Proceedings: Case-Based Reasoning Workshop, pages 25--36, Washington, D.C., 1991.

[27] Craig Stanfill and David Waltz. Towards Memory-Based Reasoning. Communications of the ACM, 29(12):1213--1228, December 1986.

[28] Katia P Sycara and D Navinchandra. Index Transformation and Generation for Case Retrieval. In Proceedings of the Case-Based Reasoning Workshop, pages 324--328. Morgan Kaufmann Publishers, 1989.

[29] Rui Feng Zhu and Tadao Takaoka. A Technique for Two-Dimensional Pattern Matching. Communications of the ACM, 32(9), September 1989.

Self-Questioning and Experimentation: An Index Vocabulary of Situated Interaction

Ruediger Oehlmann   Peter Edwards   Derek Sleeman

Department of Computing Science
University of Aberdeen
King's College
ABERDEEN, AB9 2UE,
Scotland, UK.
email: {oehlmann, pedwards, sleeman}@csd.abdn.ac.uk

Abstract

Various cognitive and computational models have addressed the use of previous experience to understand a new domain. In particular, research in case-based reasoning has explored the ideas of retrieving and adapting previous experience in the form of cases. If the cases take the form of plans, the process is referred to as case-based planning. We have developed a computational model of Exploratory Discovery which integrates case-based reasoning and case-based planning. Motivated by results from cognitive science, we incorporated into this model features for improving the learning process such as *exploration* and *self-questioning*. This paper will focus on the index vocabulary needed to accomplish the interaction between the generation of self-questions and the experimentation process. This interaction depends on questions asked, answers given, and previously performed experiments; interaction is therefore situated.

Continuous Case-Based Reasoning

When people are exposed to an unfamiliar task such as understanding a new device, they are sometimes reminded of previous experience in other domains. Cognitive models of reminding have evolved in an attempt to explain this phenomenon (e.g. Ross 1989). The concept of re-use of previous experience has been exploited in the paradigm of case-based reasoning where previous experience is usually represented as cases (see Kolodner 1993 for an overview). There is a strong mutual relationship between cognitive models of reminding and case-based reasoning. Perhaps the most crucial issues in case-based reasoning are the retrieval and modification of previous cases. Both processes use indexes which describe the content of a case and reflect the current understanding of the reasoner. Often a case contains the description of a problem and its solution. If, in contrast, the case is a plan which contains a sequence of actions, we refer to the process as case-based planning (Hammond 1989).

The idea of incorporating plans to facilitate the learning process has been supported by results from cognitive science. Schauble et al. (1991) and Sternberg (1981) suggested that learning is improved if the learner makes use of plans. Additional psychological experiments indicate that human learning can be further improved by the use of self-questions, i.e. questions which are generated and answered by the learner. We have demonstrated elsewhere that self-questions can be used to change the direction of a case-based reasoning process and to avoid reasoning failures

(Oehlmann, Edwards, & Sleeman 1994). This is accomplished by planning questions in response to a question situation characterised by previous questions, answers, and experiments which are generated by the system.

Most of the work on self-questioning investigates how self-questions can be used to improve reading abilities (see the review of Wong 1985). AI systems which read a text and attempt to understand it by generating self-questions are AQUA (Ram 1991) and its successor Meta-AQUA (Ram & Cox 1994). The influential results of Wong and Jones (1982) demonstrated that the reading comprehension of learning disabled students can be improved by self-questioning. Miyake and Norman (1979) pointed out that the generation of self-questions is constrained. One of these constraints is content knowledge. If prior knowledge is available, it enables the student to formulate a question on a given topic and to evaluate the answer. If, on the other hand, the relevant knowledge is missing, the student's ability to ask questions is restricted. Unfortunately, work which addresses issues of self-questioning does not investigate how question generation is changed by a surprising answer or a situation in which a question cannot be answered. Indirect evidence, however, is given by experiments reported by Schauble et al. (1991). Their subjects had to discover laws, such as Ohm's and Kirchhoff's laws, by self-directed experimentation in a computer circuit laboratory. The results demonstrated that good learners are characterised by two exploratory abilities; they perform more controlled experiments and they rarely use characteristic paths through the space of possible circuits. Although their subjects did not use explicit question strategies, they applied implicit strategies to the selection of circuit components and the measurement of voltage.

To date, case-based reasoning and case-based planning have largely been treated as separate research issues. Case-based reasoners do not typically interact with the environment and case-based planners do not typically interact with a case library reflecting a (partial) state of the environment. Furthermore, case-based reasoning and case-based planning have typically been implemented as "one-step" processes: a previous case is retrieved and adapted to the current situation, then the process stops. A solution generated as a result of a case-based reasoning process is not used to initiate a new case-based reasoning process. In contrast, the human reasoning process has been viewed as a continuous "stream of thoughts"(James 1981). When we follow this view, we have to regard generation of questions or experiments as being dependent on the generation of previous questions and experiments; i.e. the process of generating a question is a situated interaction24 with previous episodes of question and experiment generation.

We view the situated interaction as an instance of the theory of situated activity (Agre & Chapman 1987). A core idea in this theory is that complex behaviour can emerge from simple situation-action rules which depend on a changing world. Agre and Chapman's theory appears to be influenced by Suchman's (1987) work on situated actions and Brook's concept of emerging behaviour which has been discussed in Brooks (1991). Suchman takes the view that the nature of actions depends on a priori specifications of a given situation in which the action is to be performed. Brooks argues that the behaviour of a given system should emerge from the interactions of simple system components. Attempts to integrate the views of case-based reasoning and situated activity have been discussed by McDougal (1993) and Sooriamurthi & Leake (1994).

The situated interaction between self-questioning and experimentation motivates our approach to continuous case-based reasoning. This approach is referred to as Exploratory Discovery and has been implemented in the IULIAN system. Whereas cases in the standard case-based reasoning approach describe states, plans are descriptions of processes. The IULIAN system has to maintain states as well as processes; therefore case-based reasoning and case-based planning are integrated. In addition, the system is able to execute plans which modify the environment. Such modifications are represented in memory as new cases which, in turn, influence future planning. The planning of self-questions leads to the planning of experiments and the experimental results lead to new questions. Therefore interaction between case-based question planning and experimentation planning sustains a continuous process of reminding.

To use case-based plans, they have to be stored under suitable indexes. It has been argued that a plan index should reflect the content of a given plan (Schank & Osgood 1990). The content of the question, answer, and experimentation plans used in our Exploratory Discovery approach is related to the interaction between self-questioning and experimentation. If we wish to capture the content of this interaction, we have to ask what it means in a given situation to be able to ask a particular question or to perform a particular experiment. Moreover, we have to ask what it means when a particular piece of information is missing. Answering these questions will lead to a content-theory of interactions between question planning and experimentation planning. Similar content theories which provide appropriate index vocabularies have been developed for story indexing (Schank & Osgood 1990), multi-agent planning, (Goldweic & Hammond 1992), and indexing social situations (Domeshek 1992).

We have investigated the process of Exploratory Discovery in our system IULIAN. In Section 2, we will describe an overview of the system and its data structures. The overview will be followed by an example of continuous reminding based on self-questions and experiments (Section 3). In Section 4, we will describe the index vocabulary which describes the situated interaction between question, answer, and experimentation planning. Finally in Section 5, we will discuss the vocabulary.

The IULIAN System - A Top Level View

In this section, we describe a top-level view of our implementation IULIAN. Figure 1 shows the main modules of the system: question planner, answer planner, experiment planner, and hypothesis formation. The system attempts to generate an explanation suitable to revise an initial theory. The Question Planner module accepts a problem description as input, generates a question about the problem, and transfers control to the Answer Planner. If a question cannot be answered, the Question Planner and the 4 Experiment Planner can be used to generate additional questions and experiments which help the IULIAN system recover from this situation and to provide the knowledge needed to generate the answer. Before an experiment is performed, the Hypothesis Formation module hypothesises the experimental result. When the actual result is generated, the Hypothesis Formation module determines, when appropriate, an expectation failure as the difference between the hypothesis and the actual result.

If an expectation failure has been detected, the exploration process is initiated. At its simplest, the processes of question and answer generation are based on the Question Planner and the Answer Planner which generate a question about the problem and attempt to answer it. The answer returned should be wrong because if the correct information were known, IULIAN would have generated the correct hypothesis and the expectation failure would not have occurred. If a question cannot be answered, the Question Planner and the Experiment Planner can again be used to generate additional questions and experiments in an attempt to provide the missing knowledge.

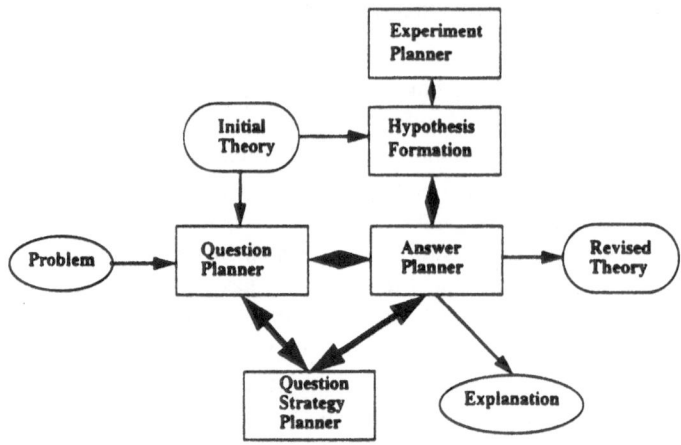

Figure 1: The IULIAN System

All the plans needed to generate questions, answers, and experiments contain indexes which are used to retrieve an appropriate plan. The indexes are the main instruments used to control the generation of sequences of questions and answers. In addition, the Question Planner can be used to generate sequences of questions and answers.

The basic data components of the IULIAN system are experiments, causal models, and plans which are used as cases. An experiment consists of two components: an experimental setting (e.g. a description of an statement that "the lamp is on when the battery is switched on". Experiments are represented electric circuit with battery, lamp, and switch) and the result of an experiment such as the by objects and relations between objects. Objects are represented as Memory Units (MU)1 which contain an object frame, a context24 frame and a content frame (Figure 2). The context frame

---

[1] MUs are similar to the Universal Index Frame (Schank & Osgood, 1990).

describes the context in which the object occurs represented by a set of relations. The content frame comprises several sets of intentional descriptor values referred to as views. The object frame comprises general information about the object. In addition to experiments, causal models are used to explain experimental results. Causal models have a similar representation to experiments. However, they are stored in a separate library and their objects are viewed as abstract concepts, e.g. the concept "lamp" rather than an actual lamp used in a given experiment (Oehlmann 1992). In addition, causal models use particular relations between concepts to represent causal links. A causal model is linked to the experiment used to generate that model. Question plans are used to apply case-based planning techniques to the generation of single questions. The elementary actions which the planner executes combine question substructures to form a complete question. For example, the question "What does the PIN-WHEEL turn?" can be built by combining the substructures "What", "does", "turn", "the", and OBJECT1. OBJECT1 is a variable which can be instantiated with the string "PIN-WHEEL ". A question plan has two main parts: the set of descriptors used for indexing the plan and a sequence of steps, see Figure 3.

The plan is retrieved by matching its index with the current situation; this is characterised by the goals the system pursues in asking the question. Additional slots in the head of each question plan contain a list of variable instantiations referred to as bindings and a set of collector slots. The bindings are used to instantiate variables in the step actions. In the collector slots, intermediate results are stored during the question formation process. Each planning step has precondition, goal, and action slots to ensure correct plan execution. If plan execution fails, the usual explanation-based repair mechanisms are employed, see Hammond, Marks, & Converse (1993). These mechanisms use pre-stored repair rules and are based on preconditions and goals.

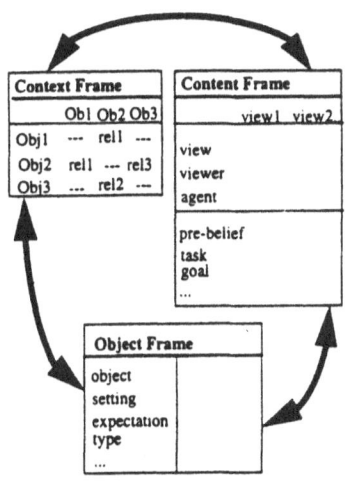

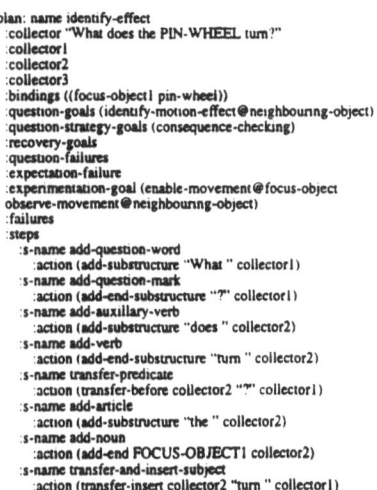

Figure 2: Memory Unit   Figure 3: Question Plan

An important advantage of the case-based planning approach is that new questions can be learned by modifying previous question plans. Answers are generated in a way similar to the generation of questions; however, steps in answer plans may have particular actions which retrieve knowledge from the case-base needed to form an answer. Question strategies are higher level plans which organise the execution of single question and answer plans to generate questions in a particular sequence. The same basic plan structure used for question and answer plans has been employed for experimentation plans, although the index vocabulary differs (Oehlmann, Sleeman, Edwards, 1993). Experimentation plans describe the steps which have to be executed to perform an experiment. The experimental setting and the result of plan execution are stored as a new experiment.

An Example of Situated Interactions

Before we describe the details of the index vocabulary, we will discuss the core of an example which illustrates question and experiment generation (Figure 4).The entire example and the questions used during the reasoning process are described in (Oehlmann, Sleeman, & Edwards 1992).

We assume that the IULIAN system receives as input the description of an electric circuit with lamp and closed switch in parallel (target domain). Associated with the description of the circuit (target case) is an experimental (target) plan to build the circuit by connecting the various components and to observe the status of the lamp. The lamp is reported as being off, as a result of this experiment. This result is inconsistent with the system's expectation based on a previous case involving a serial circuit in which the lamp was on. The situation characterised by this expectation failure (partially) matches the index of a question plan for generating a why question which would attempt to identify an explanation for the expectation failure. IULIAN is able to retrieve the question plan but not an appropriate answer plan, because the explanation has not been stored. This new situation determines an index for retrieving the question strategy ANALOGICAL MAPPING which supports analogical case retrieval between domains, see Carbonell 1993. Executing the first step of the question strategy initialises the retrieval and execution of a question plan to generate an additional top level question. An appropriate answer plan can now be retrieved and executed; the generated answer comprises a (source) case in the domain of water pipes (source domain). The interplay between the execution of question and answer plans has actually lead to case-retrieval (reminding) across domain boundaries (Oehlmann, Edwards, & Sleeman 1995).

In the source case a plain pipe and a paddle wheel are in parallel. Additionally the observation that the paddle wheel does not turn is stored in the source case, which is associated with both a causal model and the source plan. A summary of the causal model is given below:

> In order for the paddle wheel to turn, water must flow over it. There is a
> plain pipe in parallel with the paddle wheel. The smaller the resistance in a

given pipe, the greater is the water flow in this pipe. If one of two parallel pipes has a very low resistance and the other one has a very high resistance, most of the water flows through the pipe with low resistance. Since the paddle wheel offers resistance to the flow and the plain pipe does not, all of the water flow goes through the plain pipe. Since there is no water flow over the paddle wheel, the paddle wheel does not move.

The source model can not be applied to the original electric circuit, because the switch and the plain pipe are not sufficiently similar. Therefore, the source plan is transformed into a new source plan able to generate a new source case which is sufficiently similar to the target case (Oehlmann, Sleeman, & Edwards 1993)

During plan transformation, IULIAN replaces the step which refers to the insertion of a plain pipe by a step which refers to the insertion of a valve. The valve is more similar to the switch in the target domain, because both components are used to pursue the goal "select:flow interruption/flow-support". In addition, the system inserts a step which opens the valve.

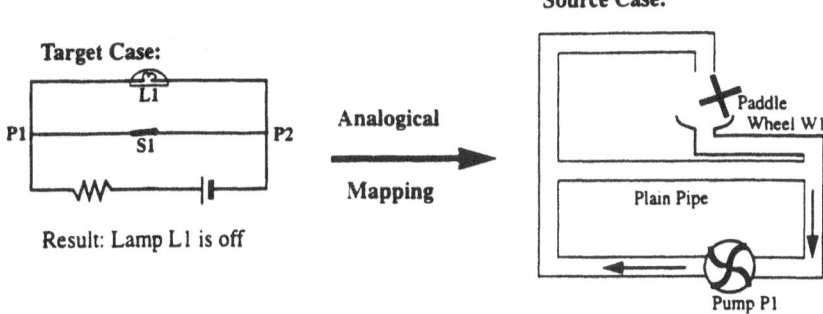

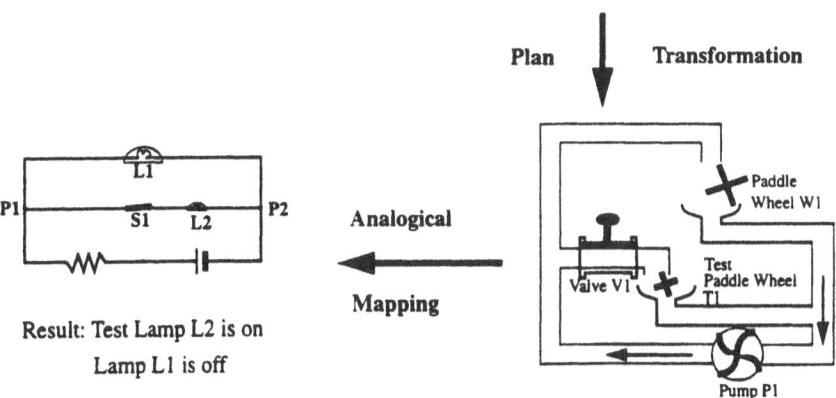

Figure 4: The Electric Circuit Example

Once the transformation process is finished, two additional reasoning stages are needed. First, the reasoner has to collect evidence that the causal model associated with the source case is valid for the transformed source case. Second, the reasoner has to modify the causal model to make it applicable to the target case, and it then has to ensure that the modified causal model is valid for this case.

The first stage can be achieved by modifying the transformed plan (Hammond1989). During the modification process, an additional step is inserted into the transformed source plan. This step has the effect that a small test paddle wheel is placed after the valve. The test paddle wheel allows the planner to test whether water runs through the valve.

In the second stage, the table of similar objects enables the system to replace all objects from the water pipe domain which appear in the causal model with similar objects from the electric circuit domain.

The validity of the modified causal model can be tested by modifying the target plan in the same way as the transformed source plan. A step is added to the plan, allowing the planner to insert a test lamp after the switch in the electric circuit in order to test whether the current flows through the path with the switch. The result of plan execution shows that the current flows through the switch rather than through the main lamp and confirms the new causal model.

A Vocabulary of Situated Interactions

If we wish to capture the content of interactions between questions and experiments, we have to ask what it means to pose a particular question or to perform a particular experiment. Moreover, we have to ask what it means when a particular piece of information is missing. Questions are often perceived as mechanisms to request information. However, our discussion of self-questioning in Section 1 revealed that questions can be used to guide the reasoning process. Similarly, experiments may play different roles in the discovery process. An experiment can be performed to confirm or reject a hypothesis. Alternatively, an experiment can be performed with a more inquisitive attitude. The IULIAN system does not know how the environment will behave under a given set of conditions. Therefore, an experiment is performed to investigate it. Experiments and questions can be described with a set of descriptors similar to the vocabulary used for story indexing (Schank & Osgood1990). This vocabulary includes descriptors such as goals, task, belief, and plan. Therefore we can describe a question or an experiment in terms of the goals the system pursues, the plans and tasks to be performed, and the beliefs the system maintains (Oehlmann, Sleeman, & Edwards 1993). However, the goal pursued in asking a self-question can be different from the goal an agent in a story pursues in interacting with other agents. This is particularly true when the question is asked because a previous question could not be answered. In such a situation which we refer to as a 4question failure, a second question may serve as a recovery tool. In addition to questions, experiments can be used to recover from a question failure.

In this section, we will discuss the issue of question failures in two stages. First, we give an example of a question failure and analyse this failure; we then derive from this analysis a set of index descriptors suitable to retrieve additional question plans, answer plans, and question strategies; all these plans can be used to overcome the failure situation. The index vocabulary developed in these sections will cover various situations in which questions can be combined to form question sequences.

The example in Section 3 involved replacing the plain pipe in the water pipe experiment with a valve (Figure 4). However, the system did not know if this replacement was adequate, i.e. if there would be water flow through the open valve. Therefore the following question was generated:

> *Q1.5*: Is there water flow through the pipe with the open valve?

This question could not be answered, because the valve had not been used in a parallel water pipe circuit before. An additional question was needed to focus on the issue of testing the existence of a water flow:

> *Q1.5.1*: What if we insert a small test paddle wheel behind the open valve? Is the test paddle wheel turning?s24

This question finally led to an experiment which revealed that there was water flow through the valve. This experimental result allowed the system to generate an answer to Question 1.5.

> *Hypothesis*: The test paddle wheel, T1, is turning.

> *Experiment*: Run an experiment with a test paddle wheel, T1, behind the open valve, V1.

> *Experimental result*: The test paddle wheel, T1, is turning and the main paddle wheel, W1, is not turning.

> *A1.5*: There is water flow through the valve, V1.

Obviously, the main reason for generating a question is to obtain an answer. If an answer cannot be generated because the necessary knowledge is not available, the question fails and the system has to recover from the failure situation. Recovering from a question failure involves the retrieval of either an appropriate single question or an entire question strategy.

In order to support the retrieval of self-questions, an appropriate indexing vocabulary has to be provided. We obtain such a vocabulary by investigating why the failure situation related to Question 1.5 has occurred and why the recovery strategy related to Question 1.5.1. has been used.

1. Why did Question 1.5 fail? It failed because:

> a) The question goal the system pursued by asking Question 1.5 can be described as checking if an entity exists which is not part of the system's experience. The entity water flow is not known because the system's experience is given in terms of experimental settings such as a system of water pipes, a paddle-wheel, an open valve and a pump and in terms of

experimental results such as paddle-wheel has state turning. This question goal is not satisfied, because the answer cannot be given.

b) The system is unable to derive the answer to Question 1.5 directly from its causal knowledge.

2. Why has Question 1.5.1 to be asked? It was asked because:

a) The system needs to recover from the failure which occurred when Question 1.5 was not satisfactorily answered.

b) As we stated above, the system has to know about the existence of an entity which is neither part of its experience nor derivable from its causal knowledge. However, if the system has previously generated an explanation, such as a small test paddle-wheel is turning, because there is water flow through the test-paddle-wheel, then it can match the entity water flow in Question 1.5 with the same entity in the explanation. This allows the system to focus on a new entity test-paddle-wheel which can be integrated into Question 1.5.1.

c) In applying a question strategy, the system may attempt to identify an analogy between electric circuits and water pipe circuits (see the example in Section 3). This strategy would not succeed if it were not possible to decide whether the entity water flow exists.

d) In Section 2, the system needs to explain the incorrect expectation that the lamp is on although the experiment revealed that the lamp is off. The existence of the water flow and the electric current would support a causal chain between experimental result and experimental setting.

An Indexing Schema for Question Plans

From our discussion in the previous section, we can derive several requirements for indexing question plans. Considering the explanations which we have given as answers to Question 1 and 2, we note that generalisations of these explanations hold for a large number of system generated questions. On the other hand, we expect the details of other question failures to be sufficiently different to allow the system to distinguish between questions and to retrieve the appropriate question.

In addition, we indicated that a question can have several functions. In general, questions have to support the acquisition of additional knowledge, represent a query about knowledge stored in memory, and support recovery from situations in which a previous question could not be answered. These requirements are reflected in the indexes of question plans. In the remainder of this section, we will list the descriptors which are used to index questions plans. In addition, we will give short descriptions of the functions these descriptors fulfil.

question goals: Questions are retrieved by the goals the system attempts to satisfy in asking a given question.

reasoning-goals: In addition to the very concrete question-goal, the system might pursue a more general reasoning-goal. For instance, the system attempts to identify the state of a paddle wheel under given conditions as part of a general process of analogical mapping. Whereas the question-goal focuses on identifying a state, the reasoning-goal addresses the entire strategy of analogical mapping.

recovery-goal: The basic strategy to recover from a question failure is the generation of additional questions and possibly an additional experiment. Whereas a question-goal focuses on a possible answer or a possible experiment, the recovery-goal focuses on the question failure and on a means to recover from this failure.

k-resource-need: A possible reason for asking a question is the need for a particular piece of knowledge referred to as a k-resource-need2 . This need can be satisfied by a k-resource-gain generated by an answer plan.

k-resource-assumption: Asking a particular question might make sense only under particular circumstances. For example, it is unreasonable to ask why a given lamp is off, when no lamp is used in an experiment. Therefore, the descriptor k-resource-assumption specifies assumptions made when asking a particular question.

An Indexing Schema for Answer Plans
Answer plans are indexed by the goals the system pursues in executing the plan and by the planning failures the system attempts to avoid.

answer-goals: Answer goals are used to retrieve an appropriate answer plan.

failures: An answer plan fails when a planning step cannot be executed.

k-resource-gain: If an answer is generated, a particular piece of knowledge is provided. This situation is described by the k-resource-gain descriptor which interacts with question plans in two ways. The k-resource-gain might satisfy a k-resource-need, i.e. the answer was successful, or the k-resource-gain might match a

bk-resource-assumption: i.e. it makes sense to generate the question whose plans contains this assumption.

An Indexing Schema for Experimentation Plans
experimentation-goals: In performing an experiment, the system may pursue goals which belong to different goal types. In the previous sections we have discussed those goal types which are related to the reasoning process. In addition, the system pursues goals which are directly related to actions, such as

---

[2] *k-resource* is an abbreviation for *knowledge-resource*.

enabling the current flow. These goals are referred to as *experimentation-goals*.

activity-goals: · This goal type has a function similar to that of reasoning-goals in question plans. In addition to the more concrete experimentation-goal, the system might pursue a more general activity-goal. For example, the objective of modifying an experiment in order to obtain a new experiment can be expressed by an activity-goal. During the modification process, an additional battery could be added to an electric circuit to increase the current. This objective establishes an *experimentation-goal* which is more specific than the *general activity-goal*.

Discussion

We have described our Exploratory Discovery system IULIAN which is based on an integration of case-based reasoning and case-based planning. Furthermore, we have argued that our approach of planning the generation of questions and experiments requires a content oriented index vocabulary. The descriptors which form the vocabulary address the situated interaction between self-questioning and experimentation and enable the system to perform case-based reasoning as a continuous process.

The interactions between question planning and experimentation planning have to address two tasks: filling a knowledge gap and supporting a reasoning or experimentation strategy. For example, Question 1.5 in Section 4 was asked because the reasoner did not know whether there was water flow through the open valve. Therefore the question leads to an experiment, i.e. the index vocabulary has to provide a link between a question which cannot be answered and an experiment.

In contrast, the first question which was asked about the plain pipe experiment in Section 3 was generated to initiate a reasoning strategy. The strategy used in the example is the analogical mapping strategy which belongs to the strategy type changing the focus. Strategies which change the focus of the reasoning process involve questions about different issues.

The task of filling a knowledge gap involves three sub-tasks: noting that a knowledge gap exists, judging that a question addresses a knowledge gap, and noting that a knowledge gap has been filled. These sub-tasks are addressed by the index descriptors k-resource-need, k-resource-gain, and k-resource-assumption.

Supporting a reasoning strategy is addressed at a local (situated) and a global (strategic) level. The local level guides the generation of the next question, answer, or experiment. Single questions, answers, and experiments modify the current situation which leads to a new situated response. The descriptors used at this level are question-goal, answer-goal, and experimentation-goal. The global level guides the generation of sequences of questions, answers, and experiments which realise entire reasoning strategies such as analogical mapping, plan transformation, changing the viewpoint, or perturbing the environment. These strategies are not implemented in the form of a single algorithm. We consider them as emerging from the situated generation of single questions, answers, and experiments. The descriptors reasoning-goal and activity-goal are used at the global level.

In contrast to the tasks discussed so far, the task of recovering from a question failure involves descriptors related to knowledge gaps as well as descriptors related to strategies. For example, the strategy changing the focus is used to address a question failure; therefore this strategy is guided by the descriptors recovery-goal and *k-resource-gain* . Using the descriptor recovery-goal initiates a new strategy, whereas the descriptor *k-resource-gain* indicates when the strategy succeeds and the knowledge gap is filled.

The index vocabulary discussed above supports the generation of single questions, answers, and experiments because it enables the system to retrieve the appropriate question, answer, or experimentation plans. Furthermore, the vocabulary supports the retrieval of question strategies and therefore the planned generation of sequences of questions and answers. Whereas the planned generation of single questions, answers, and experiments is based on case-based planning, we view the emerging strategies as closer to Agre and Chapman's concept of situated activity. In this sense, our approach integrates the concepts of case-based planning and situated activity.

References

Agre, P. & Chapman, D.(1987). An Implementation of a Theory of Activity. In *Proceedings of the 6th National Conference on Artificial Intelligence*, (pp. 268-272).

Brooks, R. (1991). Intelligence without Reason. In *Proceedings of the 12th International Joint Conference on Artificial Intelligence*, (pp. 569-595).

Carbonell, J. (1993). Learning by Analogy: Formulating and Generalizing Plans from Past Experience. In R. Michalski, J. Carbonell & T. Mitchell (Eds.), Machine Learning: *An Artificial Intelligence Approach*, Vol. I (pp. 137-161). San Mateo, CA: Morgan Kaufmann

Domeshek, E. (1992*). Do the Right Thing: A Component Theory for Indexing Stories as Social Advice*. Ph.D. Thesis, Yale University, New Haven, CT.

Goldweic, P. & Hammond. K. (1992). Multi-agent Interactions: A Vocabulary of Engagement. In *Proceedings of the 14th Annual Conference of the Cognitive Science Society*, (pp. 18 - 23).

Hammond, K. (1989). *Case-Based Planning: Viewing Planning as a Memory Task*. New York: Academic Press.

Hammond, K., Converse, T., & Marks, M. (1993). Toward a Theory of Agency. In S. Minton (ed.). *Machine Learning Methods for Planning* (pp.351-396). San Mateo, CA: Morgan Kaufmann.

James, W. (1981). *The Principles of Psychology*, 1, Cambridge, MA: Harvard University Press.

Kolodner, J. (1993). *Case-Based Reasoning*. San Mateo, CA: Morgan Kaufmann.

McDougal, T. (1993). Using Case-Based Reasoning and Situated Activity to Write Geometry Proofs. In *Proceedings of the 15th Annual Conference of the Cognitive Science Society*, (pp. 711 - 716). Hillsdale, NJ: Lawrence Erlbaum Associates.

Miyake, N. & Norman, D. (1979) To Ask a Question, One Must Know Enough to Know What is Not Known, *Journal of Verbal Learning and Verbal Behaviour*, 18:357-364.

Oehlmann, R. (1992). Learning Causal Models by Self-Questioning and Experimentation. In *Proceedings of the AAAI-92 Workshop on Communicating Scientific and Technical Knowledge*. (pp. 73-80).

Oehlmann, R., Edwards, P., & Sleeman, D. (1994). Changing the Viewpoint: Re-Indexing by Introspective Questioning. In *Proceedings of the 16th Annual Conference of the Cognitive Science Society*, (pp. 675 - 680). Hillsdale, NJ: Lawrence Erlbaum Associates.

Oehlmann, R., Edwards, P., & Sleeman, D. (1995). Introspection Planning: Representing Metacognitive Experience. In *Proceedings of the AAAI Spring Symposium on Representing Mental States and Mechanisms*, (pp. 102-110), Cambridge, MA: AAAI-Press.

Oehlmann, R., Sleeman, D. & Edwards, P. (1992). Self-Question and Experimentation in an Exploratory Discovery System, In *Proceedings of the ML-92 Workshop on Machine Discovery*, (pp. 41-50).

Oehlmann, R., Sleeman, D., & Edwards, P. (1993). Learning Plan Transformations from Self-Questions: A Memory-Based Approach. In *Proceedings of the 11th National Conference on Artificial Intelligence*, (pp. 520-525). Cambridge, MA: AAAI-Press.

Ram, A. (1991). A Theory of Questions and Question Asking. *The Journal of the Learning Sciences*, 1(3-4):273-318.

Ram, A. & Cox, M. (1994). Introspective Reasoning Using Meta-Explanations for Multistrategy Learning. In R. Michalski & G. Tecuci (Eds.), *Machine Learning: A Multistrategy Approach*, Vol. IV (pp. 349-377). San Mateo, CA: Morgan Kaufmann.

Ross, B. (1989). Remindings in Learning and Instruction. In S. Vosniadou &A. Ortony (Eds.), *Similarity and Analogical Reasoning*. Cambridge, UK: Cambridge University Press.

Schank, R. & Osgood, R. (1990). *A Content Theory of Memory Indexing*. Technical Report 2, The Institute of the Learning Sciences, Northwestern University.

Schauble, L., Glaser, R., Raghavan, K., & Reiner, M. (1991). Causal Models and Experimentation Strategies in Scientific Reasoning. *The Journal of the Learning Sciences*, 1:201-238.

Sternberg, R. (1981). Intelligence and Nontrenchment. Journal of Educational *Psychology*, 73(1):1-16.

Sooriamurthi, R. & Leake, D. (1994). Towards Situated Explanation. In, *Proceedings of the 12th National Conference on Artificial Intelligence* 24 , (p. 1492). Cambridge, MA: AAAI-Press.

Suchman, L. (1987). *Plans and Situated Actions. The Problem of Human Machine Communication*. Cambridge University Press: Cambridge, UK

Wong, B. & Jones, W. (1982). Increasing Metacomprehension in Learning Disabled and Normally Achieving Students Through Self-Questioning Training. *Learning Disability Quarterly* 5, (pp. 228 - 240).

Wong, B. (1985). Self-Questioning Instructional Research. A Review. 24 *Review of Educational Research*, 55, 227-268

Improving the Interfaces to Interactive Case Memories

Andrew M. Dearden

Department of Computer Science
University of York
York YO1 5DD
UK
andyd@minster.york.ac.uk

Abstract

An interactive case memory (ICM) is a system that interacts with a human user to gather information about a problem, interpret that information and search a store of previous cases to find cases that may be useful in solving the new problem. Many of the commercially successful products that have been derived from research on case-based reasoning could be described as ICMs. ICMs are type of advisory knowledge based system (KBS). Research on the design of interfaces to rule-based advisory KBSs has suggested that a user of such a system should be allowed to take control in interaction with the KBS. The user should be able to review their input, select the reasoning strategy used and re-direct the KBS towards particular hypotheses.

In this paper, I discuss how existing knowledge about interfaces to advisory KBSs can be applied to the design of interfaces to ICMs. I present a prototype ICM that demonstrates some of the facilities that could be incorporated into an ICM to increase the user's control over the interaction.

Introduction

Some of the most commercially successful products that have been developed from CBR research may be characterised by the term *Interactive Case Memory* (ICM). An ICM is a system which interacts with a human user to gather information about a problem, interpret that information and search a store of previous cases to find cases that may be useful in solving the new problem. Examples of ICMs are CBR Express (Klahr & Vrooman, 1991), ReMind helpdesk (Barletta & Mott, 1991), KATE and CASSYS (Manago & Conruyt, 1992), and PATDEX (Richter & Wess, 1991).

The success of any interactive knowledge based system (KBS), whether it be rule-based or case-based, is dependent not only on the quality of the knowledge encapsulated within the system but also on the quality of the interaction that the system supports. Young (1989) argues that one of the major reasons that early rule-based expert systems failed to gain wide acceptance was due to inadequate consideration of the interaction between the system and the user.

Research on the design of interfaces to other advisory KBS indicates the importance of allowing the user to take the *initiative* in the interaction. In this paper I shall show some of the implications that this advice might have for the design of ICMs. I shall illustrate these points by reference to an ICM that is designed to increase a user's control over the interaction.

Structure of this paper

In section 2, I review existing work on interfaces to other types of advisory KBS and use that work to derive requirements for interfaces to ICMs. In section 3, I describe a prototype ICM that is designed to increase the users control over interaction. In section 4, I discuss how the prototype is able to meet some of the design requirements from section 2. In section 5, I summarise the outcome of this work and describe some of the further issues that the system raises.

Interaction with KBS and ICMs

It is commonly acknowledged that the early promise of research into advisory rule-based KBS was not fully realised. Some authors have argued that a major reason for this was a lack of attention to the user interface requirements during their design (Young, 1989). A common observation from studies of human-human advisory dialogues, see e.g. Pollack (1985), Kidd (1985), Aaronson and Carrol (1987), is that the clients of advisory services often volunteer new information that is not requested by the advisor, and/or propose their own solutions for analysis by the advisor. Based on these observations it has been argued that interfaces to advisory interactive KBS should allow the user to take an active role in problem solving (Coombs & Alty, 1984; Fischer, 1990). In contrast, the interfaces to early advisory KBS enforced strict control over the dialogue with the system presenting questions that the user was expected to answer.

Roth *et al.* (1988) report that the overall problem solving performance of a human technician and an interactive KBS working together is highest when the human is an active participant in the interaction with the KBS rather than a passive data gatherer. The need for the active involvement of the technician arises because of the possibility of variations in the problem solving domain that were not anticipated when the KBS was initially designed, and the possibility of erroneous input by the technician. Where these factors arise the KBS may become `fixated' with a particular (inappropriate) hypothesis and may be unable to recover. Roth *et al.* argue that the interface to an interactive KBS should provide facilities to allow the user:

- to review and change their previously entered observations;

- to inspect and alter the state of the KBS, in particular the reasoning strategy being pursued; and

- to inspect and possibly alter the set of hypotheses being considered.

Since CBR is often recommended for use in domains where the domain knowledge is either incomplete or poorly structured, it is possible that these requirements will be very important for ICMs.

Below, I consider how these three requirements might affect the design of ICMs.

Reviewing the Input to an ICM

In a previous paper (Dearden & Bridge, 1993), I argued that one of the major advantages of case-based approaches to diagnostic tools for use in a help desk was the ease with which a help desk operator could manipulate the information about the problem they were trying to solve. For an ICM that uses a flat structure to organise a CB and makes use of a nearest neighbour approach to similarity, changes and revisions to the information about current case are easy to accommodate, and simply result in a new search of the CB. However, in the case of an ICM with a fixed indexing structure such as a decision tree, changes may be more difficult to deal with. For instance, if the user retracts the answer to the question that forms the root of a decision tree then none of the other information about the current problem can be directly used to identify cases.

ICM designers must consider carefully how to trade off the efficiency gained by using a fixed indexing structure with the loss in flexibility of interaction that results from this choice.

Choosing a reasoning strategy in interactive KBS

When starting an interactive consultation with an advisory KBS, a user will typically have only a small amount of information about the current problem. In a typical interaction, the user will begin by entering this information. The hypotheses, or the cases in an ICM, that are retrieved on the basis of this information can be used to suggest to the user which parts of the problem to investigate next. The relationship between the retrieved hypotheses and the question that the system recommends that the user ask next can be regarded as defining the 'reasoning strategy' being supported by the ICM. Various different reasoning strategies may be applied in interactive KBS. Below I list just three common strategies.

- If one particular hypothesis seems to be much better than all the others, then the KBS might suggest investigating evidence that would tend to confirm that particular hypothesis. This strategy is sometimes referred to as *pursuit*.

- If many hypotheses are judged to be of similar relevance to the current situation, then the KBS might suggest investigating features that discriminate between the hypotheses. This strategy is known as *discriminate*.

- Occasionally it may be useful to exclude one particular hypothesis by searching for evidence that will refute it. This strategy is sometimes referred to as *rule-out*.

Considering existing ICMs, it appears that most ICMs select one particular reasoning strategy and do not allow the user to change it. For instance, in CBR Express after the user has searched the CB the system presents a list of questions with the questions associated with the highest scoring case appearing first. Assuming that the user is most likely to select the first question from the list this could be interpreted as following a strategy of pursuit. KATE and CASSYS construct decision trees based on an information gain metric that prefers questions that will partition the set of cases that are currently under consideration into equal sets. Thus these ICMs may be regarded as following a strategy of discrimination. PATDEX also prefers discriminating questions, but interestingly allows a user to instruct the system to ignore particular cases. This does not precisely equate to supporting the rule-out strategy since PATDEX does not suggest questions that will help to rule-out the case, it only allows a user to try the solution associated with the case and rule-out that solution if it fails.

Interaction with ICMs might well be improved by allowing a wider range of reasoning strategies to be supported.

Changing the Hypotheses under Consideration

Equal opportunity is a design heuristic that is intended to reduce the imbalance between a user and a computer system in an interaction. Thimbleby defines equal opportunity as requiring that:

> *all that can be supplied or demanded by the machine can also be*
> *supplied or demanded by the user. Equivalently, each item of*
> *information passed across the interface can be passed in either*
> *direction.*(Thimbleby, 1990)[p.348]

In the case of graphical editors and word processors, equal opportunity may be related to direct manipulation, in that the output of the computer system, the text or figures that make up the document, can be used to generate input to the computer system, by moving, copying or pasting. Equal opportunity can also be related to the idea of solving a problem by working backwards from a desired solution state to a goal state (Polya, 1973)[p.225].

From the viewpoint of equal opportunity in ICMs, we may require that, if an ICM is able to provide as output a set of cases or an ordering over a set of cases, then the user should be able to use this ordering to input information to the ICM. To understand why such a facility might be desirable it is useful to consider some scenarios in which the user of an ICM might need to reason backwards from a stored case to develop a different understanding of the new case. Four such scenarios are noted below.

- The analysis by Roth *et al.* (1988) of interactions between a user and a rule-based diagnostic KBS suggested that in certain circumstances the interactive KBS may begin to follow an unproductive line of reasoning. Roth *et al.* recommend that the operator of the KBS should be provided with facilities to inspect and to alter the internal state of the interactive KBS so as to force the system to re-direct its attention.

- In a help desk providing computer support, a situation may arise in which the help desk operator knows of some external fault, that is beyond the scope of the ICM, and that is currently affecting the computer network being supported. The external fault may cause one case or a set of cases that are usually uncommon to become much more likely. When a new customer calls, the operator may want to start problem solving by considering this set of cases, rather than those cases that are most likely under normal circumstances. To enable the operator to do this, the ICM could allow the operator to directly select one of the problems in this set and check whether the customer is experiencing any of the symptoms associated with this case.

- An alternative scenario may arise during a problem solving session with the helpdesk ICM in which the operator may see a case that is associated with a different interpretation of the information that has been collected so far. The operator may then want to switch the attention of the ICM so that this new interpretation is the preferred one.

- Another possibility is that the user of an ICM will reach a point where the cases delivered seem very inappropriate and may want to widen their search of the CB to investigate alternative possibilities.

The examples above all suggest that it would be useful in an ICM for the user to be able to manipulate the output of the ICM so as to change the focus of problem solving, to focus in on particular cases, or to widen the search. Such a requirement may be regarded as a call for the user to be given an equal opportunity to manipulate the case ordering, to form input to the system as well as being able to input information by manipulating the statement of the current problem.

Summary
In this section, I have considered some of the recommendations that have been made for the design of interactive KBS, and what those recommendations might mean in the context of ICMs. In the rest of this paper, I shall describe an ICM that demonstrates how the user's control over a dialogue with an ICM can be increased.

A Prototype ICM

The "cars ICM" described in this section was developed in order to explore how more control could be given to a user in interaction with an ICM. The cars ICM is designed to support a user in deciding on the purchase of a new car. The CB consists of information on over 50 models of car, together with their price and the costs of possible optional features such as sunroofs, central locking, alarms, airbags etc.

```
case_fact3(case023, name(`c23 BMW 520i saloon')). case_fact3(case023, make(
`BMW' )).
case_fact3(case023, model( `520i saloon' )).
case_fact3(case023, attribute(engine_size, 1991 )).
case_fact3(case023, attribute(min_price, 20150)).
case_fact3(case023, attribute(max_price, 24285)).
case_fact3(case023, attribute(max_speed, 131)).
case_fact3(case023, attribute(fuel_consumption, 41 )).
case_fact3(case023, attribute(fuel_type, unleaded)).
case_fact3(case023, attribute(zero_sixty,10 )).
case_fact3(case023,    attribute(class,    hatchback   )).    case_fact3(case023,
attribute(seats, 4)).
case_fact3(case023, attribute(year, 1994)).
case_fact3(case023, property(safety, average )).
```

```
case_fact3(case023, property(performance, good )).
case_fact3(case023, property(running_cost, average )).
case_fact3(case023, property(comfort, average )).
case_fact3(case023, property(reliability, average )).
case_fact3(case023, feature(power_steering)).
case_fact3(case023, feature(anti_lock_brakes)).
case_fact3(case023, feature( electric_windows)).
case_fact3(case023, feature( seat_height_adjust)).
case_fact3(case023, feature( steering_wheel_adjust)).
case_fact3(case023, option(automatic_gears, 1100)).
case_fact3(case023, option( air_conditioning, 1515)).
case_fact3(case023, option( sunroof, 830)).
case_fact3(case023, option( alarm, 690)).
```

Figure 1: An example case from the cars ICM

Figure 1 shows part of the specification of a BMW 520i[1]. The specification includes:

- values for attributes such as the fuel type, miles per gallon at a steady 56mph, length and width in inches, year of manufacture etc.;

- a set of features that the BMW520i includes as standard fittings, e.g. power steering, anti_lock_brakes;

- a set of features that are optional together with the additional price in pounds sterling of incorporating these features, for the BMW520i the options are air conditioning for £1515, automatic gears for £ 1100, a sunroof for £ 830, and an alarm for £ 690;

- a list of (subjective) judgements as to certain qualities of the car[2], e.g. the degree of comfort the car affords, the overall performance of the car, the ecological impact of the car etc.

Similarity in the cars ICM

The similarity function for the cars ICM is based on two heuristics:

1. prefer cases that match more features;

2. of these prefer cases that match features earlier in the sequence input by the user.

To search the CB, the user inputs their requirements of a new car as a sequence of constraints. When a user begins interacting with the cars ICM, many cars will be able to match all their constraints. As long as any cars match all the constraints, these cars are displayed in the 'best matched' set. As the user adds constraints, fewer and fewer cars will match all the constraints and the size of the 'best matched' set will decrease. Eventually the user will enter a constraint that cannot be matched by any of the cars

---

[1] Specifications were taken from Car Week Magazine 15th December 1993

[2] A possible design enhancement would be to calculate these assessments working from the objective specifications of the vehicle.

in the `best matched' set. At this point, the ICM searches for case that match the new constraint, and from these selects the set of cases that match the new constraint, plus the earliest set of constraints from the users current input. The details of the algorithm beyond the scope this paper, the reader is referred to Dearden (1995). Below, I describe a simple interaction with the cars ICM.

A simple search in the cars ICM
Figure 2 shows the state of the cars ICM after a user has input 4 constraints:-

- the engine size of the car should be greater than or equal to 1600cc;

- the car should run on diesel fuel;

- the price of the car should be less than or equal to £12000;

- the fuel consumption should be at least 60 miles per gallon at a steady 30mph.

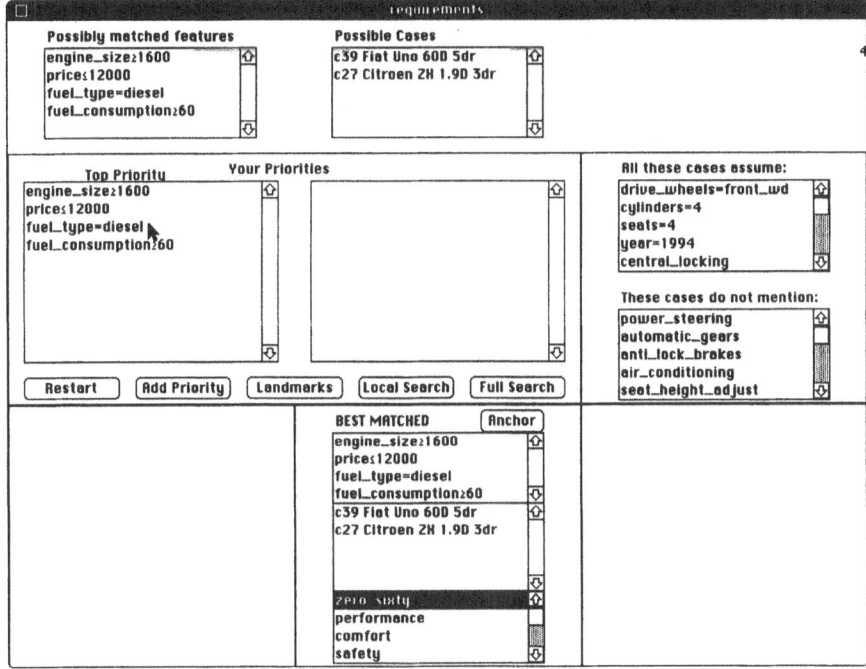

Figure 2: Searching in the cars ICM:1

The display shows that two cars in the CB match all the constraints of the specification, a Fiat Uno 650 and a Citroen ZX. This is shown by the list in the bottom centre of the display.

Below the list of matched cars a list of attributes, features, or qualities that could be used to discriminate amongst the set is displayed. The list shows that the time taken to accelerate from zero to sixty miles per hour is the most discriminating attribute, followed by the degree of comfort and degree of security. Further discriminating attributes are included in the list, and the user may choose to scroll through the list to find other possible ways of discriminating.

The user may select any one of the possible discriminators, by clicking on the attribute or feature with the mouse, in order to narrow their search. This generates a dialogue box that can be used to specify a constraint for this particular attribute or feature. By default the new constraint is appended to the end of the current list of constraints, although the user can choose to alter the point at which the constraint is inserted. The result of a new search will be that only those cars in the old `best matched' set that satisfy the new constraint will remain in the new `best matched set'. Thus the set of cases in the `best matched' set is gradually reduced.

Additional areas of the screen indicate more information. On the right hand side of the display a list of features that are common to all the cars retrieved is presented. This allows the user to see if there are any undesirable consequences of their current selection. Also displayed on the right are any features, attributes or qualities that are not mentioned by any of the cases retrieved. At the top of the screen a set of `possibly matching cars' is presented. To be included in this set a car must either match all the constraints in the input sequence, or not mention these features. Thus this set represents an interpretation of a missing attribute in the case by assuming that the car satisfies the constraint given by the user, whereas the lists presented at the bottom of the display interpret a missing attribute by assuming that the car does not satisfy the constraint.

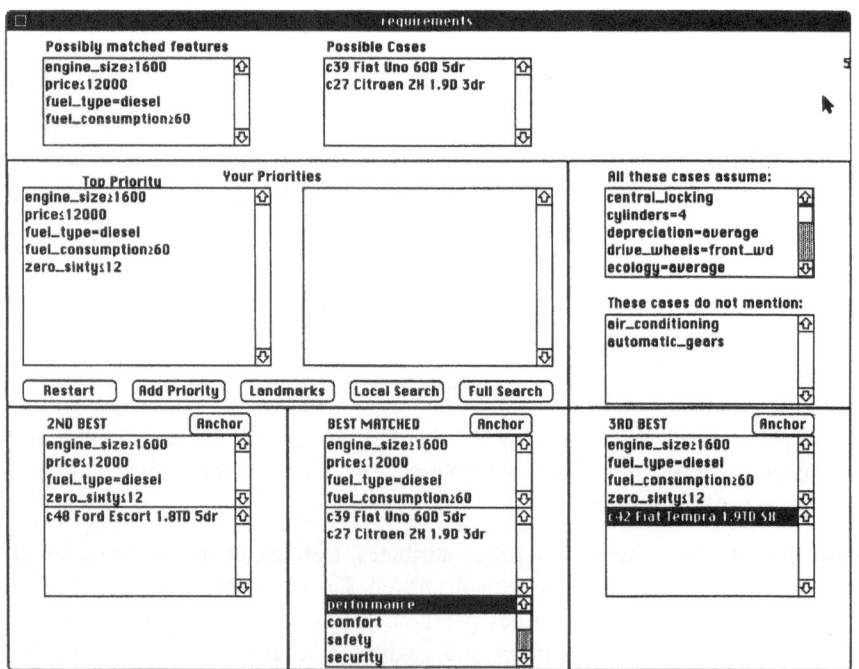

Figure 3 Searching in the cars ICM:2

As more constraints are added by the user, the specification may reach a state where no cars in the CB can satisfy all of the constraints. In this case the ICM searches for cases that match subsets of the criteria. In figure 3, the user has added an additional constraint that the car should be capable of accelerating from zero to sixty mph. in under 12 seconds. The resulting search shows that the Fiat Uno and the Citroen ZX cannot meet this additional constraint, and in fact none of the cars in the CB meet all the constraints. The ICM therefore searches for other cars that can match a subset of the constraints. The Fiat Uno and Citroen ZX are still shown as the best matching cases since they meet the first four constraints, but not the fifth. The other cases displayed are a Ford Escort 1.8TD, which satisfies the engine size, fuel type, price, and acceleration but not the fuel consumption requirements; and a Fiat Tempra that can match the engine size, fuel type, fuel consumption and acceleration, but not the price constraint.

These three sets might be seen as all equally valid responses to the user's input, since they all match subsets of the constraints in the query, and for each case it is true that: *no other case in the CB matches a superset of the features from the user's input that are matched by the retrieved case.* The three sets are ordered, however, by reference to the ordering of the constraints. The first set in the order being presented in the bottom centre of the display.

Interaction with the Prototype

In this section, I show how the prototype supports some of the requirements for interactive KBS that I introduced in section 2.

Reviewing Input
As well as being able to add constraints, the user of the cars ICM is able to change the order of the constraints, or to discard a constraint altogether. This can be done by double-clicking with the mouse on any one of the constraints. This generates a dialogue that allows the user to select a new position for that constraint in the ordering, to alter the constraint, or to discard the constraint. For instance the constraint `price < 12000' in figure 3 could be modified to `price < 10000' and moved to the top of the sequence of constraints in a single dialogue cycle.

Alternative Reasoning Strategies
In section 2, I described three possible reasoning strategies that might be implemented in an interactive KBS. The strategies were: pursue, discriminate and rule-out.

By default, the cars ICM allows a user to follow a strategy of discrimination by suggesting questions, along with each of the three displayed case sets, that can be used to discriminate between the cases in the set. The questions are ordered by an information gain metric similar to that used in ID3 (Quinlan, 1983)

If the user wants to pursue a particular case, this can be achieved by clicking on the case name. The result of this action is to generate a dialogue in which the features of

```
┌─────────────────────────────────────────────────┐
│▓▓▓▓▓▓▓▓▓▓▓▓▓▓ zoom_to_case ▓▓▓▓▓▓▓▓▓▓▓▓▓▓▓▓│
│  c39 Fiat Uno 60D 5dr                             │
│    ☒ engine_size≥1697                             │
│    ☒ price≤8544                                   │
│    ☐ max_speed≥100                                │
│    ☒ fuel_consumption≥64                          │
│    ☒ fuel_type=diesel                             │
│    ☐ cost_per_mile≤30                             │
│    ☐ tank_capacity≥10                             │
│    ☐ drive_wheels=front_wd                        │
│    ☐ zero_sixty≤17                                │
│    ☐ insurance_gp≤6                               │
│    ☐ service_interval≥10000                       │
│    ☐ value_in_yr3≥3700                            │
│    ☐ maintain_to_yr3≤1400                         │
│    ☐ cylinders=4                                  │
│    ☐ class=supermini                              │
│    ☐ seats≥3                                      │
│    ☐ length≤150                                   │
│    ☐ width≤65                                     │
│    ☐ height≥60                                    │
│    ☐ min_boot≥10                                  │
│    ☐ max_boot≥35                                  │
│    ☐ year≥1993                                    │
│    ☐ stereo                                       │
│    ☐ split_rear_seat                              │
│    ☐ tailgate                                     │
│    ☐ rear_seat_belts                              │
│    ☐ side_impact_bars                             │
│  ───────────────────────────────────────────     │
│    ☐ sunroof                    £307              │
│    ☐ central_locking            £271              │
│    ☐ electric_windows           £271              │
│       ( Cancel )  ( Select all ) ( Ok )           │
└─────────────────────────────────────────────────┘
```

Figure 4: Focusing on a single case

the case are used to suggest constraints that the user might wish to apply. Figure 4 shows an example of this type of dialogue.

By clicking on the check boxes in the dialogue box, the user can add any or all of the constraints associated with this case. The result of adding the constraints is that the next search of the CB will tend to remove from display cases that are not similar to the selected case. The dialogue is labelled `zoom_to_case' since the operation it supports is analogous to `zooming in' to a part of the CB.

The strategy of ruling out a case is not directly supported by the cars ICM, although in principle a dialogue similar to that used for pursuing cases could be applied to generate constraints that will rule the case out.

Controlling the Focus of Problem Solving
The final form of user control over interaction with an ICM that I introduced in section 2 was control of the focus of problem solving. This is achieved in the cars ICM by two facilities.

The first option that the user has to control the focus of the ICM is to shift attention from the `best matched' set of cases to the `2nd best' or `3rd best' sets. By clicking on one of the buttons marked `Anchor' in figure 3 the user can swap the associated cases to become the new focus. Assuming that the similarity function does not change, this must be achieved by finding a new value of the current problem. In the case of the cars ICM the necessary change can be made by moving the constraints associated with the selected set of cases to the beginning of the constraint sequence. This results in the selected cases becoming the `best matched' cases for the new PS. For example, if the cars ICM is in the state shown in figure 3 and the user clicks on the anchor button associated with the second best group of cases, then the new sequence of requirements will be:

$$\langle engine\_size \leq 1600, price \leq 12000, fuel\_type = diesel,$$
$$zero\_sixty \leq 12, fuel\_consumption \geq 60 \rangle$$

For other similarity functions an appropriate new value for the input problem may be difficult or even impossible to find.

The second way of redirecting the search within the cars ICM is to select one of the questions listed under `these cases do not mention' or `these cases all assume'. By answering any of these questions and inserting the answer into the current sequence of constraints, the user can ensure that a different part of the CB is investigated. By default the dialogue associated with these constraints inserts the new constraint at the position of the first constraint that is not matched by the current `best matched' set. This choice ensures that only the `2nd best' and `3rd best' case sets are changed, the `best matched' set remains constant, so the user maintains some sense of position within the CB.

Conclusions and Further Work

Previous research has shown that it is important to provide the user with facilities to control and direct dialogues with advisory KBS. Designers should take advantage of this previous work in designing interfaces to ICMs. I have presented a description of a user interface for an ICM that increases the degree of control over interaction that can be exercised by a user. The cars ICM demonstrates ways in which it is possible to implement some of the requirements arising from research into the design of interfaces to advisory KBS in the context of an ICM.

I am currently investigating the problems involved in inferring a new representation for the input problem given a request for a change of focus. It is clear that this task is much simpler for ICMs using some similarity metrics than it might be for others.

Acknowledgements

I should like to thank Tony Griffiths for his helpful comments on an earlier draft of this paper. The cars ICM was developed with the support of BT plc and EPSRC through a CASE studentship.

References

Aaronson, A. and Carroll, J. M. (1987). The answer is in the question: a protocol study of intelligent help. *Behaviour and Information Technology*, 6(4):393-402.

Barletta, R. and Mott, S. (1991). *Techniques for Employing Case Based Reasoning in Automated Customer Service Help Desks.* Advertising Literature, Cognitive Systems Inc.

Coombs, M. and Alty, J. (1984). Expert systems: an alternative paradigm. *International. Journal of. Man Machine Studies*, 20:21-43.

Dearden, A. M. and Bridge, D. G. (1993). Choosing a knowledge based system to support a help desk. *Knowledge Engineering Review*, 8(3):201-222.

Dearden, Andrew M. (1995) *The use of Formal Models in the Design of Interactive Case Memory Systems.* DPhil Thesis, University of York, Department of Computer Science.

Fischer, G. (1990). Communications requirements for co-operative problem solving systems. *Information Systems*, 15(1):21-6.

Kidd, A. L. (1985). What do users ask? Some thoughts on diagnostic advice. In *Proceedings of the 5th Technical Conference of the BCS Special Interest Group on Expert Systems*, 9-19.

Klahr, P. and Vrooman, G. (1991). Commercialising case based reasoning technology. In Graham, I. M. and Milne, R. W., editors, *Research and Development in Expert Systems VIII,* 18-24. Cambridge University Press.

Manago, M. and Conruyt, N. (1992). Using information technology to solve real world problems. In Schmalhofer, F., Strube, G., and Wetter, T., editors, *Contemporary Knowledge Acquisition and Cognition*, number 622 in Lecture Notes in Artificial Intelligence. Springer Verlag.

Pollack, M. E. (1985). Information sought and information provided: An empirical study of user/expert dialogues. In *Proceedings of the ACM/CHI* San Fransisco, 155-159.

Polya, G. (1973). *How To Solve It.* Princeton University Press.

Quinlan, J. R. (1983). Learning efficient classification procedures and their application to chess endgames.In Michalski, R., Carbonell, J., and Mitchell, T., editors, *Machine Learning: An Artificial Intelligence Approach.* Tioga Press.

Richter, M. M. and Wess, S. (1991). Similarity, uncertainty and case-based reasoning in patdex. In Boyer, R. S., editor, *Automated Reasoning: Essays in honour of Noody Bledsoe*, 249-265. Kluwer.

Roth, E. M., Bennett, K. B., and Woods, D. D. (1988). Human interaction with an `intelligent' machine. In Hollnagel, E., Mancini, G., and Woods, D. D., editors, *Cognitive Engineering in Complex Dynamic Worlds*, 23-69. Academic Press.

Thimbleby, H. (1990). *User Interface Design,* ACM Press.

Young, R. M. (1989). Human interface aspects of expert systems. In Murray, L. A. and Richardson, J. T. E., editors, *Intelligent systems in a human context*, 20-34. Oxford University Press.

Capturing and Matching Dynamic Behaviour in Case-Based Reasoning*

Peter J. Funk and Dave Robertson

Edinburgh University, Department of Artificial Intelligence
80 South Bridge, Edinburgh EH1 1HN, UK
E-mail: {peterf | dr}@aisb.ed.ac.uk

Abstract. In the telecommunications domain, reuse of service specifications is a major issue. However, it has proved difficult to modularise services because of the high degree of interaction between them. Direct application of formal logics to the specification of services has proved impractical because of the size of the services. However, much of this complexity stems from the details of implementation of the services; by contrast, the principal behaviours of a service are often approximated by simple varieties of logic which are easily accessible to users. We address the problem of determining, from a library of services, those which might be appropriate for reuse in constructing a new service. Simple behavioural sequences are used to provide features within a CBR system which matches these to behavioural examples supplied by users. By side-stepping the problem of formally specifying the entire service, we aim to promote greater reuse of services while avoiding a commitment to full logical specification.

Non-mathematicians often have difficulty in expressing requirements formally. By using a CBR approach the user can sketch out simple, familiar behaviours and with these examples the system is able to retrieve relevant cases and interactively produce a formal requirements sketch capturing the new required behaviour. A case in the case library encapsulates a particular formalised behaviour in a simple logic which is sufficient to capture the key dynamic behaviours of the domain. With a simulator the user can evaluate the behaviour without being confronted with the formal representation itself. Our domain is telephone features such as call waiting, redirect call, call back. These telephone services are stored in the case library as cases, each consisting of a set of transition rules. In previous papers we have described the general architecture of the system (see for example [Funk & Robertson 1994]). In this paper we focus on matching dynamic behaviour and the formal representation of the cases.

1. Introduction

The CABS system (see [Funk & Robertson 94]) approaches the design of formal requirements specification of telecommunication services. The user gives coarse-grained examples of the required behaviour, which are then matched against cases in a case library in order to identify similar parts of previous cases (requirements specifications). These previous cases are then used in the process of producing a new specification. This approach reduces the effort required to produce requirements

* This research was supported by the Marcus Wallenberg Foundation for Scientific Research and Education and ELLEMTEL Telecommunication Systems Laboratories, Sweden.

specifications since parts of existing specified, tested and integrated specifications may be reused to construct the requirements. This Case-Based approach relies on simple formal notation for features of the cases, capturing the required dynamic behaviour. This notation enables the comparison of cases with respect to these features, suggesting where they may exhibit the same behaviour and where they might differ.

The CABS system aims to cover a small section of the domain of telephone service requirements including the dynamic requirements of the services "redirect call", "wake up call" "call back", etc. These are examples of services which are frequently reused. The case library contain cases which capture the behaviour of the requirements of a specific telephone service. In this and similar domains, it is not merely a matter of producing a new solution to capture the required behaviour of the new functionality, we also have to specify the requirements of interaction with other services as well as behaviour in exceptional circumstances. If we can reuse a past case in such a domain, we may benefit from the fact that the case is already integrated with other services, and that the behaviour of such exceptions may already have been specified.

This paper focuses on how to represent cases which themselves represent dynamic behaviour, and also on the comparison of cases. A brief outline of the CABS system is given in Section 2. In Section 3 the requirements of cases which capture dynamic behaviour are outlined. Examples and an outline of the formal logic used to store cases are given in Section 4. Section 5 discusses dynamic similarity measurements. Finally Section 6 contains a brief summary and conclusions.

2. Brief Description of the approach taken in CABS

In Figure 1 a brief overview of CABS is given, structured according to the four REs (Retrieve, Reuse, Revise, Restore) [Aamodt & Plaza 94] in the case-based reasoning cycle. In CABS the input is given as coarse-grained examples of the new behaviour. As described in Figure 1, the input is translated into a representation in which the necessary features for the matching can easily be accessed. In the matching process we identify transition rules (explained in Section 4) capturing a similar behaviour. Thereafter the modules (sets of transition rules) are ranked according to their similarity. The most common situation will be that there is one single case in the case library close enough to the new case to be used as a starting point for constructing new requirements specification. In some situations there are sets of rules from different cases which are similar to different parts of the input. They have to be merged and might need some adaptation in order to produce a proposed solution which is consistent. The adaptation might simply be to add a transition rule connecting two states not captured in the retrieved case but captured in the input. Finally the proposed solution is tested and further adapted to conform to the input example and the user's intentions as closely as possible.

The representation of cases as used in CABS needs to meet a number of requirements, such as being able to reuse cases both in whole or in part, determine what parts of cases differ and what parts are similar, and identify inconsistency between parts of cases merged in order to produce a proposed solution. In the next Section we will outline the main features of such a representation.

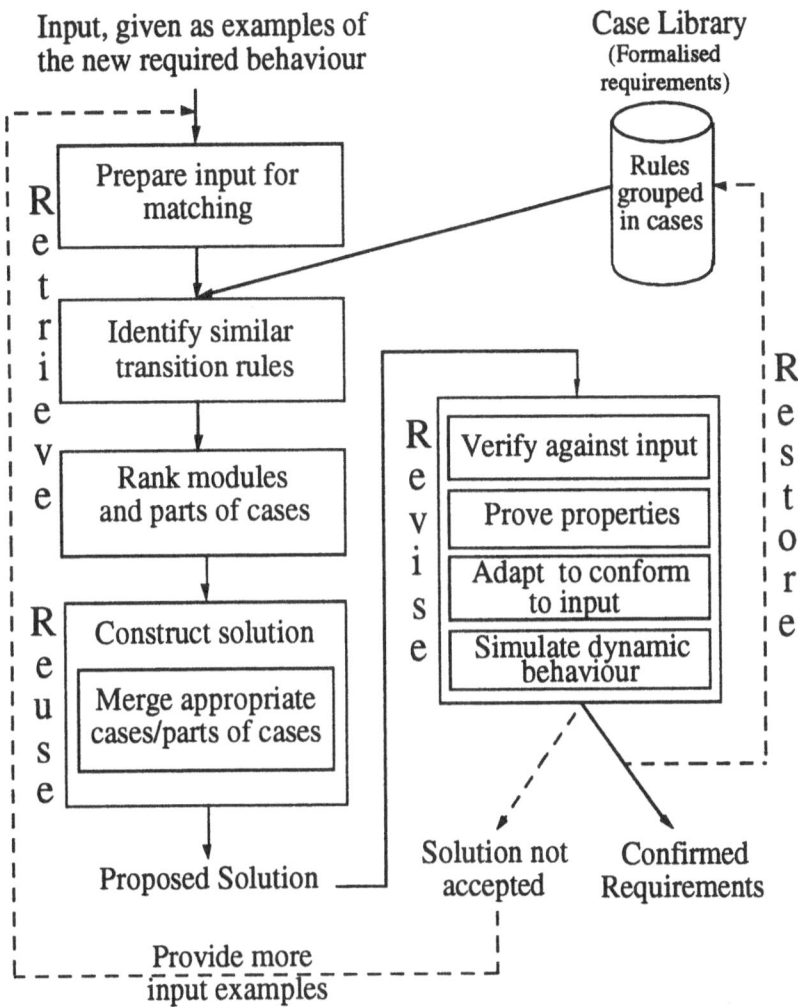

Fig. 1. Overview over the CABS system

3. Representing Dynamic Reactive Behaviour

Representing dynamic behaviour is an active research area and formalisms like event calculus, situation calculus, π-calculus, petri-nets, CCS, etc. have been widely explored in this context. These representations have the expressive power to reason about different aspects of temporal behaviour such as communicating processes, history, indeterminism, events valid in an open duration, etc. However, we are not concerned with describing all the possible behaviours of services – only an outline of the main features of their behaviour, which can assist in identifying appropriate services. It is important that the language we use should be simple enough to be communicated to non specialist users, since they must ultimately approve the service specified. If we restrict ourselves to specifying a single process which accepts discrete sequenced stimuli, a simple finite state machine represented in predicate logic (Moor-automaton, see e.g. [Lewis & Papadimitriou 81]) may be used.

This allows us to:

- store a particular behaviour in the form of a set of transition rules (a case).

- compare cases and determine if they capture the same behaviour.

- determine which parts of two compared cases correspond and which do not.

- produce a new behaviour by reusing parts of cases.

- determine which parts of the behavioural example given as input are covered by the proposed solution, and which are not.

4. A Simple Logic Capturing Change

The language we use [Funk 93, Echarti & Stålmarck 88, Gelfond & Lifschitz 93] contains transition rules (R), stimuli, (S), atomic terms (A) and states (T), which are sets of atomic terms. A stimulus is the only cause of change. Atomic terms are used to describe a state or part of a state. A rule contains a set of preconditions (atomic terms). If the stimulus S has occurred and the precondition is true, the conclusions are necessarily true in the next state.

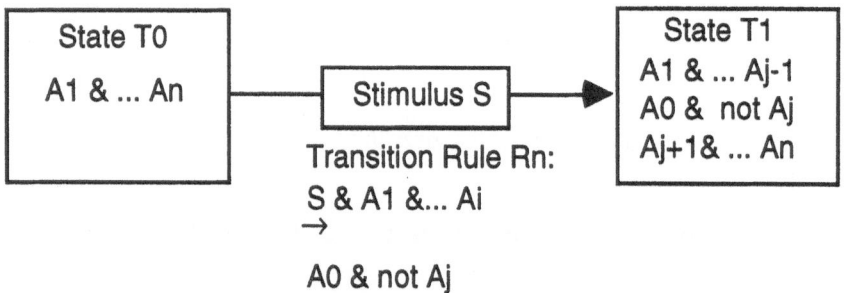

Fig. 2. Example of a transition.

State transition rules have been argued to be sufficient for outlining the main behaviour of simple telephone services [Funk & Raichman 90] and we have used these to specify 16 different services. Following is a simplified example of a transition rule:

Stimulus :	dialling(A,Nr)
Precondition at T:	answer_on(B,Nr) &
	¬ redirect(Nr,Nr2)&
	idle(B).
Conclusion at T+1:	calling(A,B) &
	ring_tone(A) &
	ring_signal(B).

Our syntax assures an ordered sequence of time points and restricts us to only having preconditions about T and conclusions about T+1. This excludes reasoning about anything other than the immediate past, but gives a simple and computationally efficient implementation. Using predicate logic gives us access to a number of validation tools for consistency checking, simulation, transformation etc. (see for example [Bundy 92]). We may also add restricted natural language and graphical notations [Dalianis & Hovy 93, Davis 90] in order to further aid the user in the validation process of a new service.

5. Similarity Measurement of Dynamic Behaviour

There are two steps in identifying useful cases: we have to identify similar cases, and thereafter rank these cases according to how easily they can be adapted in order to produce a solution (see e.g. [Smyth & Keane 93]). To identify whether a case is similar to the input behaviour we have to determine:

- which transitions of the input example are covered by the case.

- which state transitions are missing in the case.

- what extra information the case captures and whether this extra behaviour is of interest for the proposed solution.

- if state transitions in the input are not covered, are there transition rules close to the input and are these candidates for adaptation.

The input examples are translated into partial transition rules – partial since it is assumed that the input examples are not complete but merely an outline of the required behaviour. Hence the partial rules' preconditions may have missing predicates and the conclusions may be incomplete.

If the matching algorithm (see [Funk & Robertson 1994] for the algorithm) does not find an appropriate rule for a state transition we have to either adapt a similar rule from the case library or use the transition rule generated from the input to fill the gap. This allows us, at the very least, to come up with a suggestion capturing the same behaviour as the input.

6. Conclusions

This paper has provided an overview of the different parts of a case-based reasoning system supporting the reuse of telecommunication services based on requirements expressed as dynamic behaviour. It has focused in particular on the representation of cases and the matching of dynamic behaviour.

We have outlined how a simple logic is used to capture the behaviour of cases. Cases are indexed using transition rules as features, which enables us to capture simple forms of dynamic behaviour and compare cases with respect to their behaviour. This allows us to reuse cases or parts of cases in order to produce a proposed solution.

References

Aamodt, A. and Plaza, E., (1994). Case-Based Reasoning: Foundational Issues, Methodological Variations, and System Approaches. *AI Communications*, Vol. 7, No 1, pp 39-59.

Bundy, A., (1992). Tutorial notes: reasoning about logic programs. *Second International Logic Programming Summer School, LPSS '92*. Proceedings, pp. 252-77, Comyn G., Fuchs N.E., & Ratcliffe M.J. (eds.), Springer-Verlag.

Dalianis H. and Hovy E. (1993). Aggregation in Natural Language Generation, *The Fourth European Workshop on Natural Language Generation, Proceedings*, Pisa, Italy.

Davis, E., (1990). *Representations of Commonsense Knowledge*, chapters 2 and 3. Morgan Kaufmann.

Echarti, J. P. and Stålmarck, G., (1988). A logical framework for specifying discrete dynamic systems, Technical Report, Ellemtel Telecommunication Systems Laboratories.

Engstedt, M., (1991). A Flexible Specification Language using Natural Language and Graphics. MSc thesis, University of Edinburgh.

Funk, P. J. and Robertson D., (1994). Case-Based Selection of Requirements Specifications for Telecommunication Systems. *Second European Workshop on Case-Based Reasoning, Proceedings*, Keane M., Haton J. P., Manago, M. (eds.), Chantilly, France, pp. 293-301.

Funk, P. J., (1993). Development and Maintenance of Large Formal Specifications Supported by Case-Based Reasoning. TP26. University of Edinburgh.

Funk, P. J., Raichman, S., (1990) ROS, An Implementation Independent Specification for ISDN, Technical Report, Ellemtel Telecommunication Systems Laboratories.

Gelfond, M. and Lifschitz, V. (1993). Representing action and change by logic programs, *Logic Programming*, pp. 301-321.

Lewis, H. R. and Papadimitriou C. H., (1981). *Elements of theTheory of Computation*, Prentice-Hall.

Smyth, B. and Keane M. T., (1993). Retrieving Adaptable Cases, In K-D. Althoff, K. Richter, & S. Wess (eds.), *First European Workshop on Case-Based Reasoning*. Kaiserslauten: Germany.

INCREMENTAL CONCEPT LEARNING AND CASE-BASED REASONING : FOR A CO-OPERATIVE APPROACH.

Isabelle Bichindaritz[1]

[1] LIAP-5, U.F.R. de Mathématiques et Informatique, 45 rue des Saints-Pères, 75270 Paris Cedex 06, France

Abstract. In case-based reasoning systems, the hierarchical memory organization presents the same set of problems as conceptual clustering learnt hierarchies. The co-operation between these two artificial intelligence methodologies gives several advantages. In case-based reasoning, memory and reasoning are closely linked. So the quality of the reasoning process is highly dependent upon that of the memory. Incremental concept learning permits to optimize the memory structures and organization. It also enlarges the application range of case-based reasoning. In incremental concept learning, case-based reasoning proposes its whole architecture, and above all its memory, from which the learning process can benefit, particularly for remedying the problem of the dependence upon the order of presentation of the instances, which is a crucial problem for this type of learning. It also permits the use of theoretical knowledge to explain the concepts learnt. This article presents a case-based reasoning system taking advantage from this co-operative approach.

1   Introduction

Case-based reasoning is often presented as an artificial intelligence methodology meant for processing empirical knowledge. It achieves this goal by studying how to conceive and how to implement memories dedicated to the realization of a precise cognitive task [1]. The memories of case-based reasoning systems are characterized by their ability to interact tightly with the reasoning and learning processes [24].

In this paper, a *cognitive task* is a task that a system can perform, such as diagnosis or planning. A cognitive task can be characterized by an initial space, containing the initial state, a final space, containing the final state, and a path between these two states. When the final state is well-defined from the start, a cognitive task can be called an *analysis task* [7]. On the contrary, when the final state is unknown at the beginning, it must be constructed by the reasoning process, and the cognitive task is called a *synthesis task*.

The general principle of case-based reasoning is to perform a given cognitive task, whether analytic or synthetic, by replacing it with an analytic task : choosing, among all the cases in the memory, the most useful case for performing the given task. Nevertheless, some case-based reasoning systems also use synthetic learning strategies, which are kinds of synthetic tasks. For example, the problems related to the construction of the memory organizing structures, which can be called concepts, meet those related to incremental concept learning in artificial intelligence. These problems have actually been in common from a longer time, since concepts have been used in case-based reasoning from the start to organize the memory.

This article proposes to join these two sets of problems, and to present some advantages of a co-operation between them. This co-operative approach is implemented in a case-based reasoning system, which is also presented .

The second part presents the set of problems related to case-based reasoning, and the third part that related to incremental concept learning. In the fourth part, some advantages of a co-operation between these two methodologies are explained. The fifth part proposes a co-operative system implementing this co-operation. Some result examples are set out in the sixth part. It is followed by the conclusion.

2 Case-based Reasoning

2.1 Definitions

First of all, a *case* is a set of empirical data, which are data met by a computer system during one of its experiences. It can simply represent a case existing in the application domain, for instance a patient case in a medical domain, or be constructed by the system, for instance to represent a problem-solving experience.

A *case-based reasoning system* is a system using, in order to process a new case, one or several previously met cases.

2.2 Methodology

Thus case-based reasoning is an artificial intelligence methodology the principle of which is that it is preferable, in order to process a new case, to use one or several previously met cases.

The set of cases previously met by a case-based reasoning system is a case-base, also called a *memory*. This memory comprises its accessing and its updating processes. Moreover, the processing of a new case presented to the system is realized by a set of processes closely linked to the memory [24]. These are :

1. the *interpretation* of the input data for the new case in order to match the indexes of the memory (when it is an indexed memory) ;
2. the *extraction* from the memory of the cases potentially useful for the reasoning process ;
3. the *selection* of the set of cases that will serve as a basis for the reasoning process ;
4. the *proposition* of a processing for the new case according to these extracted and selected cases ;
5. the *use* of these cases ;
6. the processing *evaluation* ;
7. the *learning* process in response to this evaluation.

The tasks realized by such a system may be various, and cover mainly two categories [15] : *problem-solving*, the goal of which is to find a solution for the terms of a problem contained in the representation of the new case, and *interpretation*, the goal of which is to construct an argumentation around the new case, based on the selected case(s).

2.3   Cognitive Modeling

Case-based reasoning also proposes a *cognitive model* of memory-based reasoning, such that memory and intelligence are closely linked. The precursory works of case-based reasoning are Schank's theories, that have progressively established the importance of memory for reasoning [23, 25]. The outcome of this work, the theory of dynamic memory [24], has laid out the path followed by the first case-based reasoning systems [16]. These systems study how memory, reasoning and learning can be made inseparable.

2.4   Learning

Learning in a case-based reasoning system is a memory-based learning prior to being an inference-based learning. If an *inference-based theory of learning* has been proposed [12] to classify symbolical machine learning systems, learning in case-based reasoning systems comes more under a *memory-based classification* than under an inference-based classification.

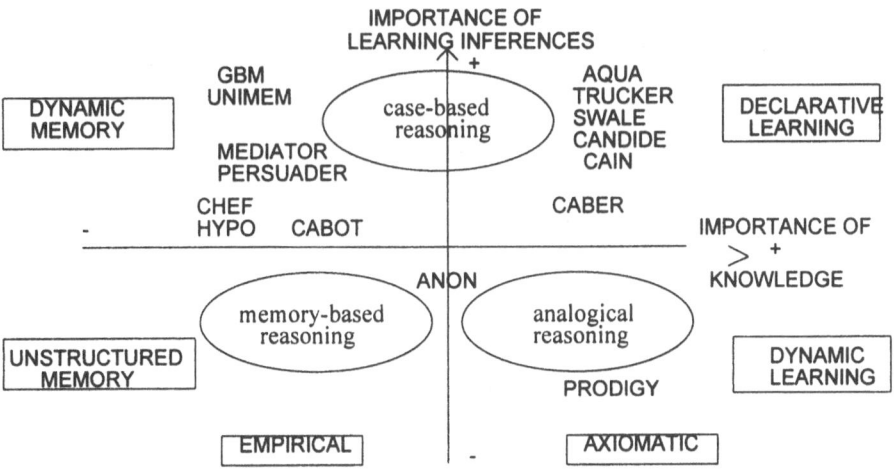

Fig.1. A memory-based classification of case-based reasoning systems.

In fact, learning in these systems consists in the construction and the refinement of the structures in memory, in their organization in an indexed memory, and in the modification of memory accessing and updating processes, that are part of it.

Nevertheless, several approaches have been used by a family of systems all sharing the use of passed experiences to reason about new experiences : memory-based reasoning systems, analogical reasoning systems, and case-based reasoning systems. Memory-based reasoning systems are characterized by unstructured memories, preferring a massive parallel search, and have difficulties for using background knowledge. Analogical reasoning systems are concentrated upon the *use* stage of the reasoning cycle, and thus deal as little as possible with the memory organization. They often rely upon substantial background knowledge to perform their reasoning process. Case-based reasoning systems focus their efforts towards the interrelation between memory and reasoning. Thus they incorporate as much as possible from the reasoning inferences to the memory, by the way of declarative learning inferences.

Two dimensions permit, among other, to classify these systems :

- the importance of *background knowledge* during the reasoning process ;
- the importance of *declarative learning inferences* : these can be defined as learning inferences the result of which is expressed in a declarative way, so that it can be kept in memory.

Figure 1 shows these dimensions, and positions case-based reasoning systems with regard to them, as well as some other systems families.

2.5   Set of Problems

The quality of the new case processing proposed by a case-based reasoning system depends upon the following principal criteria :

- the *usefulness* of the case(s) extracted and selected for the reasoning process;
- the *ease* of use of this(these) case(s) ;
- the *validity* of the reasoning process, a priori (before the experimentation) and a posteriori (after the experimentation) ;
- the *improvement* of knowledge through experience.

As stated before, case-based reasoning methodology views these criteria from the memory point of view, and studies what structures in memory, and what memory organization are advantageous for these problems.

These systems evolution favors hierarchically structured memories, either in shared-features networks (such as in IPP [17]), or in discrimination networks (such as in CYRUS [13, 14]). These organization variants are similar, and can be turned into one another. They rely upon the construction of clusters of similar cases in the memory, indexed under a common structure, generalized from them (a MOP [24]). To remedy the problem of uncomplete new cases descriptions, they also propose redundant networks, such that cases are indexed under several clusters. These clusters, or MOPs, are kinds of concepts, and the algorithms used in case-based reasoning to create and organize them are close to incremental concept learning, or conceptual clustering, algorithms in artificial intelligence.

The advantage of these hierarchically structured memories is that they ease the search for the most similar cases, when the size of the memory increases. Instead of traversing all the cases in the memory, only the most general, limited in number, structures (the MOPs), are traversed in a first step. Then, progressively, more specific structures are traversed, until the most specific structure matching the new case is found, conversely with the set of cases indexed under it. If the general structures ease the extraction and the selection of cases, the utmost specificity of the cases selected facilitates their use. Moreover, this type of memory faces the future. Learning occurs whenever a new case is processed, and following its results. Thus the memory keeps track of each of its experiences, whether success or failure, in a declarative way ; it is then as ready as possible to take advantage from future experiences.

The drawbacks of these memories are first the place needed to store the network of these general structures, secondly the amount of learning inferences necessary to keep this network to date, finally the lack of guarantee to lead to the most similar case [15].

3   Incremental concept learning

3.1   Definition

Incremental concept learning, also called conceptual clustering, is a variety of empirical learning that clusters a set of instances descriptions in classes, also called concepts. It uses inductive inferences to derive operational (which means in a language close to that describing the examples) definitions of the concepts from the examples.

Each concept has a particular characterization, generally expressed by a set of attributes, the values of which may be symbolical or numerical, and by relations between these attributes. Moreover, the concepts are organized in a hierarchy.

Incremental concept learning systems classify instances and construct taxonomies.

3.2   Methodology

Incremental concept learning systems are presented in [10]. The following formalization sums up this methodology [10] :

1. Giving a set I of instances to present sequentially, and their descriptions d_i :
$$I = \{ d_i \}.$$
3. Find conceptual classes Cj that cluster these instances in categories.
4. Find an intensional definition Dj for each category, that characterizes it.
5. Find a hierarchy H that organizes theses classes.

GBM [18] is an incremental concept learning system which is particularly interesting for the present research because its methodology can also be considered as case-based. As a matter of fact, this author proposed an implementation of the theory of dynamic memory, IPP [17], which was a true precursor of case-based reasoning systems, before working on empirical generalization.

The memory of GBM is composed of GEN-NODES, also called concepts, and instances. The GEN-NODES, similar to MOPs, are constructed by gathering the common features, (attribute, value) pairs, of all instances indexed under them. Attribute values are qualitative. Moreover, a discrimination network, or D-NET, is associated to each GEN-NODE, as in IPP, and indexes the depending instances by the features differing from the norm stored in the GEN-NODE.

A problem for the memory of this system is the dependence of the concepts learnt upon the order of presentation of the instances. A remedy for it was proposed : to defer as much as possible the construction of the concepts [20]. From then, whenever a new instance can not be linked to a concept, the system prefers to wait before rejecting this concept that its evolution permits it to definitely incorporate, or not incorporate, the instance.

Finally, the COBWEB system [9] uses another approach of conceptual clustering, by measuring a concept utility with a probability function. The aim of this numerical function is to minimize inter-classes differences and to maximize intra-classes similarities. The concepts learnt are conjunctions of disjunctions of (attribute, value) pairs. And more, an improvement of COBWEB, that dealt only with qualitative numerical values, is the CLASSIT system, that also deals with continuous numerical values.

3.3   Cognitive Modeling

Forming concepts, or categories, is one of the essential characteristics of human intelligence. Concepts are presented in psychology as the building blocks of human cognition and behavior [21]. In addition, the hierarchical organization of the concepts that humans constantly learn is the outcome of human categorization evolution [11], and the tendency to impose over-constraining structures on the examples plays a leading role [26], even if these structures are far more complex than those proposed in machine learning.

3.4   Learning

In the GBM system [18] for example, learning occurs at the level of each element, or feature, of the description of a concept. By the means of a counter associated to each feature of a concept, each one of them may be confirmed, by incrementing, or unconfirmed, by decrementing, during the search for a new instance through the memory. When a minimal threshold, which is a system parameter, is reached, the corresponding feature is withdrawn from the concept ; if the concept carries no more feature, it is withdrawn. Inversely the system constantly searches for new concepts to create.

Thus this system memory is a dynamic memory, containing both instances and concepts. It has been used by two systems, UNIMEM [19] and RESEARCHER.

3.5   Set of Problems

The quality of the proposed clustering, or classification, can be evaluated through the following criteria :

- the *fineness of the classification* : the instances of a same concept must be as similar as possible, and those of different concepts as dissimilar as possible ;
- the *ability to evolve* : if necessary, the partition must be dynamically updated each time a new instance is added : learning is then incremental ;
- the *utility of the classification* : for uncomplete instances, the classification should add new features coming from the description of the class to which they belong ;
- the *independence from the order of presentation of the instances* : an important problem for these systems is that they are dependent upon the order of presentation of the instances. UNIMEM as well as COBWEB deal with this problem, but don't avoid it [26]. Some authors [8] put the stress on the difficulty to achieve the independence from the order of presentation of the instances when learning is unsupervised, and proposes research directions.

4   Advantages of a Co-operation

4.1   Improving Case-based Reasoning through Concept Learning

The incremental concept learning practiced in many case-based reasoning systems deserves a thorough investigation. In fact, the concepts learnt during the case-based reasoning may play several roles :

- to *facilitate the extraction* when the case-base grows ; as pointed before, the search through a hierarchy is more efficient than an exhaustive search through the whole case-base : it is a heuristic search ;
- to *facilitate the selection* of the cases the most useful for the reasoning process : these are indexed under the concepts retrieved ; the comparison of these cases is reduced to their differences, and is thus more simple ;
- to *guide the use* of these cases : concepts provide general knowledge able to guide the use of the cases, for instance the adaptation ;
- to *increase the reasoning validity* : when similar cases are clustered together in the memory, the structure imposed by a common concept is an additional guarantee of the reasoning validity ;
- to *facilitate learning*, and thus the improvement through experience : it is in fact localized in the extracted concepts, and in the cases depending upon them ; a more global restructuring is achieved only if local restructuring is judged insufficient.

It appears that the construction of concepts, if it involves more learning inferences at each new case processing, facilitates, and increases the validity of the reasoning process for subsequent cases. This advantage may be summarized by this property of dynamic memories, as quoted earlier : they face the future.

Another advantage is that concepts, which are learnt structures, remain in memory, and can be used later throughout the reasoning process ; not only to improve case-based reasoning in its field of application, but also to *broaden this field*. As a matter of fact, if the general methodology of case-based reasoning can be characterized as a *heuristic classification*, achieving an analytic or a synthetic task by an *analytic strategy* (choosing a case among all those of the memory), the concepts learnt during reasoning may serve as a basis for a *synthetic strategy* [4]. The concepts learnt are thus similar to elaborated cases created by the system, as in some other case-based reasoning systems, such as CABOT [6].

4.2 Improving Concept Learning through Case-based Reasoning

Integrating a conceptual clustering algorithm in a case-based reasoning system permits it to benefit from its whole methodology. The memory accessing and updating processes, and other reasoning processes, are placed at the disposal of the concept learning sub-task, and of its whole set of problems. Thus keeping the cases indexed under some concepts permits to remedy the problem of the dependence upon the order of presentation of the instances, faced by these systems when they forget all of them, without falling into the opposite excess of reconsidering all instances whenever a new instance is processed.

Moreover, when the case-based memory also contains theoretical knowledge, concept learning can profit from these by turning to an explanation-based generalization [22]. Another example of co-operation is the proposition of an explanation for the concepts learnt, either based solely on the cases, or equally based on the theoretical knowledge in memory [2]. In case-based reasoning, the explanation generation is indeed unseparable from the reasoning, therefore from the memory.

5   A Co-operative System

5.1   General Architecture of the System

The general architecture of the system presented here is a current case-based reasoner architecture (Figure 2). Its main peculiarity is essentially to be able to reason from concepts as well as from cases. The realization of an analysis task turns it towards the search for the most specific cases. But the realization of a synthesis task turns it on the contrary towards the search for the most specific concepts, and for the cases depending on those. It is then able to adapt to the task it performs [5].

Its memory is divided into two parts, an experimental memory, and a theoretical memory [4]. In this paper, only the experimental part of the memory is presented, because this is where the concepts are located.

99

5.2   Knowledge Representation

The *experimental memory* of the system is composed of *cases*, from a particular application domain, and of *concepts* learnt from the cases by incremental concept learning. Thus both the cases and the concepts are the *entities* composing the experimental memory.

Each entity in memory is represented by a conjunction of $<El_i, arg_i>$ pairs, where the El_i are either *attributes* (in which case the arg_i are values), or *relations* (in which case the arg_i are entities in memory).

So an entity E is expressed this way :

$$E = \bigwedge_i <El_i, arg_i> \qquad\qquad (1)$$

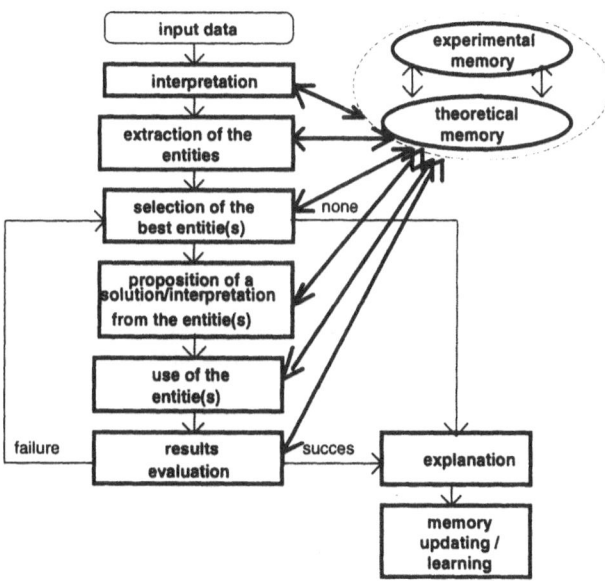

Fig.2. Functional architecture of the system.

5.3   Memory Organization

These structures are organized in hierarchies which are dependent upon points of view in the theoretical memory. Each cognitive task performed by the system is associated with a particular point of view. There are also other types of points of view, all corresponding to coherent sub-domains of the application domain. Finally, a neutral point of view is also defined, meaning that it is independent from the cognitive task realized. The concepts hierarchies depending on this point of view are constructed by a totally empirical conceptual clustering. On the contrary, the concepts hierarchies depending on the points of view associated to the cognitive tasks are ordered according to this task.

More precisely, a *point of view* is a filter for the description elements associated with each entity in memory. It can be expressed in the form of a conjunction of $<El_i, n_{i,pert}>$ pairs, where $n_{i,pert}$ is *a pertinence weighted variable* associated with the description element El_i. This pertinence weight is all the more increased as this element is important according to this point of view. The El_i element may be either an $<Att_i, val_i>$ pair, or a $<Rel_i, arg_i>$ pair, or simply an attribute Att_i or a relation Rel_i.

Consequently a point of view is expressed in this form :

$$P = \bigwedge_i <El_i, n_{i,pert}> \tag{2}$$

Each point of view element El_i is then associated with a set of entities Ent_j in memory, all sharing this element. Moreover, a *predictivity weighted variable* $n_{j,pred}$ is here also associated with each entity in memory. This predictivity weight is the more increased as the corresponding element permitted to favorably select a case, and the more decreased as this selection leaded to a failure.

So each element El_i drives the search towards a set of entities in memory :

$$El_i \rightarrow \bigwedge_j <Ent_j, n_{j,pred}> \tag{3}$$

Then, each entity in memory is a conjunction of $<El_k, arg_k>$ pairs. In addition, a concept associates to each description element El_k two discrimination weighted variables, a positive one $n_{k,disc+}$, and a negative one $n_{k,disc-}$. These variables are updated by learning.

5.4 Extraction of the Entities

The extraction of the entities potentially interesting for the reasoning is realized following the several indexing levels from the point of view. The extracted entities do correspond to the Ent_j previously presented, and more precisely :

$$\{ Ent_k \} = \cup \cup \{ Ent_{j,i} \} \tag{4}$$

5.5 Selection of the Entities

The step of the selection of the entities upon which reasoning will be based is essential, because it is here that the notion of similarity between the entities in memory is applied.

Let Ent_e be a new case presented to the system.

Two similarities are defined, one according to *a proximity measure*, and the other one according to *a classification reasoning*.

The similarity by proximity is calculated by the following scoring function :

$$sim(Ent_e, Ent_j) = \frac{\sum_{k=1}^{n} \alpha * sim(El_{i,k}, El_{l,k}) + \sum_{k=1}^{n} n_{k,i,pred} * n_{i,pert} * sim(El_{i,k}, El_{l,k})}{\alpha * n + \sum_{k=1}^{n} n_{k,i,pred} * n_{i,pert}} \quad (5)$$

According to this measure, the set of entities extracted is ordered by decreasing order of similarity, in a set that is the set *CA* of the potential candidates for the reasoning process. Nevertheless, these entities belong to different types : some are cases, others are concepts.

The concepts held in the set *{ Ent_k }* are the heads of hierarchies in memory. The similarity according to a classification reasoning is defined by a traversal algorithm through the hierarchies of concepts. For each concept C_k in the set *{ Ent_k }*, a set of cases similar to the input case Ent_e is formed after the results from the traversal algorithm *SEARCH(Ent_e , C_k)*. Returning from this traversal, the set of the most specific concepts in which Ent_e is substitutable is returned, and the cases the most similar to Ent_e are the cases directly indexed under these concepts.

The algorithm *SEARCH(Ent_e , C_k)* is that of GBM [18]. Depending on the cognitive task, the selected cases are either the most similar according to proximity (analytic task), or the most similar according to classification (synthetic task). Unfortunately, these sets are not always equivalent, and this comes from the dependence of GBM upon the order of presentation of the instances.

5.6 Use of the Selected Entity

The entity(ies) selected is(are) then used for the reasoning process. For an analytic task, the cases, or a part of their representation, are adapted. For a synthetic task, the concepts, or a part of their representation, most of the time serve as a basis for constructing an argumentation. Yet other types of reasoning are possible.

5.7 A Priori Evaluation

An a priori evaluation of the validity of the inferences realized is possible, taking into account the adequacy between the most similar cases according to the proximity measure, and according to the classification. The more these sets of cases coincide with one another, the more valid are the inferences made.

5.8 Learning

Learning consists first of all in taking into account the results from the fulfillment of the processing proposed for the new case, and secondly in modifying the hierarchy of concepts according to it.

Learning of Predictivity Variables. The predictivity variables are dependent on the point of view, and thus on the cognitive task realized by the system. They are modified according to the results from the experimentation of the processing proposed (a posteriori evaluation). It is essentially a *credit and blame assignment*. If the processing is successful, the predictivity variables are incremented for the description elements in common between the selected case and the new case. If the processing fails, the predictivity variables are decremented for the description elements in common between the selected case and the new case.

Concept Learning. Before inserting a new case under the extracted concept, the system uses an improvement of GBM algorithm to remedy the problem of the order of presentation of the instances. It is at this point in the reasoning process that the incremental concept learning takes the most advantage from a co-operation with case-based reasoning.

Let Ent_e be a new entity to insert in memory, and let Ent_k be the entity in memory selected as the most similar according to the similarity measure *(5)*. SEARCH(Ent_e , C_k) returns a set of concepts $\{C_m\}$,which are the most specific concepts under which to index Ent_e. In the same way, *SEARCH(Ent_k , C_k)* returns a set of concepts $\{ C_j \}$, which are the most specific concepts under which to insert Ent_k.

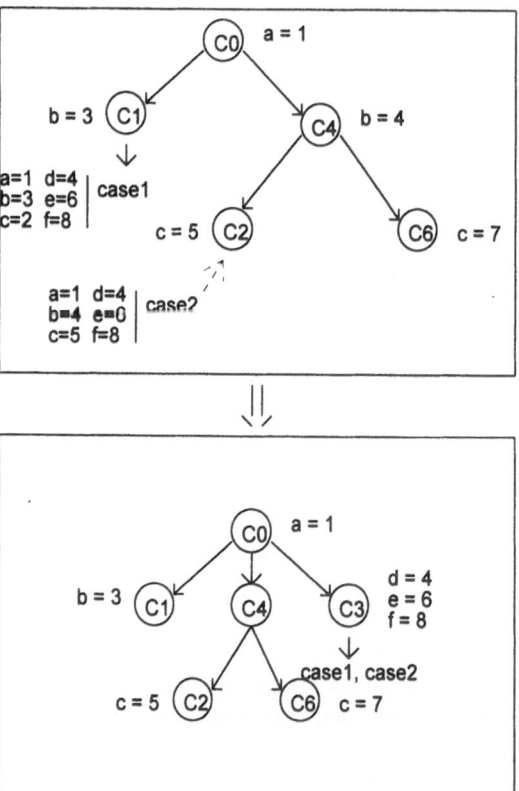

Fig.3. Example of a concepts adjustment where *case1* and *case2* are finally indexed under a new concept C_j directly indexed under the most subsuming concept C_0.

The problem is then to adjust the C_j to the C_m so that both cases are indexed under the same concept. This *adjustment* proceeds in several steps :

1. *concept matching* : first of all, the C_j are matched against the C_m, with the same similarity measure *(5)* as for the selection of the most similar case according to proximity ; the algorithm then proceeds with each pair of concepts formed ;
2. *search for the most specific subsuming concept* up in the hierarchy : let (C_1, C_2) be a pair of concepts, the most specific subsuming concept common to these concepts is searched for up in the hierarchy ;
3. *concepts adjustment* : when the most specific subsuming concept is C_1, a concept subsumed by C_1 is created, under which both cases are indexed ; the case indexed under C_2 is removed from it, and the hierarchy is updated accordingly (in particular, the discrimination variables are modified, and the concepts may need to be suppressed, starting with C_2) ; when the most specific subsuming concept is C_2, a processing analogous to the preceding is realized, where the roles of C_1 and C_2 are reversed ; when the most specific subsuming concept is neither C_1 nor C_2, but C_0, then a new concept C_3 is created under C_0, and both cases are indexed under this concept ; moreover, the index from C_2 to the recalled case is removed, and the hierarchy between C_0 and C_2 is reorganized following the modification of the discrimination variables. Figure 3 illustrates this last configuration.

Then the insertion of the new case under the concepts modified this way follows the general insertion algorithm of GBM [18].

6   Application

6.1   Domain

The application domain having benefited from this co-operation between case-based reasoning and incremental concept learning is *eating disorders in psychiatry*. A restricted validation of the system has been realized on the alimentary questionnaires of the patients. These questionnaires, filled by the patients themselves, contain three types of information, about 232 foods :

1. *the appreciation* of the food, having three values possible : "I like it", "I am indifferent to it" and "It disgusts me" ;
2. *the avoidance* of the food, having two values possible : "I avoid it" and "I don't avoid it" ;
3. *the reason of the avoidance* of the food, for each avoided food, with 22 values possible, such as "Sugar", "Fat" or "Taste" for instance.

The cognitive tasks realized by the system are *diagnosis* and *treatment* (analysis tasks), and *research assistance* (synthesis task). They are more detailed in [3, 4].

104

6.2   Results

The results presented here are about one *analysis task*, *diagnosis*, and the *synthesis task*.

For *diagnosis*, Figure 4 presents the results graphically.

Diagnosis

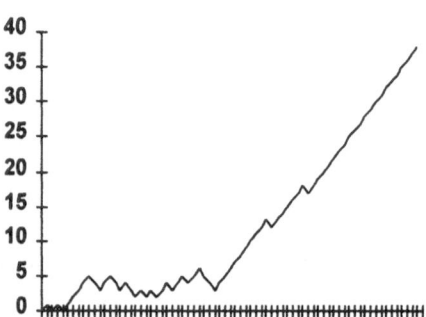

Fig.4. Accuracy of diagnosis : each ascending line between two X-axis points is a diagnosis success, and each descending line is a diagnosis failure.

For *clinical research assistance*, an example of a concept learnt by the system is given here for the neutral point of view, where learning is totally empirical. The case-based reasoning system gives an explanation for this concept learnt, on one hand from the theoretical knowledge contained in the memory about foods composition, and on the other hand by comparing this concept with those learnt from a control, that is to say non pathological, case-base. This explanation process is presented in [2].

```
Concept C38

    Diagnosis1(anorexia-nervosa)
    Prawn-appreciation(I-appreciate-it)
    Tripe-appreciation(It-disgusts-me)
    Rillettes-appreciation(It-disgusts-me)
    Dry-sausage-appreciation(It-disgusts-me)
    French-beans-appreciation(I-appreciate-it)
    Zucchini-appreciation(I-appreciate-it)
    Low-fat-fish-appreciation(I-appreciate-it)
    Milk-chocolate-avoidance(I-avoid-it)
    French-fries-avoidance(I-avoid-it)

This concept groups 19 patients.
The patients directly indexed under this concept
are Mrs. A and Mrs. G.
```

```
The foods appreciated share :
    calories( very-low)
    water( high)
    carbohydrates( very-low)
    lipids( very-low)
    magnesium( very-high)
    potassium( high)
    lipids( very-low)
    vitamin-B6( normal) ...
```

They are also appreciated by the control subjects(in the same proportion for {French-beans, Zucchini, low-fat-fish}, but in a higher proportion (90%) for {prawn}.

```
    They can be separated in 2 sub-groups( with:
    group 1 = {prawn( low-fat-fish}
        proteins( very-high)
        sodium( high)
        cholesterol( very-high)
        phosphor( very-high) ...
    group 2 = {French-beans( courgette}
        proteins( very-low)
        sodium( very-low)
        cholesterol( very-low)
        phosphor( very-low) ...


The foods in disgust share : ...

The sub-concepts are :

Concept C36
...
```

Conclusion

The system presented here shows how incremental concept learning and case-based reasoning can co-operate advantageously in a same system. On one hand the composition and the organization of the memory in a hierarchical memory, also called a dynamic memory, direct the case-based reasoning process, and so the quality of the concept learning process constrains strongly the case-based reasoning quality. In addition, case-based reasoning enlarges its methodology to the realization of true synthesis tasks, for which the concepts learnt by conceptual clustering form the basis for the reasoning process. On the other hand, incremental concept learning can also benefit from the contribution of the case-based reasoning methodology, as the example of the GBM algorithm shows in this article. It does so by questioning the concepts learnt incrementally during the case-based reasoning, and by explaining these concepts. More research is needed to take a better advantage from this reciprocal contribution.

References

1. Aamodt, A., Plaza, E.: Case-based reasoning : foundational issues, methodological variations, and system approaches. AI Communications 7(1) (1994)

2. Bichindaritz, I.: A case-based reasoning system using a control case-base. In : Proceedings ECAI-94, T. Cohn (Edt.) (1994) 38-42
3. Bichindaritz, I.: A case-based assistant for clinical psychiatry expertise. In : Proceedings 18th Symposium on Computer Applications in Medical Care, AMIA, Washington DC (1994) 673-677
4. Bichindaritz, I.: Apprentissage de concepts dans une mémoire dynamique : raisonnement à partir de cas adaptable à la tâche cognitive. Ph.D. thesis of University René Descartes Paris (1994)
5. Bichindaritz, I.: A case-based reasoner adaptive to different cognitive tasks. In : Proceedings ICCBR, A. Aamodt and M. Veloso (Edts.), Springer-Verlag LNCS/LNAI (to appear)
6. Callan, J., Fawcett T., Rissland E.: CABOT : an adaptive approach to case-based search. In: Proceedings of AAAI-92, Cambridge, MA (1992) 803-808
7. Clancey, W.: Heuristic classification. Artificial Intelligence 27 (1985) 289-350
8. Cornuéjols, A.: Getting order independence in incremental learning. In: Proceedings of the European Working Session on Learning (1993) 196-212
9. Fisher, D.: Knowledge acquisition via incremental conceptual clustering. Machine Learning 2 (1987) 139-172
10. Gennari, J., Langley P., Fisher D.: Models of incremental concept formation. Artificial Intelligence 40 (1989) 11-61
11. Houdé, O.: Catégorisation et développement cognitif. Presses Universitaires de France Paris (1992)
12. Kodratoff, Y., Michalski, R. (Edts.): Machine learning : an artificial intelligence approach Volume 3. Morgan Kaufmann Publishers Inc. San Mateo CA (1990)
13. Kolodner, J.: Maintaining organization in a dynamic long-term memory. Cognitive Science 7 (1983) 243-280
14. Kolodner, J.: Reconstructive memory : a computer model. Cognitive Science 7 (1983) 281-328
15. Kolodner, J.: Case-based reasoning. Morgan Kaufmann Publishers San Mateo California (1993)
16. Kolodner, J., Riesbeck, C. (Edts.): Experience, memory and reasoning. Lawrence Erlbaum Associates Hillsdale New Jersey (1986)
17. Lebowitz, M.: Generalization from natural language text. Cognitive Science 7 (1983) 1-40
18. Lebowitz, M.: Concept learning in a rich input domain : generalization-based memory. In : machine learning : an artificial intelligence approach Vol 2, Michalski, R., Carbonell, J., Mitchell, T. (Edts.) Morgan Kaufmann Los Altos CA (1986)
19. Lebowitz, M.: Experiments with incremental concept formation : UNIMEM. Machine learning 2 (1987) 103-138
20. Lebowitz, M.: Deferred commitment in UNIMEM : waiting to learn. In : Proceedings 5th Machine Learning Conference. Ann Arbor Michigan (1988) 80-86
21. Medin, D.: Concepts and conceptual structure. American Psychologist Vol. 44 No. 12 (1989) 1461-1481
22. Ram, A.: Indexing, elaboration and refinement : incremental learning of explanatory cases. In : Case-based learning, Kolodner J. (Edt.) Kluwer Academic Publishers Boston (1993) 7-54
23. Schank, R.: Conceptual information processing. North-Holland Amsterdam (1975)
24. Schank, R.: Dynamic memory. A theory of reminding and learning in computers and people. Camdridge University Press Cambridge (1982)
25. Schank, R., Abelson, R.: Scripts, plans, goals and understanding. Lawrence Erlbaum Associates Hillsdale New Jersey (1977)
26. Woo-Kyoung, A., Medin, D.: A two-stage model of category construction. Cognitive Science 16 (1992) 81-121

Can CBR imitate human intelligence and are such systems easy to design and maintain? A critique.

Farhi Marir and Ian Watson

Department of Surveying, University of Salford, Salford, M5 4WT, UK

1. Introduction

"Human intelligence is approximately ninety nine percent pattern recognition and one percent reasoning" (Forsyth 1984).

This paper discusses the design and development expert systems that imitate human intelligence by solving discrete problems. This imitation has tended to focus on reasoning methods and the knowledge required to solve problems rather than focusing on the way problems are routinely solved. That is, reasoning rather than problem recognition. Case-based reasoning (CBR) is claimed to be a new paradigm that is more akin to the human way of solving problems. It has consequently been claimed that CBR systems will be easier to design and develop than model-based expert systems. This paper highlights some problems that exist with the model-based approach and asks if CBR really does address these problems. Our findings are based both on CBR literature and an investigation into the design of an expert system for housing refurbishment.

2. Evolution of Expert Systems

An important aim of AI is to imitate human intelligence in resolving, interpreting and explaining problems in real world domains. Designing expert systems requires building an explicit model of the knowledge needed to solve a problem *second generation* systems [Clancey, 85] using a *deep* causal model that enables a system to reason using first principles. But whether the knowledge is shallow or deep an explicit model of the domain must still be elicited and implemented often in the form of rules or perhaps more recently as object models.

Expert systems built using rules have been the predominant commercial applications of AI in the last decade [DTI, 1992]. These systems contain hundreds of rules that represent a causal model of the problem domain. In a complex domain, particularly one that involves quantitative or experimental judgement, eliciting and encoding this knowledge into a rule-set can present great problem for the knowledge engineers. Moreover, such systems can be brittle [Hart, 1985] and are difficult to modify or maintain as knowledge changes [Bachant & McDermot, 84; Coenen & Bench-Capon, 1992; Watson et al., 1992b]. Moreover, they are often slow and are unable to access or manage large volumes of information [Minker 1988, Marir 1993].

Solutions to these problems have been sought through better elicitation techniques and tools [Motta et al., 89; Brooke & Jackson, 91], better KBS shells and environments, improved development methodologies [Diaper, 89; Watson et al., 92a; Wielinga et al., 1992], knowledge modelling languages and ontologies [Alexander et al., 86; Steels, 90;

Chandraskaren 86 & 90; Wielinga et al., 92], and tools for maintaining systems [Bench-Capon & Coenen, 92, Watson et al., 92b].

Despite these efforts, several classes of potential applications ranging from computer-aided design to medical applications could not be implemented as they require efficient systems that have both the ability to manage large volumes of information and to perform deductions [Lai 1992; Meyer et al. 1991 and Kuhara et al. 1991]. Attempts have been made to integrate database technologies with artificial intelligence (Minker 1988, Marir and Yip 1992). In such integrated systems, the database management systems (DBMS) can be used more intelligently and efficiently if enhanced with logic system features such as the inference capabilities, while logic systems can effectively be made to access and share very large database through existing DBMS technology. The concurrency control, integrity constraint management and security enforcement of the database management systems will be very beneficial for the large and expensive knowledge bases that need to be shared and protected.

However, there is a more fundamental problem that has been overlooked. KBS practitioners did not consider how to build a KBS when there was no model available for complex domains. Overlooking this problem reflects the heritage of KBS in academic research laboratories. The early KBS (e.g., DENDRAL, MYCIN, PROSPECTOR) all operated in domains where there were good underlying models (either from first principles or statistical) - scientists are comfortable with working with models, they build them for a living. Unfortunately, in a commercial environment and outside of the Universities many people solve problems using previous experiences without reference to first principles and underlying causal or statistical models. It is no surprise that *expert* and *experience* derive from the same root. We posit that the KBS community was seduced by rules and neglected the truism that experts solve problems by applying their experience, whilst only novices attempt to solve problems by applying rules they have recently acquired. The application of experience to problem solving is the hallmark of CBR. CBR is proposed by some as a psychological theory of human cognition [Slade, 91] and one that provides a cognitive model of how people solve problems [Kolodner, 91]. It offers a paradigm that is claimed to be close to the way people solve problems and one that overcomes the brittleness of MBR systems [Barletta, 91; Helton, 91]. Also, CBR is attracting attention because it seems to directly addresses the problems faced in knowledge elicitation and maintenance outlined above, and integrate both database and AI techniques in storing, retrieving and reasoning upon the knowledge of the domain.

3. The CBRefurb Case-Based Expert System

This section describes a case-based reasoning expert system (*CBRefurb*) that estimate the cost of house refurbishment using the ReMind CBR shell. Refurbishment represents a substantial part of the UK construction programmes (on the year 2000 around 90% of the UK property will be over 20 years old) and is seen as an economic alternative to new build [Douglas and Peter 1990; Cedric 1990]. In addition, unlike new building, in this domain there are two interrelated source of complexity: the building's condition, which may not be accurately known until after a detailed building condition survey and the client's requirements, which may not be completely defined at the feasibility stage. The choice of CBR for this domain follows results from an investigation amongst the North West of England Councils and contractors that shows the complexity of this domain. This makes it difficult to build an explicit model of the domain and to implement it using rules or object models. This claim has been consolidated by the fact that even the domain experts use previous work on items of the house e.g. foundation, walls and roof to estimate new work.

CBRefurb project responds to this crucial need for the real world strategy of cost estimation by using previous experience as a base for estimating where uncertainty exists along with the use of estimation techniques and rules where appropriate[Smith 1992]. However, the design of such CBR system is still requiring an extensive knowledge acquisition from the experts in the domain. This is due to the variation of the expert views on the importance of parameters that have an impact on the cost and the methods used to adapt similar cases and also the aim of the construction institution.

3.1 Case Representation
At least three classes of factors have been identified as having an impact on the price. The *house specification factors* e.g. the age, the place, the items to be repaired and the structure of the house which reflect the state of the house, and the extent and the quality of the work required. The *external factors* which reflect the state of the market, technological innovations of new and cheaper materials and the personal experience of the estimator. Finally, the *item specific factors* which describe the state, type and size of the item, and the quality of materials to be used for its repair. It follows that each case of the system will be composed of two main parts. A flat representation for the generalised features like house specification features, the different item involved in the work, the external factors and the real costs for the whole work, and a hierarchical representation as sub-cases for the specific features of each item of the house.

3.2 Case Indexing
In the same manner two levels of domain knowledge are associated to the case and its sub-cases. General knowledge of the domain, its construction regulations and other constraints are represented in ReMind inductive decision tree and production rules. Such general knowledge is used to classify similar cases into sets of *Context-Cases* that share similar knowledge. Specific Knowledge of the item, its specific construction regulations are represented by rules enabling weights to be associated with specific features of items. In addition a mechanism have been implemented to allow the user to change the rules, the importance of the features in indexing and the case classification as the knowledge evolves.

3.3 Cases Retrieval

Due to the complexity of the domain and the fact that the cost estimation of a new house may involve pieces of several old cases, a strategy of multiple features and multiple case retrieval is retained. First context-cases are retrieved using as a similarity measure the general knowledge of the domain represented by rules and the inductive decision tree. Then further selection amongst the Context-cases based on similarity at sub-case level. This last retrieval is based on the specific knowledge of each item and the performance of the nearest neighbour techniques that uses the weight provided for the item specific features. If no similar cases exist, another mechanism has been implemented to allow backtracking up the hierarchy to return to context-cases or even to its nearest class of cases and perform a search for cases that match the remaining unmatched features.

3.4 Case Adaptation

Case adaptation processes will be implemented using a combination of procedural programming, rule-based and CBR techniques. It starts at the level of the item sub-cases. If the item is similar then adaptation of the price can be performed. However if no similar sub-cases exist, a computation technique that implement one of the new building cost estimation techniques [Smith 1992] will be used and its result adapted. A similar approach of adaptation will be used for each item sub-case and extended to the whole case.

4. A Critique of CBR

We found during the investigation of cost estimation in building refurbishment that most of the estimators in the North West of England use previous case estimation as a basis for any new refurbishment work. They also confirm that they use other estimation techniques only when previous similar cases are not existent, and always these techniques give results far from reality in contrast to the close estimations to the reality when using previous real cases.

To this end, this section presents a comparison between model-based and case-based reasoning, from the aspect of the imitation of human expertise and the practical design of expert systems.

4.1 Imitating Human Expertise

Expert systems are designed to imitate human expertise; they can solve problems and explaining their reasoning by explicitly representing and managing large amount of complex knowledge.

4.1.1 Problem Solving

However, People do not solve problems using conceptual models of the world and the knowledge of an expert can not be entirely embodied in a set of rules or various hypothetical models. People do not reason about each problem they face from first principles as if they nor anyone else had ever faced a problem like it before. Instead, they try to find the best plan they have heard of, or previously used, that is the closest to the problem at hand and attempt to adapt the plan to the current situations (Riesbeck & Schank 1989). These are the reason why much of the AI community agrees that CBR is more close to the way people solve problems and thus as a psychological theory of human cognition [Slade, 1991] and one that provides a cognitive model of how people solve problems [Kolodner, 1991].

Comparing case-based reasoning to model-based reasoning from the human imitation aspect, is in fact comparing the use of experience and models as a way of solving problems. CBR is more efficient than model-based since reasoning from first principles is often a very complex way to come to an answer. Many steps must be followed through and often many assumptions must be made and checked. If human expertise was based on this method then everyday tasks would require a huge intellectual effort. However, using past experience is often a quicker and simpler method of reaching a solution. An illustrative example of the importance of previous experience is found in some councils who often refurbish a single house and use the resulting experience as an estimate for refurbishing large schemes of similar houses.

However, claims by the CBR community should not deny that model-based reasoning can provide accurate and precise results for well formulated problems as compared to the often approximate results of CBR. The techniques of CBR can be made more accurate only if it integrates MBR into the techniques of retrieval and adaptation. We found that even in weak domains, like refurbishment, parts of these domains can be modelled and implemented using rules and object-oriented methods alongside CBR techniques.

4.1.2 Explanation

Many questions arise whether most current model-based systems can really claim to be *experts* in their domains. One of the main areas of criticism is the quality and depth of the explanation of their reasoning in complex domains. A main cause of inadequate explanation is that a system while containing sufficient knowledge to infer a useful answer, lacks the underlying expertise upon which the performance is based. A human expert can explain his behaviour, not merely retrace his steps, by motivating and validating his decision and relating them to the domain as necessary. However, people generally prefer to reason from past experience rather than from theoretical knowledge because solutions derived from past experiences have precedents. Thus, answers given by case-based system can be explained and justified with precedents and not by listing the rules that fired or summarising the principals used to arrive at the answer. This is supported by our study. Many refurbishment experts found it easy to explain and convince their executive managers using real cases when making decisions ranging from minor ones (e.g., using one material instead of another) to strategic decisions (e.g., deciding between redeveloping or refurbishing a scheme).

4.1.3 Managing Large and Complex Knowledge

Many expert systems focus on inferencing and can not manage large volumes of complex knowledge (Minker 1988, Marir and Yip 1992). Due to such limitations, several classes of potential applications, ranging from computer-aided design to medical applications, can not be implemented since they require efficient systems that have both the ability to manage large volume of information and to perform deductions [Lai 1992; Meyer et al. 1991 and Kuhara et al. 1991]. However, in integrated database and AI systems, the database management systems (DBMS) can be used more intelligently and efficiently if enhanced with logic system features such as inference capabilities. While logic systems can effectively be made to access and share very large database through existing DBMS technology. The concurrency control, integrity constraint management and security enforcement of the database management systems will be very beneficial for the large and expensive knowledge bases that need to be shared and protected. The ability of an integrated system to reasons and manage large and complex knowledge-bases is claimed to be a characteristic of CBR. However, there is little research that shows that CBR systems can manage and reason with massive case-bases. The *saleability* of CBR is an pressing research issue.

4.1.4 Learning Process
It might seems from the literature that the learning process in CBR involves simply adding new cases to the case base. However we believe that the process is not so simple and must involve the following processes:
- Check the validity of the case instead of simply adding it, since incorrect cases may cause system to work improperly and redundant cases may cause inefficiency Relying on previous experience without validation may result in inefficient or incorrect solutions being recommended causing an increase in problem-solving time or errors that may have negative effects on the process of learning.
- Forget unused cases in order to maintain case-base efficiency.
- learn about the emergence of any indices that had not previously been thought significant. It is very important to have a dynamic mechanism for indexing features where some features who used to be meaningless can be very important. For example, in construction some buildings may have to demolished instead of refurbished because the cost of meeting modern building standards would be prohibitively high.

4.2 Design, Development and Operation
Although expert systems, especially rule-based and object-based are popular, they are, however, still regarded by many as an expensive luxury and they still face several problems during their design, development and operation. Namely:
- knowledge elicitation is a difficult process, often being referred to as the *knowledge elicitation bottleneck*;
- implementing KBS is a difficult process requiring special skills and often taking many man years;
- once implemented model-based KBS are often slow and are unable to access or manage large volumes of information; and
- once implemented they are difficult to maintain [Bachant & McDermot, 84; Coenen & Bench-Capon, 92; Watson et al., 92b].

Facing these problems the AI community is attracted to CBR because it claims to directly address the problems outlined above:

- CBR does not require an explicit domain model and so elicitation becomes a simple task of gathering case histories,
- implementation is reduced to identifying significant features that describe a case, an easier task than creating an explicit model,
- by applying database techniques largely volumes of information can be managed, and
- CBR systems can learn by acquiring new knowledge as cases thus making maintenance easier.

4.2.1 Knowledge Elicitation and Acquisition

The process of elicitation and acquiring knowledge usually require both a domain expert and a knowledge engineer. A large amount of time is needed to obtain and process the knowledge required for any reasonable sized domain. This stage represents an expensive *knowledge elicitation bottleneck* [Hayes-Roth et al., 1983]. Moreover, the engineer will meet a lot of problems in acquiring knowledge even in a domain that is based on a strong theory.

The fact that CBR systems use knowledge in a form familiar to the expert makes knowledge transfer between the domain expert and the system simpler. In domains that already have much of the required knowledge in the form of cases, CBR systems are easy to develop. Prior examples are compiled, analysed and input into a case base, instead of having to acquire and represent knowledge in the form of rules. CBR is expected to overcome the knowledge acquisition problem [Kobayshi 92]. However, it should be mentioned that CBR does not necessarily remove the need for knowledge acquisition altogether. What is being suggested is that there could be a major saving in the amount of knowledge engineering required to produce a CBR system compared to a MBR systems [Hennessey et al., 92].

Although, there may already be existing cases, choosing the attributes that are used to describe cases may require specialised knowledge engineering skills [Dearden et al., 93]. We face this problem in the refurbishment domain where the records we collected are in standard format but the emphasise on the features is very different from one enterprise to another. Moreover, If MBR faced the problem in eliciting and acquiring knowledge to build their models, case-based systems will face similar problems when using rules or formulae for adaptation. Since some items in our refurbishment domain will be modelled and presented using rules or objects. The elicitation and acquisition of this domain knowledge will obviously meet the same elicitation problems as faced in model-based systems.

4.2.2 Expert Systems Development

A CBR application can help the developer get the application running quickly, even though there is an incomplete case library [Hennessey, 92]. An incomplete rule-based system provides little value. This is because rule-based systems mach rules to a problem description, a missing rule will halt the reasoning process. The problem will not be solved. However, partial matching and 'best guessing" are built into the case-based strategy, because it is seldom that two complex situations match completely [Slator et al., 92]. Other nearly matching cases can compensate for a missing case. Therefore, the system can find and adapt at least a partial solution. However, difficulties may still arise regarding the confidence in the data collected for individual cases [Dearden et al., 93]. Moreover, Inference, who have considerable experience in fielding case-bases have reported that if a system can not solve most problems adequately there can be a very negative response from users. This can jeopardise the success of the system.

The claim that CBR systems can be implemented faster than MBR systems was supported by a study conducted by Cognitive Systems which stated that it took two weeks to develop a case-based version of a system that took four months to build in rule-based form [Goodman 89]. Also, and more recently, developers at Digital Equipment Corporation confirmed that a rule-based system called CANASTA took more than eight times longer to develop than CASCADE a case-based system with the same functionality [Simoudis, 92; Simoudis et al., 93]. However, claims such as these should be treated with cautions. The fact that the knowledge acquisition and elicitation have been performed when first developing these systems using rules, may contribute to the speed of developing them using CBR.

4.2.3 Maintenance

By their very nature expert systems require regular updates and maintenance. In all but the most static domains knowledge is continually changing. This need for regular maintenance is in addition to the general requirement to debug or expand computer systems in general. For many years practitioners believed that expert systems were easy to maintain - almost all books on expert systems development written during the eighties will contain a quote similar to "maintaining a rule-base is easy, being simply a matter of adding or subtracting rules from the knowledge-base" Easier than maintaining procedural C or FORTRAN code true, but not *easy*. Unfortunately, the experience of XCON/R1 [Bachant & McDermot, 84] and others [Coenen, & Bench-Capon, 92; Vargas & Raj, 93] has shown that maintaining model-based systems is not as simple as adding or subtracted rules or objects. As a knowledge-base grows it becomes a complex debugging task. The maintenance of the knowledge-base in expert systems usually requires the re-employment of a knowledge engineer and in larger systems the splitting of control knowledge and data can hamper maintenance. Introducing a new rule or modifying an existing one where the rule-base is large may lead to clashes of rules. There are no widely accepted techniques or procedures for maintenance of these systems. However, cases are easier to maintain [Slator, 92] since there is no requirement to edit a rule set or construct a decision tree; the system easily absorbs new experiences. Indeed a CBR system can grow as it gains experience of more cases.

Another major benefit claimed for CBR is a case-base may be updated and modified by the expert without the assistance of a knowledge engineer or developer. The effort of maintaining the knowledge base and the consequent cost and time are therefore greatly reduced. However, such *user-maintenance* has only been reported with Inference's tool CBR Express.

The above claims for CBR are still to be proven. As mentioned above it is unwise to blindly add cases to a case-base. Moreover, if developers have integrated rules into their CBR systems for adaptation, there will be a need to maintain the rules.

5. Conclusion and Future Work

The investigation and the prototyping of *CBRefurb* have been useful in acquiring experience of theoretical and practical aspects of case-based reasoning. This paper critiques the claims made for CBR. As with many claims there is often some truth. CBR does seem to mimic human reasoning. CBR systems do seem to ease the knowledge elicitation bottleneck, they may be easier and quicker to implement and they can learn. However, our work shows that developers of CBR systems do face real problems. It is necessary to integrate CBR fully with other reasoning paradigms and information systems. Methods for analysing and maintaining cases need formulating and importantly the effectiveness of CBR in commercial applications must be critically evaluated.

6. Acknowledgements
This work was partially funded by EPSRC project number GR/J42496.

7. References

Alexander, J.H., Freiling, M.J., Shulman, S.J., Staley, J.L., Rehfuss, S. & Messick, S.L. (1986). Knowledge Level Engineering: ontological analysis. *AAAI-86*, 2: pp963-68.

Bachant, J., & McDermott, J., (1984). R1 Revisited: Four years in the Trenches. *The AI Magazine,* 5(iii).

Barletta, R., (1991). An introduction to case-based reasoning. *AI Expert*, August 1991, pp.42-49.

Brooke, S. & Jackson, C. (1991). Advances in elicitation by exception. In, *Proc. 1st SGES Int. Workshop on Knowledge Based Systems Methodologies*. British Computer Society SGES, pp.70-8.

Chandrasekaran, B. (1986). Generic tasks in knowledge-based reasoning: high level building blocks for expert system design. *IEEE Expert*, 1(iii): pp.23-30.

Chandrasekaran, B. (1990). Design problem solving: a task analysis. *AI Magazine*, Winter 1990: pp.59-73.

Cedric Pugh [1990]. The costs and benefits of rehabilitation and refurbishment Proc. of Int. Symposium on Property Maintenance, management and modernisation, 7-9 March 1990, Singapore, Ed. Quah, Lee Kiang.

Clancey, W.J., (1985). Heurestic Classification. *Artificial Intelligence*, 27: pp289-350.

Coenen, F. & Bench-Capon, T.J.M. (1992). Maintenance and Maintainability in Regulation Based Systems. *ICL Technical Journal*, May 1992, pp.76-84.

Dearden, A.M. & Bridge, D.G. (1993). Choosing a reasoning style for a knowledge-based system: lessons from supporting a help desk. *The knowledge engineering review*, 8(iii): pp.210-22.

Diaper, D. (1989). Knowledge Elicitation: Principles, Techniques and Applications.Ellis Horwood Ltd.

Douglas J.F. and Peter S.B. (1991). Cost Planning of Buildings (6th Edition). BSP Professional Books.

DTI (1992). *Knowledge-Based Systems Survey of UK Applications*. Department of Trade & Industry, UK.

Forsyth, R. [1984]. Expert Systems: Principles and Cases Studies. Chapman and Hall Computing. London , UK.

Goodman, M. (1989). CBR in battle planning. In *Proceedings of the Second Workshop on Case-Based Reasoning*, Pensacola Beach, FL, US.

Hart , A. (1988). *Expert Systems: An introduction for Managers,* Kogan Page.

Hayes-Roth, F., Waterman, D. & Lenat D., eds. (1983). *Building expert systems*. Addison Wesley, Reading, MA, US.

Helton, T., (1991). The Hottest New AI Technology- Case-Based Reasoning. *The Spang Robinson Report on Artificial Intelligence*, Vol. 7, No. 8.

Hennessy, D. & Hinkle D., (1992). Applying Case-Based Reasoning to Autoclave Loading. *IEEE Expert*, 7(v): pp.21-6.

Kobaych, [1992]. Case-Based Reasoning and Knoweledge acquisition from cases. Japanese Journal of Fuzzy theory and systems, Vol. 4, No 4., USA.

Kolodner, J. L., (1991). Improving Human decision making through case-based decision aiding. *AI Magazine 12(ii), pp: 52-68.*

Kuhara, S. et al., [1991]. A Deductive database system PACADE for three dimensional structure of protein. Proceeding of the Twenty-Fourth Annual Hawaii International Conference on Systems Science. IEEE Comput. Soc. Press, Los Alamitos, CA, USA Vol.1, pp.653-9.

Kuntajoro, W. et al. [1994]. *Application of Case-based reasoning for setting-up optimization strategies*. Proceedings of Expert System 94. the fourth annual technical conference of British Computer Societ Specialist Group on Expert Systems, Cambridge, Dec. 1994.

Lai, E. et al., [1992]. The implementation of a deductive database for engineering *correlations*. Journal of Engineering Applications of Artificial Intelligence, Vol. 5,no.2,pp145-53, Marsh 1992.

Marir, F. & Yip Y.J.(1992) An Inference System Based on the Compiled Approach for the Relational Database Systems. *In the ITI Papers of the University of Salford*, :, pp.47-72, May 1992.

Marir, F. (1993). *An Integration approach for the deductive database systems: Enhancing the relational database system with a logic inference based on a compiled approach*. Ph.D. Thesis, University of Salford, UK.

Marir, F., & Watson, I.D. (1994). Case-Based Reasoning: A Categorised Bibliography. *The Knowledge Engineering Review*, Vol. 9 No. 4.

Meyer, R., Schlageter, G.,[1991]. *Knowledge base management system in the field of high energy physics. In DEXA 91*. Database and Expert Systems Applications. Proceeding of the International Conference, Berlin , Germany, 21-23 aug. 1991.

Motta, E., Rajan, T. & Eisenstadt, M. (1989). A methodology and tool for knowledge acquisition in KEATS-2. In, *Topics in Expert System Design: Methodologies and Tools*. Guida, G. & Tasso, C. (eds.), pp.297-322. North-Holland.

Reisbeck, C.K, & Schank, R.C. (1989). *Inside Case-Based Reasoning*. Lawrence Erlbaum Associates, Hillsdale, NJ, US.

Simoudis, E. (1992a). Using Case-Based Retrieval for Customer Technical Support. *IEEE Expert*, 7(v): pp.7-13.

Simoudis, E. , et al. [1992b]. *Knowledge Acquisition in Case-Based Reasonong: '... and then a miracle happens'*.   The 5th Symposium Proceedings Artificila Intelligence Research Fort Lauderdale, FL. USA, 7-9 Apr,pp. 273-7.

Simoudis, E., Mendall, A. & Miller, P. (1993). Automated support for developing retrieve-and-propose systems. In *Proceedings of Artificial Intelligence XI Conference*, Orlando, Florida.

Slade S.,(1991). Qualitative Decision Theory. *In Proceedings , see Bareiss R.,(Ed.) 1991*.

Smith, R.C., [1992]. Estimating and tendering for building work. Longman Scientific & Technical.

Steels, L. (1990). Components of expertise. *AI Magazine*, Summer 1990: pp.28-50.

Vargas, J.E., & Raj, S. (1993). Developing maintainable expert systems using case-based reasoning. *Expert Systems,* 10(iv): pp.219-25.

Watson, I.D., Basden, A. & Brandon, P.S. (1992a). The Client Centred Approach: Expert System Development. *Expert Systems* 9(iv): pp.181-88.

Watson, I.D., Basden, A. & Brandon, P.S. (1992b). The Client Centred Approach: Expert System Maintenance. *Expert Systems* 9(iv): pp189-96.

Part Two

Case-Based Reasoning: Application

Deciding Parameter Values with Case-based Reasoning

C. J. Price and I. S. Pegler

Centre for Intelligent Systems Department of Computer Science,
University of Wales, Aberystwyth, Dyfed, SY23 3DB, United Kingdom.
Email: cjp@aber.ac.uk

Abstract. This paper describes an industrial application of case-based reasoning (CBR) in the aluminium die-casting industry: the setting of parameters of a pressure die-casting machine for a specific die. As well as describing the application, the paper shows how the system has evolved. The use of cases has given the system a flexibility which has enabled it to be used in ways that were not foreseen at the outset of the project. The pressure die-casting application is a good example of a common problem: the correct setting of system parameters depending on a set of input values. The paper discusses the general use of CBR for deciding on parameter values, and describes the lessons that have been learned through the construction of the die casting parameter setting system.

1 Introduction

This paper describes Wayland, a computer program which applies case-based reasoning [3] to the problem of setting parameter values on an aluminium pressure die-casting machine.

There have been previous applications of CBR for deciding how companies should operate machinery, notably Clavier [1, 2]. Wayland differs from Clavier in two important ways. Firstly, it performs approximate numerical matching to past cases, where Clavier only does exact textual matching. Secondly, adaptation of the result is an important part of Wayland, whereas it seems to have been dropped from Clavier.

Wayland has been deployed for two years, and demonstrates the clear benefits that such a system can provide. The paper describes the mechanics of the Wayland program and the foundry's experience in using it. Finally, the paper considers the wider possibilities of applying case-based reasoning to deciding on parameter values, and draws out the lessons learned from implementing the pressure die-casting system and from observing how different types of user access it.

2 The Pressure Die Design Problem

Pressure die casting involves injecting molten metal at very high pressure into a mould (a die), where it cools to make a casting. Figure 1 illustrates many of the main objects involved in the process. Some of the key concepts are:

Gate. The hole through which the molten metal enters the impression part of a die (the shape of the casting to be made). The gate is usually kept to a narrow slit to reduce the cost of the casting. It has to be removed from the casting, and if the gate is more than about 3mm deep, the excess has to be sawn off rather than clipped. Consequently, both the gate depth and the gate cross sectional area are of interest.

Sleeve. The tube into which the molten aluminium is poured so that it can be pushed by the plunger into the die.

Tip. The tip is the end of the plunger by which the metal is pushed into the die. Smaller tips allow higher pressures to be exerted on the die. Larger tips allow quicker filling of the die.

Number of impressions. Some dies make more than one component per casting. For example a die which makes four components from a single casting is referred to as a four impression die.

Cycle time. This is the total time to make a casting, from one injection of metal to the next. It includes filling the casting (cavity fill time), cooling time, and extraction of the component from the die.

The terms given here are those used in die casting of aluminium. Some terms and concepts will vary in the casting of other metals.

Machine settings are critical for successful pressure die casting, and will always be a compromise between factors such as cost of producing the casting, maximizing the die life, and quality of the final product.

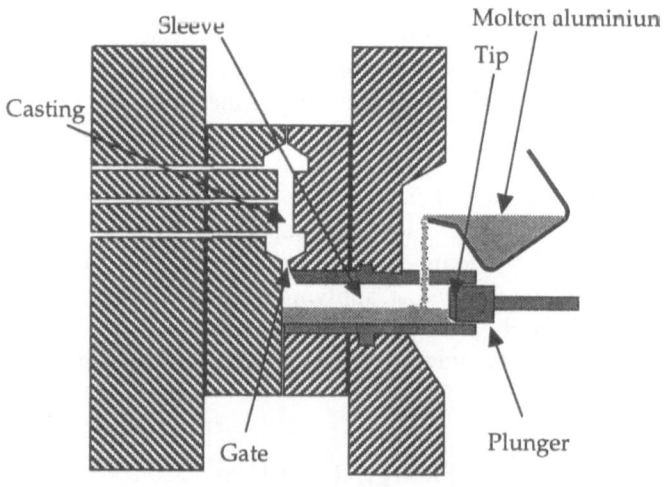

Fig. 1. A typical pressure die-casting situation

If the machine settings for a new die are badly wrong, then that fact can affect safety. For example, the combination of small tip size, high pressure and small casting can cause the die to "splash", i.e. the die opens momentarily, spraying molten aluminium at temperatures in excess of 500 degC. The ability to calculate values for machine settings during die design also has commercial implications when bidding for a new casting contract.

There are no generally applicable formulae for calculating values for pressure on metal, gate velocity, cycle time etc. for a given set of conditions, although different engineering bodies have attempted to present formulae to rationalise the process. The different formulae give vastly differing results even for identical operating conditions, so there is no agreed algorithm for calculating results.

The reason for the discrepancies between these formulae is that there are a number of sets of conditions under which a casting can be made. The die parameters are strongly interrelated, making the problem non-decomposable. A change in one parameter can be compensated for by altering another.

Case-based reasoning is an appropriate technology for this problem, because a foundry will tend to have a particular way of working. Foundries which have not built up a body of experience about particular types of casting might use the formulae provided by one of the engineering bodies, but foundries with rather more experience will rely on their own experience. Engineers will refer to records of previous dies with similar input requirements, and adjust the parameters for a similar die to reflect the different requirements of the new die being built. The records of previous dies are good examples of working compromises between the different operating requirements: such compromises might well have been found by costly adjustments performed in the foundry after the die was built.

The Wayland system, described in the following section, automates the identification of past dies with similar characteristics, alters the die settings to take into account the differences between the past die and the new one being designed, and validates that the new solution is within all design limits.

3 What Wayland Does

Wayland is available on the foundry computer network, and so users can quickly obtain answers about die design at their own desks. When they start running Wayland, they are presented with a form which they can tab through, filling in the requirements of the new casting: weight, size, number of castings made at one time and the characteristics of the shape. Figure 2 is a screen dump of a filled in form with values specified for each of the input fields.

Clicking on the Search button shown in figure 2 will cause Wayland to produce the best matching previous case. This is shown in figure 3, and is presented in three windows:

1. Details of the previous case that best matched. This window contains the requirements of the previous case plus the machine setting values being used for that die.

2. An adapted version of the previous case with the best values for this new die. This window is placed on top of the window with details of the previous case, and slightly to the left of it. This allows the user to compare the two sets of values and to see how the different input requirements have altered the output specification.

3. A picture of the previous casting. The values input in figure 1 do not specify the new die perfectly (they only give an approximation of its shape). The picture allows the user to decide whether the previous case that was selected really is like their new design.

If the user is not happy with the past case that was matched with their problem, then they can press the Next button to look at how further cases match their problem. Each time the user presses the Next button, the next best matching case will be displayed until the system has shown all matching cases.

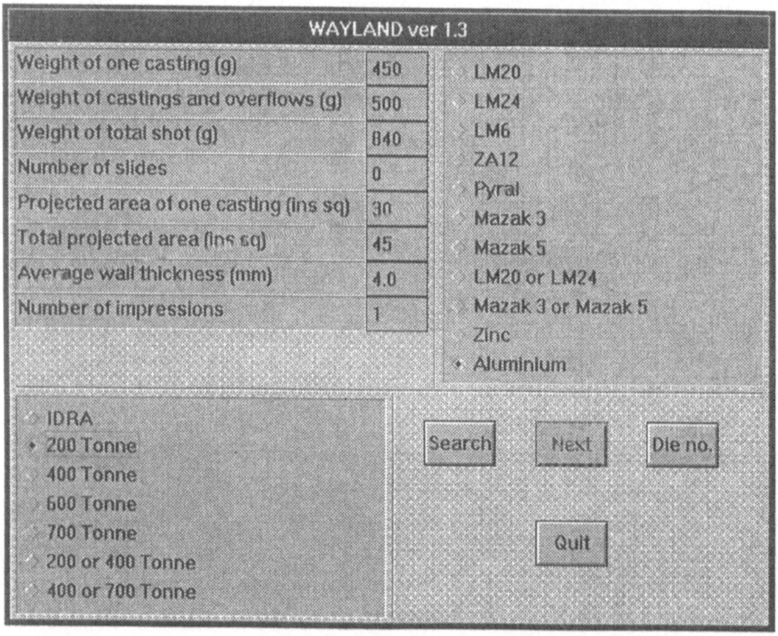

Fig. 2. Wayland input form with values filled in

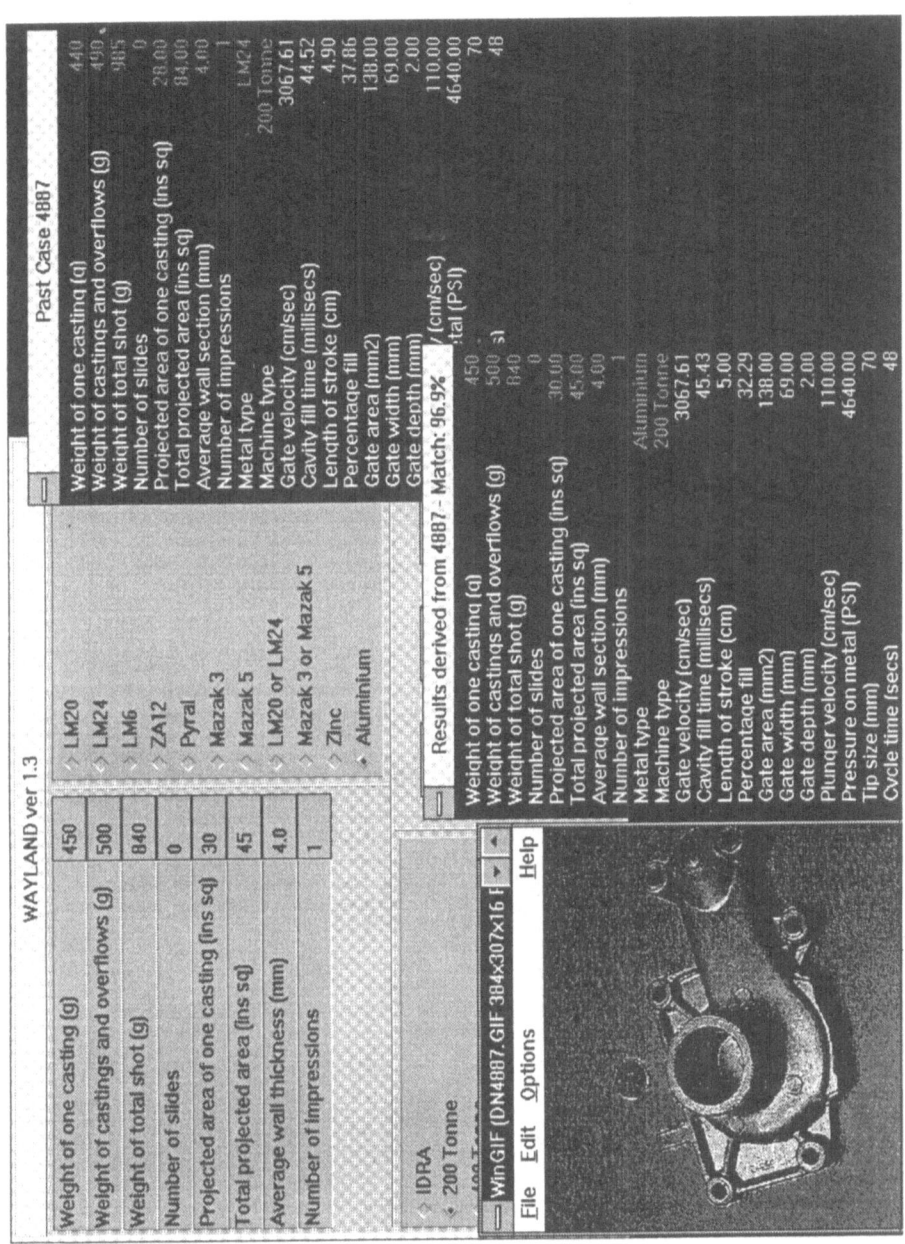

Fig. 3. Output information from Wayland

4   How Wayland Works

When the user runs the Wayland program to obtain parameter settings for a new
die, the specifications of the die are input as in the example shown in figure 2.
The input details are matched against the details of previous dies, and the most
appropriate past case is selected from the case base. Finally, rules are then
applied to make sure that the best possible solution for the new die is reached.
The rest of this section describes the details of this process, giving examples of
cases and rules.

4.1   Finding the Best Matching Case

Wayland has a case base of some 200 previous die designs, extracted from a
database of records of actual die performance maintained at the foundry. Only
dies with satisfactory performance have their values entered into the case base,
so the foundry personnel are confident that each case provides a good basis for
calculating new solutions.

Cases are fixed format records, with a field for each of the values shown in
figure 3. Some of the fields may be blank, if complete records for a die have not
been available. Here is the format of a typical case record.

```
CASE INSTANCE die_no_5014 IS
    weight_of_casting = 240.00;
    weight_of_casting_and_overflows = 310.00;
    weight_of_total_shot = 520.00;
    no_of_slides = 0.00;
    projected_area_of_casting = 19.50;
    total_projected_area = 35.50;
    average_wall_thickness = 2.75;
    no_of_impressions = 1.00;
    machine_type = t400;
    metal_type = lm24;
SOLUTION IS
    imagefile = 'dn5014.gif';
    gate_velocity = 6414.09;
    cavity_fill_time = 13.77;
    length_of_stroke = 3.10;
    percentage_fill = 16.24;
    gate_area = 135.00;
    gate_width = 90.00;
    gate_depth = 1.50;
    plunger_velocity = 225.00;
    pressure_on_metal = 8000.00;
    tip_size = 70.00;
    cycle_time = 35.00;
END;
```

Preliminary pruning of the case base is done by only retrieving cases for the same type of die-casting machine (e.g. only dies used on the 400 ton machine). Each of the retrieved cases is then assigned an overall match value. This is done by assigning a matching mark to each field and summing the total. Each field is given a weight which expresses its significance (e.g. number of impressions is an important field to match: it specifies how many of the parts are made at once in the die). Matches can be specified as exact (e.g. for number of impressions) or approximate (for items such as weight of casting) where the mark awarded will depend on how close the match is.

The case with the highest overall mark is the best match, and will then have rules applied to it in order to produce the kind of answers shown in figure 3.

4.2 Adapting the Best Case to Fit the New Circumstances

Rules are applied to the specification values and to the answers from the past case in order to:

- calculate further information from the specification
- take account of the differences between the past case and the new problem
- change parameters when safety criteria are violated
- decide whether the final result is good enough

This section explains what each kind of rule does, and gives an example of such a rule in Wayland.

Calculating Further Information from the Specification. The simplest type of rule calculates a necessary value directly from the information that the user has given. For example, the total volume of the metal in the casting and overflows is needed in order to calculate other values such as length of plunger stroke. It can be calculated by the following rule:

```
REPAIR RULE find_volume_of_casting_and_overflows IS
    WHEN volume_of_casting_and_overflows IS UNDEFINED THEN
        EVALUATE volume_of_casting_and_overflows TO
                weight_of_casting_and_overflows / 0.0026;
END;
```

Adapting Values from the Past Case for the New Die. This type of rule takes results from the past case and adapts them to the differing circumstances of the new die. For example, the following rule uses the length of the plunger stroke for filling the new die (calculated by the first kind of rule) and the value for plunger velocity taken from the past case, and calculates the time it takes to push the metal into the die.

```
REPAIR RULE find_cavity_fill_time IS
    WHEN cavity_fill_time IS UNDEFINED THEN
        EVALUATE cavity_fill_time TO
                    (length_of_stroke / plunger_velocity) * 1000;
END;
```

Changing Parameters when Safety Criteria are Violated. Some of the rules check whether the operating values are within safe boundaries and change them if they are not. The following example checks that the velocity of the metal through the gate is not too high. If it is, then it increases the size of the gate, so that the velocity will be reduced. The command "REPAIR" states that all rules should then be re-evaluated. This enables the rule to fire more than once if the gate velocity is still too high.

```
REPAIR RULE gate_velocity_too_big IS
    WHEN gate_velocity >= 5000 THEN
        EVALUATE gate_area TO gate_area + 10;
        EVALUATE gate_depth TO
                (gate_area / gate_width) / no_of_impressions;
        pr(['Warning: changed gate area: gate velocity too big']);
        pr(['Warning: changed gate depth: gate velocity too big']);
        REPAIR;
END;
```

Deciding Whether the Final Solution is Safe. Some problems caused by the difference between the past case and the new die are too complex for the Wayland program to deal with in the way shown above for gate velocity. In those cases, the user is warned about the problem. The following example warns that the job is too large to run on any of the machines in the foundry.

```
REPAIR RULE no_machine_big_enough IS
    WHEN total_projected_area >= 160 THEN
    pr(['Warning: projected area too big for 700 tonne machine.']);
END;
```

5   Benefits of Wayland

Wayland has been available at the foundry for more than two years, and is used by several different kinds of foundry personnel. They are interested in different information from the case base. For some users, the information that they actually want is not held on-line in the case base, but the best matching case can be used to index further information that is held not on computer but in manual files. Such users still find this much faster and more effective than browsing through paper records of past dies to find relevant information.

The main types of user can be categorized as:

- Sales staff
- Die designers
- Foundry engineers

5.1 Sales Staff

Wayland is in daily use to provide estimates of the cost of producing a new component. Sales staff are most interested in cycle time, although close matches in the case base are also used to access off-line information such as the cost of building the die to manufacturing such a component.

Before Wayland was available, sales staff had either to obtain an accurate estimate from an experienced engineer (taking several hours), or give a 'finger in the air' estimate: very unsatisfactory in the highly competitive foundry industry.

5.2 Die Designers

A close match with an existing die design can be helpful when designing a new die. It can enable the designer to reuse an existing design for 'running and gating' (the layout for metal feeding into and overflowing from a die). This can save several days work. More importantly, it bases the new design on a previous design known to be successful, and so minimises the risk that the new design will not work properly, or will have a short lifespan.

5.3 Foundry Engineers

This is the area where Wayland was originally intended to be used. By providing the most accurate available values for parameter settings, it can save significant setup time when a new die is first being installed. Previously, several days might have been spent experimenting with settings such as plunger velocity, in order to produce acceptable castings. In some cases, the physical shape of the die needed to be altered in order to produce acceptable results, causing further expense and loss of production. The use of Wayland has significantly reduced this time.

The Wayland case base is maintained by one of the foundry engineers, and perhaps the best measure of its success is that he is happy to have the task of maintenance. The amount of time it saves him and his colleagues far outweighs the effort of occasionally adding further cases.

The engineers are imaginative in their use of Wayland and produce new ways in which it can help them. One of the most recent innovations was using Wayland in troubleshooting. The engineers had had problems with one particular die for some time, and had been unable to make it work well consistently. An engineer decided to enter its parameters to Wayland. There was a good match on an existing case, and Wayland recommended a larger gate area than there was on the problem die. The gate on the problem die was altered accordingly, and the problems went away.

5.4 Summary of Benefits

The benefits of Wayland can be broken into four main areas:

It replaces opinion with reference to actual experience. In the trouble-shooting example just quoted, different engineers had different opinions of how to fix the problems. Wayland referred to a good previous solution and used that as a basis for its recommendations.

It saves engineer time. Much less time needs to be spent altering dies or changing parameters.

It reduces scrap. Less bad castings are made, because the parameters are correct.

It produces accurate estimates. This could be done before, but only by expending engineer time on a very speculative exercise. The foundry can produce much more competitive tenders in a fiercely competitive market.

Perhaps the most telling item in favour of the system us that the benefits clear enough to decide to use Wayland elsewhere. The foundry where the system has been deployed is part of a group of three foundries, and the system is also being deployed in the other two foundries in the group. This will be done using their own case bases, as their methods of working and typical dies are different.

6 Lessons for this type of System

This section draws together the lessons that have been learned from the development of Wayland, and discusses how generally applicable they are.

6.1 Characteristics of the Problem

Wayland has a database of input values and corresponding output values, where the relationship between the two has been obtained from past experience of correct solutions to similar problems. The further characteristics that made case-based reasoning a good solution to the problem were:

Large value space for inputs and outputs. Many of the input variables are continuous. and can vary quite widely, giving an infinite combination of possible sets of inputs.

Relationship between inputs and outputs unclear. There are no complete algorithms to give reliable output values for all inputs. The multi-dimensional nature of the problem would make it very difficult to discover such an algorithm.

Adjustment of individual parameters works well for near-miss answers. While there are no global algorithms for providing correct answers, it is possible to adjust an answer locally so that the new solution works correctly for the new problem.

A completely accurate solution is not needed. There is a space of correct solutions, where the system will work adequately.

Wayland is effective because its case base provides local reference points in the global space of all possible casting problems. The repair rules then provide both local adjustment, and verification checks that the new answer does not violate any global constraints.

The task which Wayland carries out can be identified in other industries as well. Obvious examples are in related industries. For example, we are constructing a system for a similar problem in a plastic injection moulding company. However, in order to illustrate that such problems are common throughout engineering, we will give two further examples:

Design of standard highway bridges. Highway bridges are the most common type of bridge built in modern times, and large construction companies have designs for many such bridges. A bridge design only tends to be reused where an engineer has specific experience of a previous similar design. We have constructed a prototype working in a similar way to Wayland, which accesses previous designs with similar characteristics [4]. This would enable many of the same features that Wayland does (accurate estimating, method of construction for previous design).

Deciding on mix when making steel. When scrap steel is added to a blast furnace, it is necessary to decide how much lime and iron to mix together in order to make the right quality of steel. The answer will depend on the type and amount of scrap being added. Deciding on the correct mix seems to be an arcane skill, where previous experience counts for much. Such experience is available in abundance in the form of previous records of mixes and whether they were successful or not. Again, minor repairs to the closest solution would give a fairly accurate answer.

6.2 Case-based Reasoning is an Effective Solution

It is reasonable to consider whether other technologies might not provide a better solution to the kinds of problem just described.

The Minimalist Approach. Does this problem need case-based reasoning? Could it not be solved by putting past cases in a spreadsheet or database and writing some macros or C code to access relevant cases.

The answer is undoubtedly "yes, it could be solved with more conventional technology". The advantage of CBR is that it makes the knowledge explicit. Both the matching rules and the repair rules are written in an understandable and maintainable way.

The Subsymbolic Approach. Why not use a neural net for this type of problem? Nets are excellent at learning to make associations.

It is not clear what examples could be given to a net to train it. A number of past examples of good solutions exist, but no examples of what is a good match.

In effect, the person constructing the net would still be generating weights for fields in order to produce examples to give to the net, so that it could produce an overall matching expression. It seems easier to keep the allocation of weights explicit, so that the system is more accountable.

The Symbolic Approach. Something like this could be built in a knowledge representation language.

Indeed it could. Each case would be an object of class "case type", and you could write a number of rules to do the matching and adaptation of cases. This would provide a reasonable solution. The argument against doing this is the same as the argument against using a spreadsheet. Case-based reasoning provides a more specific paradigm for building such systems. The case-based reasoning concepts of having a case, performing matching on the case and then adapting the resultant solution are identifiable in this type of application. It is reasonable to use a tool which explicitly supports those concepts.

6.3   Design Lessons

Given that such tasks exist in different branches of engineering, and that case-based reasoning with repair rules is an effective solution for such applications, this subsection discusses issues that arise when building such an application.

Provide Flexibility. Wayland was originally designed for one type of user, foundry engineers. Early versions of the system expected users to enter values for all input fields and to take the best result provided and use it.

In fact, users have different ways of working. Some do work in the way described (salesmen, for instance). Engineers prefer to browse through several of the best matches looking at the information, so we provided the Next button for them. Both foundry engineers and die designers like the ability to look at all examples of solutions to a particular kind of problem — all three impression dies with two sliders, for example — so it is important that they should be able to do this more traditional database retrieval as well.

Provide the Maximum Amount of Information. Such systems are of maximum benefit when users can access all of the information related to the case. Technical users will want to see the original case as well as the set of adapted answers that are the new solution. They may want details of the original case which are not part of the adapted answer. Cost of producing a die is an example of that in Wayland. If that information is not in the case itself, it is important that the case at least provides a pointer to where it can be found.

Provide Guidelines for Interpreting Answers. Technical users will have their own opinions as to whether an answer from the system is valid. For salesmen and other less technical users, it is important to provide guidelines on how the system should be used. The match has a weight attached to it: what values are good matches? Warnings are provided when altering significant values in previous cases: when should the user decide that the warnings mean that the case is not valid. We have provided a set of written guidelines for the users on these matters. In hindsight, it would have been better to provide further repair rules which did this interpretation automatically.

Acknowledgements:

This work was carried out at Kaye (Presteigne) Ltd on SERC TCS grant GR/H50043.

References

1. Hinkle, D., Toomey, C.: Clavier: applying case-based reasoning to composite part fabrication, Proceedings 6th Innovative Applications of Artificial Intelligence Conference, Seattle, Washington, pp55–62, AAAI Press, 1994.
2. D. Hennessy, D. Hinkle, Applying case-based reasoning to autoclave loading, IEEE Expert 7(5), pp21–26, 1992.
3. Kolodner, J. L.: Case-based reasoning, Morgan Kaufmann, 1993.
4. Moore, C. J., Lehane, M., Price, C. J.: Procs IEE Colloquium on Case Based Reasoning, London, February 1993.
5. Price, C. Pegler, I. S., Bell, F.: Case-based reasoning in the melting pot, International Journal of Applied Expert Systems, volume 1(2), 1993.

An Application of Case Based Reasoning to Object Oriented Database Retrieval.

Jeremy Ellman
MARI COMPUTER SYSTEMS LIMITED
MARI House, Old Town Hall
Gateshead, Tyne & Wear
NE8 1HE
Jeremy.Ellman@mari.co.uk

Abstract

In the near future, a potentially huge number of telecommunication services will be available to the public. Information about these services will be stored by suppliers in large object oriented databases. Users will be able to locate services that suit their requirements by retrieving objects from these databases. However the user's decision concerning the most appropriate service will not necessarily be simple: It will involve value judgements that seek to balance the desired service characteristics with other factors, such as availability, preferred supplier, and cost. One approach to this problem is to treat potential services as cases. This permits the application of CBR techniques, where the user's service requirement acts as the match target.

The ASCOT project followed this approach. CBR has the key advantage that the user is given a choice of matched services to select among. He may then refine his requirements appropriately. The implementation highlighted the need for "explanation" capabilities that allow the user to understand why one match is preferred over others.

KEYWORDS: Case Based Reasoning, Object Oriented Databases, User
Requirements Capture.

Introduction

ASCOT is a project in the CEC's RACE program running from 1992-1995. Its principal goal was specifying and demonstrating a set of software tools for end-user configuration of advanced telecommunications services. The primary purpose of these tools was to maximise service usability and hence promote use of new telecomms services. The toolset specification was influenced one the one hand by work on the architecture of telecommunication services and on the other by human factors considerations. These aim to improve usability by decreasing the number of "enabling tasks", or complex mental actions, (Whitefield et al 1992) that a user has to perform in order to use a service.

Implementation commenced in 1993, and a public demonstration and user evaluation of the toolset were held in 1994. The project is currently disseminating and generalising the toolset results.

ASCOT's key principles

An early principle that ASCOT decided was that user's service requirements should not be restricted to those offered by telecomms providers. There were two reasons for this: Firstly, it permits users to be flexible: Thus, if they must compromise over what services they accept on one occasion, they retain the flexibility to immediately exploit new services as they become available. The second reason concerns mobility. Since the services offered in any particular country or location will vary depending on its infrastructure, so a user may very well find his service requirements satisfied in different ways as he travels. Consequently the separation of user requirements is a key project element.

Another key element of ASCOT was the simplification of the user interface. We therefore created a graphical tool to simplify the requirements capture process -- particularly so that it was acceptable to non-technical service consumers. These diagrams called *Reference for User Services* (RUS, for details see Byerley and Bruins, 1992) describe the communicating entities and the channels that link them iconically (Beardon et al 1993): That is, the tool represents advanced services using different kinds of graphical links between iconic people and terminal devices. The tool produces user level service descriptions that are approximated into service objects using a simple rule based program.

The service objects obtained from the user may now be matched against those available. This module (known as the Service Unifier) uses Case Based Reasoning (CBR) techniques to offer the user a choice of several possible services. If the user does not find any of the services appropriate, he may refine the RUS diagram he used to specify them until a suitable service is located. Once selected, the service is started, and all the appropriate connections are made. The service may then be configured and controlled as the user uses it. (Figure 1 shows the toolset interface with a RUS diagram, and matched service)

The ASCOT toolset also includes a full set of facilities for the control of services in-call. Whilst these are technically interesting (in that they allow the change of Quality of Service, and the making and breaking of connections), there is no doubt that this would not have been possible without the Service Unifier. We shall now go on to look at its implementation in more detail, highlighting the more CBR specific elements.

The Implementation

The Service Unifier is a RETRIEVAL tool (Aamodt & Plaza 1994), and what it does is quite clear in principle: It creates a case base of possible services to be matched against a user's specification. Implementation was non trivial however due to the size and complexity of the Service Provider's object oriented database (OODB). This database was designed to support telecomm's planning and consequently includes far too much detail for the average service consumer.[1]

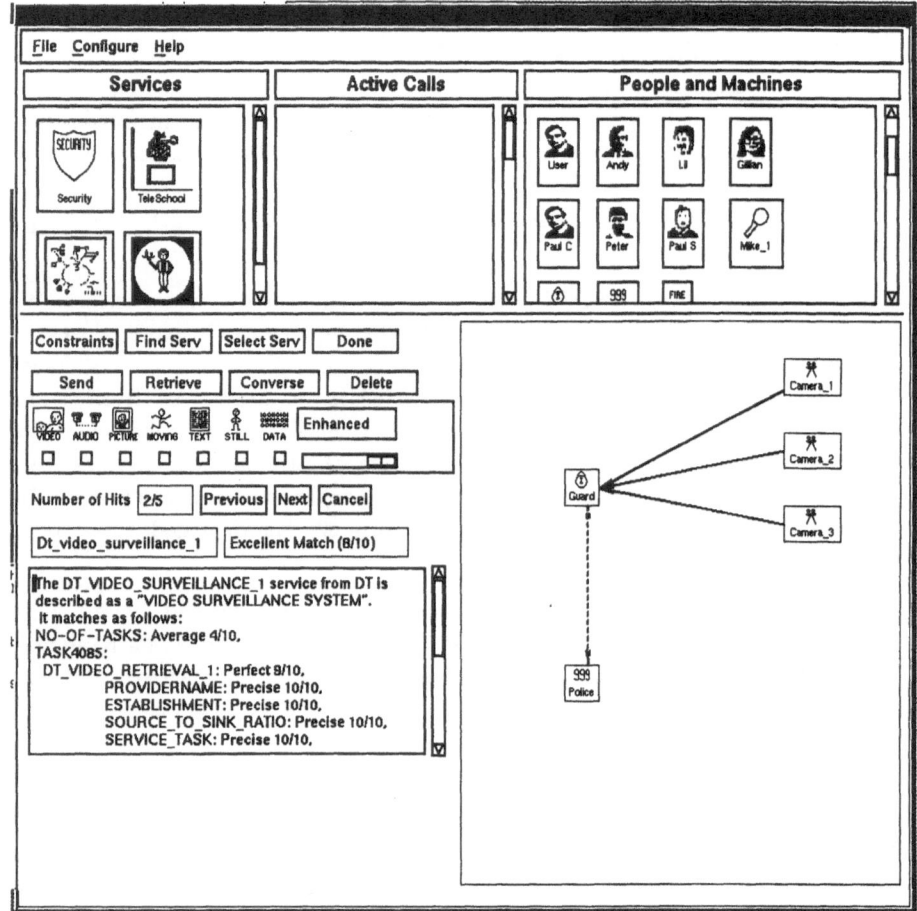

Figure 1. The ASCOT User Interface

Even if when we ignore the complexity of the OODB, future telecomms services are complex objects. Matching a user specification to one of this service involves taking into account factors at several levels of the object hierarchy of differing importance. Since the user requirements may change with each query, creating a static case base is inappropriate. The alternative, dynamically indexing the whole OODB for each query was equally unrealistic on performance grounds. Therefore, a mixed two stage

---

[1]   In fact, the database links to a model of an ATM telecomms network model that allows change in network bandwidth over particular links to be predicted as user's plan to use services.

approach was devised. Since this is domain dependent (though the approach will have wider applicability), I shall first discuss the nature of Broadband Service Objects.

Each service object is made up of service tasks, that in turn include service components. These correspond to what is usually understood be a telecomms service. For example an ordinary phone call would be an audio service component. Other service component types are video, data, still graphics, etc. These service components are modified by their quality of service, which for audio could be standard, hi-fi, or CD quality.

A video phone service would be a single service task made up of both an audio and video service component of particular qualities. A complex service may be made up of several service tasks: For example, a video conference where notes are made via a shared white board and an on-line database is available for consultation.

Component types are not the only factor in matching a user's requirements. The availability of the service is a factor, as is cost, and most importantly who provides the service. Indeed the service components in a complex service may be provided by different companies, and packaged together by a value added service provider.

Typically, this means that matching the user's task requirements is as important as matching his overall service preferences. Indeed, the same task may be included in several possible complex services that we must select among. The implication here is that the overall best service match may be a compromise and not include any best task matches. Alternatively the user may greatly prefer a good match on one task in an overall inferior service. In the interests of usability, the user must be made aware of both options and choose himself.

The principal here is that matching tasks is fairly straightforward, but matching services is not. This is because services can contain different number of tasks, and there is often no definitive correct solution to find. Therefore we match the tasks separately, and use these to index candidate service matches. Since there are fewer of these than in the whole OODB we avoid search time growing exponentially with regard to the number of tasks.

The steps in the process are as follows:-

> ¬ INITIALISE Task Case Base from the OODB
> - CAPTURE user's service requirement
> ® RETRIEVE matching tasks from Task Case Base
> ¯ LOOK-UP services that contain these tasks from the OODB
> ° CREATE Case Base of these services
> ± MODIFY user's service requirement to be a query
> ² RETRIEVE matching services
> ³ CONFIRM user selection, or GOTO -

Looking at this in more detail, the first step in matching tasks is to create a case base of available service tasks. Here we face an indexing problem, since service tasks are complex objects. Since the CBR system used (ART-IM) matches strings, words, or number we need to process the service task objects into a suitable form. This takes the service components and their qualities and combines them into complex strings for each task. For example, "STANDARD#AUDIO HIGH#VIDEO ". Additional processing also ensures that service type plays a larger role than quality in matching. Since building the task case base requires considerable processing it is only done once when the system is initialised.

Steps 5, 6 and 7 above are the next relevant ones for CBR. In step 5 we collected the services that best matched users tasks, and also kept numeric scores indicating the quality of these matches. Therefore in matching services, we can reduce the users requirement for task matches to a numeric match. That is, the user would like a service whose tasks matched his specification perfectly (1.0)

Essentially this solution reduces the problem of complex object matching to a two step process: Flatten the complex task structure, and find matches of these against the user's required tasks; Copy and simplify the services that contain these tasks dynamically into a new, small, case base that can be used to select a best overall service match.

This breakdown was needed since the CBR system used did not deal with complex objects in both source and target cases. It also has the additional advantage of *Strength Reduction*, in that services with multiple tasks increase work linearly, not exponentially. Our approach did not however solve problems that we call over-matching, under-matching and multiple task matches.

Multiple task matching occurs when the user specifies several similar tasks. Here one service task may match each user task very well, however it can not match them both simultaneously. The solution here is mechanical, and simply involves preventing the creation of multiple case base entries where a task slot is multiply assigned.

Over matching is a more interesting problem: Since some services may contain more tasks than the user requires, they are clearly less preferable (not least on the grounds of cost). However, if there are no better choices he should be told about this service.

Under matching is a closely related problem. Here one (or more) tasks match the user's specification very well. However the service does not contain enough tasks to satisfy all his requirements. If no other service matches as well, the user would like to be offered this as one of his options. Clearly, some kind of compromise is required.

The solution adapted in the Service Unifier is to explicitly count the number of tasks in a service and to include this in the generated case base. Over matching (and under matching) are consequently penalised, but not excluded. This is a satisfactory approach for users, who accept it if it is appropriately explained.

Explanation

Early on in the system's development both potential users and developers were often puzzled by the services (or cases) retrieved. This was due to an interaction between the complexity of the database and the matching process. Simply, some cases would be preferentially retrieved based on slight numeric differences. It was therefore important to reduce the effect of these since a user would be recommended some case over another due to an artifact of the matching process.

It was therefore decided to implement a minimal *explanation facility*. This simply shows the user the quality of a (service and task) match using one of the terms "NO MATCH, VERY POOR, POOR AVERAGE, FAIR, GOOD, VERY GOOD, EXCELLENT, PERFECT & PRECISE."

An essential first step was to understand the calculations carried out by ART-IM. We found that the weight assigned to any one parameter is influenced by the total weights assigned to the match. Consequently we needed to convert this match value into a simple fraction. This then allowed a straightforward index the set of match terms.

This explanation of match quality was a key aspect of the system's success. Users had no trouble differentiating between say good and poor matches, and were not inhibited in selecting other than the *best* match if they could see there was minimal difference between that and the second best.

Discussion

Frequently Case Based Reasoning is seen as a research paradigm (Slade 1991) into the structure of memory (ie following Schank and his group). Alternatively CBR is often used for applications such as building a help desk (Kriegsman and Barletta 1993). In both of these areas implementations follow what Aamodt & Plaza1994 calls a CBR cycle.

This CBR cycle is made up of four steps:-

   ¬ RETRIEVE the most similar cases
   - REUSE the knowledge in those cases to solve the problem
   ® REVISE the proposed solution
   ‾ RETAIN the parts of the experience likely to be useful for future work

This cyclic description applies equally to ASCOT. The majority of the work reported here (ie the Service Unifier) has dealt with RETRIEVAL, and how to implement this for a large OODB. Uses also have the services found automatically stored for later use. Indeed the RUS diagrams used can also be REVISED later if a modified service is needed. Work to date does not however RETAIN appropriate elements of the experience. This would in essence require the tuning the parameters used in matching, so that peoples preferences were better reflected.

In this implementation, the match weights were decided in advance, and were not modifiable by the system user. This is a simplification of the true situation. Firstly, the user may wish to prioritise some particular aspect of the service, or may have to respond to external constraints. These may be simple technological issues, such as restrictions in his terminal equipment, or policy issues. For example, his employer may have some preferred supplier relationship with a particular service provider.

In a more complete implementation, the system user should be able to tune these parameters, and should also have the capability of prioritising some particular communications channel.

Whilst the work described here has been fairly domain specific, the problems encountered have often been quite general. Essentially the ASCOT Service Unifier applied CBR to the problem of retrieval from OODBs. The approach chosen (flattening the query structure, and doing retrieval in stages) has the advantage reducing the problem from an exponential one to a series of linear steps. The creation of a smaller intermediate case base was also effective in that the most complex matching was only needed on a subset of the OODB.

Related Work

Aamodt and Plaza 1994 give a considerable number of references to all areas of CBR. However, with regard to database retrieval, Shimazu et al. 1993 describe a wholly more ambitious scheme that uses the corporate RDBMS as their case base. This approach allows CBR to be incorporated into enterprise wide systems, and brings with it the advantages of data security, integrity and so on. The essential aspect of their work is the application of SQL to achieve nearest neighbour matching. A major difference is the relatively simple nature of their queries, and the fact that queries and cases are essentially expressed in the same way.

Conclusion

Case Based Reasoning was an essential part of the ASCOT project. It increased the toolset's potential usability by separating user's requirements from the engineering requirements of the telecommunication service providers.

Case Based Reasoning allowed this to be achieved cleanly and naturally. No lengthy on-line user interrogation was needed. Additionally the user's involvement in the process was not compromised. This was because he always has the final choice over which service to select, or could choose to further refine his requirements.

References

Aamodt A and Plaza E 1994 "Case Based Reasoning: Foundational Issues, Methodological Variations and System Approaches" AI Communication Vol 7, 1 March 1994

Beardon P Dormann C Mealing S, and Yazdani M 1993 "Talking with Pictures: Exploring the possibilities of Iconic Communication" AISB Quarterly Issue 83/84

Byerley P., & Bruins, R,. Conceptual Framework for Usage of Telecommunication Services. In: P. Byerley and S. Connell. (Eds).

Byerley P. and Connell. S. (Eds) 1992. *Integrated Broadband Communications: Views from RACE - Usage Aspects* North-Holland Studies in Telecommunication Volume 18. Elsevier

Kriegsman M. Barletta R 1993 "Building a Case Based Help Desk Application" IEEE Expert Vol 8 no 6 December 1993

Shimazu H. Kitano H, and Shibata G "Retrieving Cases from Relational Databases: Another Stride to Corporate Wide Case Based Systems Proc IJCAI 1993

Slade S 1991 "Case Based Reasoning: A Research Paradigm" AI Magazine Vol. 12 no 1. Spring 1991

Whitefield A.D., Byerley, P., Denley, I., Esgate, A., and May, J., 1992, Integration of services for human end-users 1: Design principles, enabling states analysis and a design method. In: P. Byerley and S. Connell (Eds):

Case-Based Reasoning: A Technique for 'Decision Support Systems' in Residential Valuation and the Construction of Residential Housing.

Ilesh Dattani and Max Bramer, Artificial Intelligence Research Group, Department of Information Science, Faculty of Technology, University of Portsmouth.
Email: DATTANII@sis.port.ac.uk and BRAMERMA@cv.port.ac.uk

1 Introduction

Information Technology techniques; such as case-based reasoning, Adaptive search techniques and constraint modelling are being commercially implemented within dynamic support structures to aid decision making. Case-Based Reasoning is a relatively 'new research paradigm' to both problem solving and learning; in that we have not reached the kind of 'commanding heights' stage yet where we are able to 'brag' about the numerous wonderful commercial applications that have been developed.

The analysis of house price data to establish the effect of variations in locational and physical attributes has been attempted by the use of statistical techniques such as Multivariate regression. The aim is usually to establish which attributes can then be used to synthesise valuations of a range of different properties. Statistical techniques appear to have achieved only a limited degree of success despite the relatively complex calculations involved. We propose a methodology that incorporates both CBR and statistical methods. We are looking to consider whether statistics, induction and CBR can complement one another within a "hybrid system". Within such a system statistical techniques can be used to perform Exploratory Data Analysis (EDA) on large datasets and both induction and CBR can allow use of background domain knowledge when it is available: integrating both symbolic and numeric techniques.

1.1 Application Domain

We are considering the possibilities for applying Case-Based Reasoning to the valuation and construction of residential housing. Two datasets have been used to construct models, using Remind, within which the data is organised and analysed. The first dataset was collated from the 1970 US Census and included fourteen attributes (the outcome variable being the 'median value of the property).[1] The dataset includes 506 cases

---

[1] Original dataset held in the UCI Repository of Machine Learning Databases and Domain Theories

The data concerns housing values in the suburbs of Boston. Their are 506 instances all with 14 attributes, (13 continuous attributes (including "class" attribute "MEDV"), one is a binary-valued attribute. The attributes are:

CRIM	per capita crime rate by town
ZN	proportion of land zoned for lots over 25,000 sq. ft.
INDUS	proportion of non-retail business acres per town
CHAS^2	Charles River dummy variable
	(=1 <if tract bounds river>
	else
	=0)
NOX	nitric oxides concentration (parts per 10 million)
RM	average number of rooms per dwelling
AGE	average number of owner-occupied units built prior to 1940
DIS	weighted distances to five Boston employment centres
RAD	index of accessibility to radial highways
TAX	full-value property-tax rate per $10,000
PTRATIO	pupil-teacher ratio by town
B	*1000(Bk - 0.63)^2* (Bk represents proportion of blacks by town)
LSTAT	% lower status of the population
MEDV	Median value of owner-occupied homes in $1000's

There are no missing attribute values and all the data generated is in numerical format.

2 Implementation Methods and Results

2.1 Statistical techniques

"Pearsons Product Moment Correlation", "Multiple Regression" and "Principal Component Analysis" are techniques used for exploratory data analysis and attribute reduction prior to using Remind.[3]

---

[2] CHAS represents a binary attribute, all the rest being continuous.
[3] Remind™ Solutions from prior experience: A case-based reasoning development shell. Copyright © 1992, Cognitive Systems, Inc.

	MEDV	
MEDV	1.00	Represents correlation
RM	0.70	coefficient for
AGE	0.38(-)	$X_1...X_{13}$
DIS	0.30	against dependent
RAD	0.38(-)	variable **MEDV**
TAX	0.46(-)	
PTRATIO	0.50(-)	
B	0.30(-)	
LSTAT	0.74(-)	
CRIM	0.38(-)	
INDUS	0.48(-)	
ZN	0.36	
CHAS	0.18	
NOX	0.42(-)	

A correlational analysis was done in order to identify appropriate weightings for the variables within the dataset when applying the nearest neighbour retrieval.

The Correlation Coefficient is generally used when we are concerned with relationships, however, the independent variable (X) usually has many quantitative levels (i.e. X_1, X_2, ..., X_i) and the experimenter is interested in showing that the dependent variable is some function of the independent variables. (Howell.,87)

$$r = \frac{N\sum xy - \sum x \sum y}{\sqrt{[N\sum x^2 - (\sum x)^2][N\sum y^2 - (\sum y)^2]}}$$

Figure 1 Computational formulae for 'The Pearson Product-Moment Correlation Coefficient (r)

In defining the respective weightings of the 'match fields', regression analysis is a method we intend to apply in order to estimate how good a predictor 'X_1 is of Y in comparison to X_i' (where i=2, 3,.....,n). The aim of this is to derive the most appropriate methodology for EDA within this domain.

The technique of Principal Component Analysis (Pearson.,1901. Hotteling.,1933) attempts to achieve some degree of economy in that within any respective CBR model '20 or 30 original variables can be adequately represented by two or three principal components'.

The steps in a principal component analysis can be stated as:

[1] Make sure that the assumptions of 'a normal distribution' and 'homogeneity of variance' can be applied to the dataset.

[2] Calculate the covariance matrix

$$COV_{XY} = \frac{\sum (X - \bar{X})(Y - \bar{Y})}{N - 1}$$

Figure 2 The formula for calculating the covariance

This would be a correlation matrix if the assumptions for step 1 can be met.

[3] Find the eigenvalues $\lambda_1, \lambda_2, ..., \lambda_p$ and the corresponding eigenvectors $a_1, a_2, ..., a_p$. The coefficients of the ith principal component are then given by a_i while λ_i is its variance.

[4] Discard any components that only account for a small proportion of the variation in the data.

2.2 Models developed in Remind

The Nearest Neighbour algorithm and Inductive retrieval were both retrieval methods that were used for further analysis at varying levels of complexity.

$$\frac{\sum_{i=1}^{n} W_i \times sim\left(f_i^1, f_i^R \right)}{\sum_{i=1}^{n} W_i}$$

Figure 3 A Nearest Neighbour Algorithm

Such a representation of a qualitative model, as shown below, illustrates the causal relationships between attributes indicated by the virtual q-nodes within the model. They represent attributes derived as combinations of existing attributes and the respective data. As already suggested, at a simplistic level, the system uses a qualitative model to guide induction with additional knowledge. The theoretical hypothesis behind such a framework is to improve the accuracy of finding the closest match from the past instances and also to make the solution explainable using the qualitative model which would be highly desirable for practical applications.

146

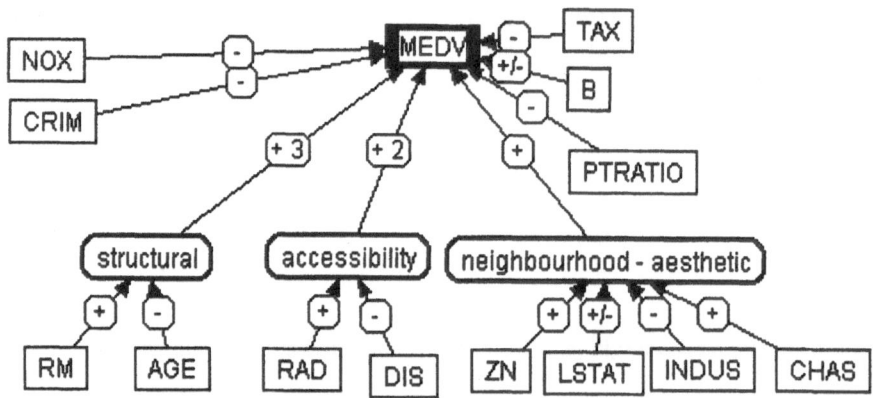

Accuracy of prediction of the variable MEDV within residential valuation appears to improve when the weightings for the respective virtual Q-nodes, which are derived from sub-sets of the set of attributes representing the cases, are increased and also when Combination retrievals are used. A Combination retrieval incorporates the use of Inductive Retrieval in tandem with a Nearest Neighbour algorithm. It is apparent that retrieval and indexing techniques can be incorporated into the system at varying levels of complexity through the use of Qualitative models, Virtual Q-nodes and Prototypes all of which can be used to represent domain specific knowledge and to accommodate knowledge guided induction within the retrieval process.

	EDA	WEIGHTING	
B =	-0.30	2	(7%)
CRIM =	-0.38	4	(14%)
DIS =	0.30	2	(7%)
LSTAT =	-0.74	8	(29%)
RAD =	-0.38	4	(14%)
RM =	0.70	8	(29%)

Qualitative Model (Virtual Q-Nodes)

Structural (11%)	Accessibility (5%)	Neighbourhood Aesthetic (11%)
RM = 0.70	RAD = -0.38	ZN = 0.36
AGE = -0.38	DIS = 0.30	LSTAT = -0.74
		CHAS = 0.18
		INDUS = -0.48

The weightings are proportional and when the virtual q-nodes are introduced into the 'weight matrix' the weightings attached to the six individual attributes are proportionally reduced.

The second dataset is a library of 34 cases from the "Inland Revenue Valuation Office (Southern Region)". This data has been applied using Neural Networks and we are comparing these results from results in Remind. Two weight vectors have been applied using six of the attributes that are considered as being the most significant in terms of there respective relationship to the outcome variable (property variable).

The variables within this second dataset are; [1] Location, [2] VO Code, [3] Type, [4] Format, [5] Constructed, [6] Reduced Covered Area, [7] Central Heating, [8] Garage, [9] Car space and the outcome variable [10] Value. The variables within this dataset are both numeric and symbolic and the development of a CBR framework using this dataset includes the use of symbol hierarchies within which the respective symbols are used to represent data that can be classified and ranked.

The symbol hierarchy is a branching graph structure of "parents" (generalisations) and "children" (specialisations). The generalised symbols allow the system to consider groupings of symbols when making splits. In a generalised symbol hierarchy, the clustering can choose between making splits on a specific value or on the generalised value, based on which value would be the best split. Illustrations of this might therefore be

　　Dwelling (generalisation): Bungalow, Cottage, House, Flat etc...(specialisations)

　　Type (generalisation): Detached, Semi-detached, Terraced etc...(specialisations)

This implementation includes the use of the CART algorithm (Breiman, 84) as the underlying mechanism for the inductive retrieval engine within Remind. CART belongs to the family of algorithms that incorporate a tree augmented strategy. Historically the major guide that has been used in the construction of classifiers is Bayes Theorem which provides a method for performing optimal classifications. Given enough information, it shows how to classify a new example with the maximum probability of success.

The use of classification trees by (Breiman 1984) did not emerge as some abstract exercise. To a large extent they evolved out of the problems that arose from some of the earlier methods.

At each node the tree algorithm searches through the variables one by one, beginning with X_1 and continuing up to X_M. For each variable it finds the best split. Then it compares the M best single variable splits and selects the best of the best. CART incorporates this standardised set of splits and has become a flexible and widely used tool.

When fixed-dimensional data have only ordered variables, another way of looking at the tree structured procedure is as a recursive partitioning of the data space into rectangles. Consider a two class tree using data consisting of two ordered variables X_1 and X_2 with $0 \leq x_i \leq 1$, $i = 1, 2$. Suppose that the tree diagram looks like Figure 4. An equivalent way of looking at this tree is that it divides the unit square (see Figure

5)[4]. From this geometric viewpoint, the tree procedure recursively partitions X into rectangles such that the populations within each rectangle become more and more class homogeneous.

3 Prospects for application

The main purpose of this project is the evaluation of a 'hybrid system' that would involve the use of a mathematical model , namely principal component analysis (PCA), with the results being applied to a CBR system incorporating CART, ID3, c4.5 (and their respective derivatives).
Steps [1] & [2] of PCA have been applied and have then to some extent been applied to a CBR tool, Remind, which incorporates CART as an underlying algorithm in its 'Inductive Retrieval Engine'.

Results to date indicate that this could be used in the development of a 'decision support system' for applications to determine taxation valuation, particularly the new Council Tax, or for loan security purposes. It could be used as an additional tool in the valuation process within which the system could gather comparables and adjust for differences relating to specific indicators. Such a system might also identify patterns based on similarities, interdependencies and relationships between pre-determined identifiers within the data. This might be useful for preliminary valuation prior to inspection. It would highlight non-conforming figures for further investigation and in some cases suggest 'a figure on which to work'. This might be suitable for application where bulk valuations might be required.

4 References

[1]Agnar Aamodt and Enric Plaza.,Case-Based Reasoning: Foundational Issues, Methodological Variations, and System Approaches. *AICOM* **Vol.7 Nr.1.** 39-59. March 1994.
[2]Barletta. R, et al.,ReMind: Developer's Reference Manual. *Cognitive Systems Inc,* 1993.
[3]Brieman. L, et al.,Classification and Regression Trees. *Belmont, CA: Wadsworth,* 1984.
[4]Dattani. I and Bramer. M.A., Case-Based Reasoning: Theoretical Principles, Development tools and the prospects for applications. *Artificial Intelligence Research Group, University of Portsmouth*: Technical Report, 1995.
[5]Evans. A, James. H and Collins. A.,Artificial Neural Networks: an application to Residential Valuation in the UK. *Journal of Property Valuation and Investment*: **11**, 195-204, Computer Briefing 1992
[6]Harrison, D. and Rubinfeld, D.L. 'Hedonic prices and the demand for clean air', *J. Environ. Economics & Management*: **Vol.5**, 81-102, 1978.

---

[4]Figures 2 and 3 are taken from (Breiman et al., 1984) and appear in the appendices.

[7]Hotelling, H. Analysis of a complex of statistical variables into principal components. *Journal of Educational Psychology* **24**, 471-41, 498-520, 1933.

[8]Howell, D.C.,Statistical Methods for Psychology, 2nd Edition.PWS-Kent Publishing Company, 1987.

[9]Pearson, K.,On lines and planes of closest fit to a system of points in space. *Philosophical Magazine* **2**, 557-72, 1901.

[10]Quinlan, R.,Combining Instance-Based and Model-Based Learning. *Proceedings of the tenth International Conference on Machine Learning. Morgan Kaufman Pub Inc,* 1993a, 236-243.

[11]Quinlan, R.,C4.5:Programs for Machine Learning. *Morgan Kaufman Pub Inc,* 1993b.

[12]Schank, R., Dynamic memory; a theory of reminding and learning in computers and people. *Cambridge University Press,* 1982.

[13]Tay, D.P.H. and Ho, D.K.K.,Artificial Intelligence and the Mass Appraisal of Residential Apartments. **10** *Journal of Property Valuation and Investment:* **2**, 1992, 525-540.

[14]Watson, I.,The Case for Case-Based Reasoning in Engineering Decision Support. *Proceedings of Information Technology Awareness in Engineering: Informing Technologies to Support Engineering Decision Making. (Edited by James A. Powell),* 55-64. Institute of Civil Engineers, London. November 1994.

[15]Watson, I and Marir, F.,Case-Based Reasoning: A Review. *The Knowledge Engineering Review:* **Vol.9, No.4,** 1994.

5 Appendices

5.1 Title: Boston Housing Data

Sources:
  (a) Origin: This dataset was taken from the StatLib library which is maintained at Carnegie Mellon University.
  (b) Creator: Harrison, D. and Rubinfeld, D.L. 'Hedonic prices and the demand for clean air', J. Environ. Economics & Management,vol.5, 81-102, 1978.
  (c) Date: July 7, 1993

Past Usage:
  - Used in Belsley, Kuh & Welsch, 'Regression diagnostics ...', Wiley, 1980. N.B. Various transformations are used in the table on pages 244-261.
  - Quinlan,R. (1993). Combining Instance-Based and Model-Based Learning. In Proceedings on the Tenth International Conference of Machine Learning, 236-243, University of Massachusetts, Amherst. Morgan Kaufmann.

Relevant Information:
Concerns housing values in suburbs of Boston.

5.2 Remind: A case-based reasoning development shell

Sources:
(a) Creator: Cognitive Systems.,Inc. Boston, MA.,United States.
(b) Date: 1992.,Version 1.1
(c) European Distributors: Intelligent Applications.,Ltd. W. Lothian, Scotland.

5.3 Residential Valuation Dataset

Sources:
(a) Origin: The Inland Revenue Valuation Office (Southern Region)

Relevant Information:

Relates to actual house price information from a number of streets in the Midlands. It covers a range of 34 post-1960 houses and bungalows (and one flat) in 14 different streets. Some particulars about the dataset at the time of undertaking the research cannot be stated because of Official Secrets Act requirements.

5.4 Initial Tree Growing Methodology

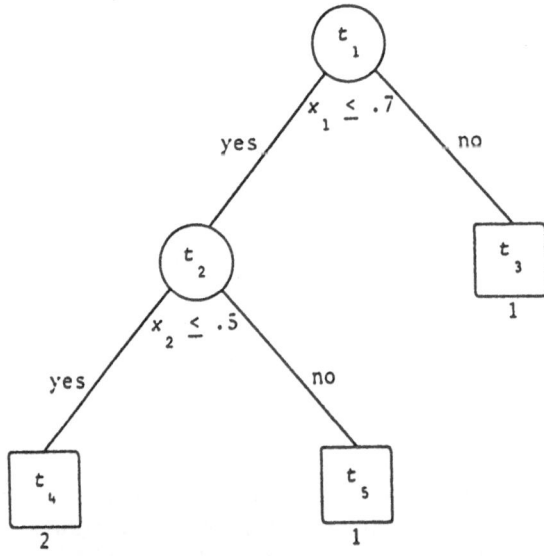

Figure 4

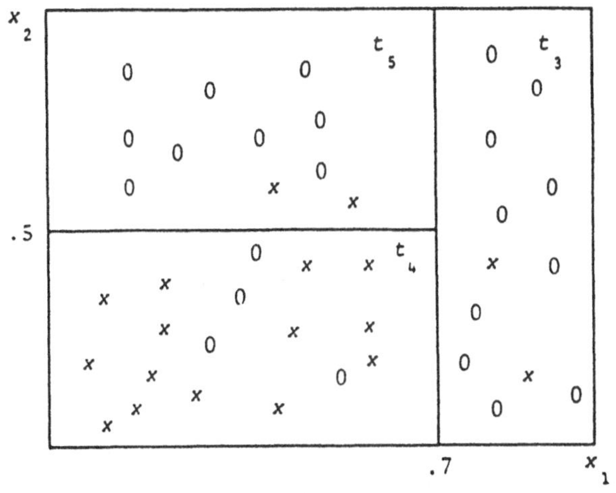

0 = class 1, x = class 2

Figure 5

A Hybrid System For Decision-Making About Assets In English Divorce Cases

Kamalendu Pal and John A Campbell
Department of Computer Science
University College London
Gower Street
London WC1E 6BT, UK
e-mail: P.Pal, J.Campbell@cs.ucl.ac.uk

Abstract. A hybrid knowledge-based (combining rule-based and case-based material) system for settling the disposition of the matrimonial home after divorce, according to relevant English law, is described. Development of such a hybrid system is significant because on their own neither rules nor past cases are sufficient for problem-solving even in such a supposedly simple legal area. A multi-layered representation is used for the case material. In responding to a new case, the system can produce initial advice using its rule-base, which may be full-fledged or partial advice, or indicate similar past cases and their decisions. The system is also designed to produce a similarity assessment to explore the best precedents to reach a final solution, taking into account the most relevant knowledge from either representation.

1 Introduction

The goal of this project is to develop a computer-based system that can use previous legal cases to suggest decisions on new cases which are similar, by exploiting both general legal rules and specific 'case-based' information. In law, 'statutory interpretation' refers to the process of determining the meaning of a legal rule, which involves determining the meaning of its constituent terms, and then applying it to a particular set of facts [Levi, 1949]. However, rules often have unspoken qualifications and exceptions. Therefore one needs to go beyond the statute itself to other sources of knowledge, particularly cases, and even to historical background about statutes. This drawback forces one to reason with precedents relevant to the statute. The advantage of case-based reasoning in this context is that it uses the results of previously-decided cases to analyse or solve a new problem. But on its own, case-based reasoning is not comprehensive for every case, and an approach is needed to encompass the relevant principles from both paradigms and apply these with additional interpretation to find a more appropriate solution.

This system takes as input a description of a current situation and produces initial advice for the user, providing that at least one of the rules from the rule base has fired. If none of the rules from the rule base fires, then the computation can suggest some particular or tentative advice by identifying the rules that come

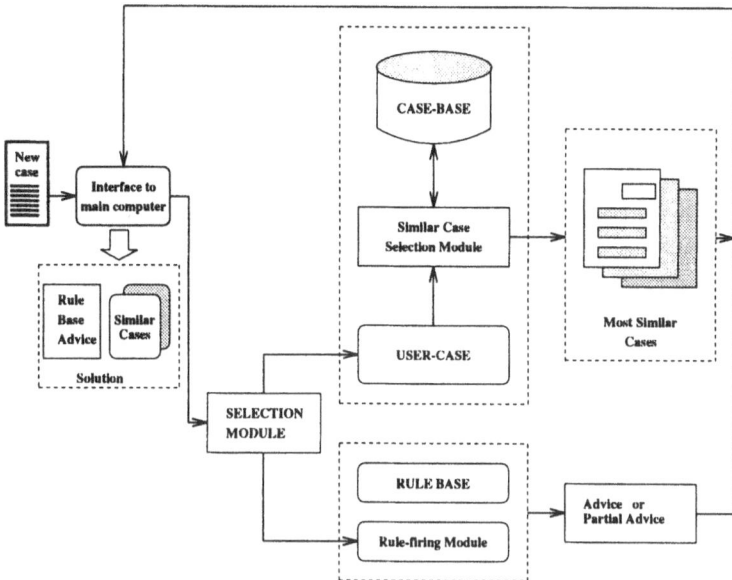

Fig. 1. System layout

closest to being valid for the situation. The computation also exploits features of the new case being considered, to choose similar cases from a relevant case-base, and displays their decisions to the user in a way that should facilitate the final decision.

2 Why a Hybrid System?

Many researchers ([Ashley, 1990]; [Ashley, 1991]; [Branting, 1991]; [Rissland, 1990]; [Gardner, 1987]) have advocated *case-based reasoning* (CBR) in the legal domain, and a few of them have attempted to design hybrid systems like CABARET [Rissland, 1990] and GREBE [Branting, 1991]. As indicated before in many legal situations, it is difficult for the decision-maker to reach final decisions using the legal rules of thumb. Any such rules may have unspoken prerequisites or may depend on a totally different situation. Therefore, the role of CBR in the system architecture is to improve on the effectiveness of a purely rule-based approach. It follows that the only cases from which useful analogies can be drawn are the exceptions. Cases that confirm the rules do not lead to any new behaviours. Notably, in the area of 'matrimonial home settlement in divorce (family) law' the application of such a hybrid system is clearly appropriate. The system layout is shown in Figure 1.

For example, the *Mesher Order*[1] is well known in English matrimonial home

---

[1] Mesher v Mesher and Hall [1980] 1 All ER 126n, CA (originally 1973). This form of order, which derives its name from the case in which it was made, requires that the home be held on trust for sale in equal shares, and the sale postponed until the dependent child(ren) of the family reach a certain age (say, 17 years), during which time the custodial parent would be able to live in the matrimonial home.

settlement after divorce. It is rule-like, although to call it a rule is something of a misnomer - it has never been more than a general rule of thumb. Initially the English courts adopted the *Mesher Order* approach as a guide to preserve the home for the child(ren) of the family during minority. However, this form of compromise between retention and sale of the family home is only appropriate under certain circumstances, and the boundary between appropriate and inappropriate conditions is still being refined after 20 years of case-based experience.

The courts have given much attention to satisfying the need of the parties for a secure home. Time and again[2], the *Mesher Order* has been out of favour with the courts in individual cases. Nevertheless, it is still currently in widespread use.

3 Knowledge Representation and Organisation

The legal knowledge for this project is represented in two forms as discussed below:

3.1 Legal Knowledge in Rule Form

The primary task of the rule-base designer is the acquisition and representation of domain-specific knowledge. Statute law has for a long time been the primary source of knowledge acquisition to arrive at rules in the IF <*condition(s)*> THEN <*conclusion*> format. For example, a small portion of the Matrimonial Home Act 1983 is represented in the rule form as shown below:

IF	the matrimonial home is rented
AND	there are dependent children
AND	the tenancy is transferable
THEN	transfer the tenancy to the custodian spouse.

If the given facts of a new case satisfy the conditions of legal rules, we can draw legal conclusions by applying such rules deductively. However, in actual cases, it is rare for legal consequences to be obtained by deductive reasoning alone. The reasons for this are as follows:

- Legal rules are written in natural language and thus often contain grammatical ambiguities. Therefore, they require precise interpretation for a particular situation.

---

[2] See, for example, the following cases where it has been decided not to apply the Mesher Order: Martin v Martin [1978] Fam 12; Chadwick v Chadwick [1985] FLR 606; Clutton v Clutton [1991] 1 FLR 242, Knibb v Knibb [1987] 2 FLR 396.

- Multiple rules may be applicable to a new case and inconsistent decisions may be reached as a result.
- The interpretation of legal rules depends on the socio-economic conditions of the society.
- Some obsolete rules may be applied to new cases.

Though legal rules involve the above problems, lawyers can draw conclusions by following legal reasoning. In applying legal rules to actual facts, lawyers interpret them according to the situation. If two rules are inconsistent, lawyers may extend or reduce the meaning of a legal rule, i.e. adjust the effect of each rule. In extreme situations, they may have to make a temporary rule to resolve the difficulty.

Because of the reasons above, the task of automating the relevant legal knowledge has taken two distinct paths. The first involves translation of legal statutes into IF *<condition(s)>* THEN *<conclusion>* format clause by clause, with additional knowledge being inserted to fill in obvious gaps in this method. The second approach involves acquiring from an expert those rules which come from an abstraction of the statute, or a workable way through the knowledge obtained from the text. In this project, we have spent considerable time to formalise a particular part of the Matrimonial Home Act 1983 from textbooks ([Cretney, 1984]; [Pritchard, 1985]).

3.2 Legal Knowledge in Case Form

It is necessary to represent the case law in some form which may be manipulated by programs. There have been two major approaches to representing legal cases for case-based reasoning: representing the entire case as a single frame, and providing a formal (non-frame; especially logic-based) representation for all the facts of the case ([Ashley, 1991]; [Branting, 1991]). Each approach has its drawbacks and strengths. Also, there is a lack of consensus as to what information should be represented in a case. One reason for this is the multiplicity of functional requirements on a case representation. The result has been that case representations range from flat lists of features to rich causally-annotated descriptions of reasoning processes. When lawyers compare cases, they compare the facts, each side's interpretation of the facts, each side's arguments, and disagreements about those arguments. Representing the case as a single flat record or similar structure does not support reasoning about the underlying themes in the case because it does not represent interconnections among the facts and themes of the case. Our multi-layer representation has implications for much of the case-based reasoning process including case comparison, selection and retrieval mechanisms.

The items of information that our software *ASHSD* (Advisory Support for Home Settlement in Divorces) represents include the following:

- the participants involved
- relationships among the participants
- commonsense knowledge

- temporal and causal relationships of the events
- the legal issues
- the decisions of past cases

3.3 ASHSD - Case Knowledge Representation and Organisation

In our work, cases are viewed as a collections of facts which are represented in a graph-based scheme that relies on the hypernode model [Levene, 1995]. We have encoded the cases manually in ASHSD - keeping in mind the need to capture a lawyer's notion of the 'facts' of a case. The main component of the hypernode graph model consists of a data structure called the Hypernode Model, whose single data structure is the *hypernode*, a directed graph whose nodes may themselves reference further directed graphs.

A hypernode case-base is a finite set of hypernodes which are used to represent real-world objects. A hypernode can be defined as :

$$G = (N, E)$$

where (N, E) is the directed graph (or simply a digraph) of the hypernode and G is the unique defining *label* of the hypernode. A digraph is an ordered pair (N, E), such that N is a finite set of nodes containing primitive nodes and labels and $E \subseteq (N \times N)$ is a set of arcs which are ordered pairs of nodes from N. In our model we assume the following domain:

1. A domain of labels L of hypernodes, whose elements are denoted by strings beginning with an uppercase letter. The labels are unique and act as object identifiers.
2. A domain of primitive nodes P which are partitioned into two disjoint domains, namely Atomic Values AV, and Attribute Names AN. AV is denoted by strings with double quotes, and attributes by strings beginning with $ - followed by a lowercase letter for naming purposes.
3. A domain of atomic values AV contains a distinguished value which is unknown and means 'value exists but not known'. This is denoted by *'unknown'*.

A *hypernode case-base* (or simply a case-base), HCB, is a finite set of hypernodes satisfying the following conditions:

CON1: No two hypernodes in HCB have the same defining label, i.e. labels are unique.

CON2: For any label (say G) in the node set of a digraph of a hypernode in HCB there exists a hypernode in HCB whose defining label is G.

The hypernodes shown in Figure 2 comprise a portion of a hypernode case-base. We note that by condition CON1 each hypernode representing one of the objects in the case-base has a unique label. Furthermore, the defining labels of the participant hypernodes are part of the hypernode with the defining label 'participants'. Thus, by condition CON2 there must be one hypernode in the case-base for each participant. Each event, participant or object in a past case has an associated unique label.

ASHSD represents participants as instances of the appropriate general class, such as *adult, child, legal* or *group* with associated properties. For example, the properties for the class 'adult participant' are *name, age, sex, qualifications*, etc. A case does not have to contain values of all the properties for a specific participant. Thus, for example, the proposed data structure for representing the participant 'Tony Smith, aged 40' is shown in Figure 2.

In this representation each participant has a unique defining label. In the example, Tony Smith's hypernode defining label is APARTICIPANT0101. The first two digits in this definition represent the case number and the last two digits represent the participant number in the particular case.

Each hypernode is composed of attribute names expressing the properties of that particular hypernode. For example, the hypernode APARTICIPANT0101 (see Figure 2) possesses the attributes $name, $age, $sex, $marital_status, $any_previo -us_marriage, $dependent, $qualifications, $occupation, $any_disability, $monthly _income and $realisable_assets_value. Whenever there is no information relating to the atomic value of any attribute, in the case report, the value is denoted by *unknown.*

The other information we gain from this representation is that Tony Smith is a graduate in science (e.g.B.Sc.) and that he is in a technical profession. He has no disability, e.g. mental or physical. His monthly income and realisable assets are 1000 pounds and 20000 pounds respectively.

Sometimes groups of participants perform actions or decisions together, and all members of the group are legally responsible for the results of those actions or decisions. For example, a group of judges in the *high_court* or *court_of_appeal* generally takes the final decision. ASHSD represents groups of participants as *gparticipants.*

The cases may contain explicit references to relationships or may contain enough information for one to be able to infer that a relationship exists, e.g. a relationship such as *divorced_couple, cohabiting_couple, stepfather, stepmother*, etc. ASHSD represents relationships as instances of a class of relationship with associated properties.

ASHSD groups all the information structures used to represent the facts and legal constructs in a case-base. The overall organisation of a case-base is shown in Figure 3, where CASE01 illustrates some of the structure that occurs in each of the cases named in the left-hand part of the figure.

The *case_index* attribute refers to the unique characteristic associated with the case. The *case_name* attribute is the unique name associated with a particular case. The *source* attribute represents the source of the case report. The *court_name* attribute is the name of the court that ruled on the case. The *participants_and_relations* attributes contain all the information associated with the participants and the relationships among them. Finally, the *facts, mat_home,* and *cause_and_actions* attributes stand for the names of the legal constructs associated with the case.

PARTICIPANTS01	
APARTICIPANT0101	APARTICIPANT0102
APARTICIPANT0103	CPARTICIPANT0101
CPARTICIPANT0102	CPARTICIPANT0102
CPARTICIPANT0103	CPARTICIPANT0104
LPARTICIPANT0101	LPARTICIPANT0102
LPARTICIPANT0103	GPARTICIPANT0101

A PARTICIPANT0101	
$name ⟶	"Tony Smith"
$age ⟶	40
$sex ⟶	"male"
$marital_status ⟶	"divorced"
$any_previous_marriage ⟶	"no"
$dependents ⟶	"unknown"
$qualifications ⟶	"B.Sc."
$occupation ⟶	"technical profession"
$any_disability ⟶	"no"
$monthly_income ⟶	"1000 pounds"
$realisable_assets_value ⟶	"20000 pounds"

Fig. 2. A portion of the 'participants' hypernode

CASE_BASE			
CASE01	CASE02	CASE03	CASE04
CASE05	CASE06	CASE07	CASE08
CASE09	CASE10	CASE11	CASE12
CASE13	CASE14	············	CASE$_n$

CASE01	
$case_index ⟶	INDEX01
$case_name ⟶	"Bassett v Bassett"
$source ⟶	"[1975] 1 All ER 513"
$court_name ⟶	COURT001
$participants_and_relations ⟶	PRELATIONS01
$facts ⟶	FACTS01
$mat_home ⟶	MATHOME01
$cause_and_actions ⟶	CACTIONS01

Fig. 3. Hypernode case-base

3.4 Case-base Management and Case Retrieval

A hypernode case-base is a set of interconnected graphs. The case-base contains
a section of heterogeneous (in size and in structure) cases. The hypernode model
provides inherent support for the nesting of information, e.g., a graph whose
nodes can themselves be graphs. This feature gives straightforward support for
case abstraction and allows each real object to be represented as a separate
graph.

In *case-based* reasoning, a new problem is solved by estimating out its similarity to a specific previously-decided problem and then adapting the solution of
the known problem to the new one. Similarity depends on the construction of a
metric that takes in a number of characteristics (e.g., goals, knowledge, context,
common features) of the problem domain. In general, the performance of CBR
systems relies heavily on a proper indexing schema and organisation for their
case-bases. Our case-base consists of two parts: a *case library*, which serves as a
repository for cases, and a set of *access procedures*.

One of the main issues in case-based reasoning systems development is the formation of a proper case-indexing schema. The *indices* of a case act like a card catalogue in a library to direct readers towards books that are likely to fulfill their reading needs. Case indices are the salient features, i.e. the choice of features that distinguish it from other cases. The *indexing problem* is one of making sure that a case is accessed whenever appropriate. Much research ([Goldman et al., 1988]; [Kolodner, 1989]; [Montazeri, 1994]; [Nitta, 1992]) has been devoted to effectiveness in the area of case indexing.

The relevant similarity is judged by matching of features of the cases. Thus in a matrimonial home settlement case, both the problem and the precedent are characterised in terms of the financial and personal facts; such as the parties' financial position, the length of stay in the home, the ownership of the home, financial needs, and other social aspects.

Our approach to retrieval based on multiple features involves using a three-step algorithm.

- First, the system reacts according to a choice made by the user on an abstraction hierarchy of the given $FIRST\_INDEX_{id}$ and then selects only cases whose $FIRST\_INDEX_{id}$ matches with the new case. For example, if the new case is dealing with an injunction order (e.g. to exclude a spouse from the matrimonial home), then the first step is to select all the cases from the case-base that have already been decided to include an injunction.
- The second step is to compare the cases selected from the case-base with the new case. This involves a similarity-assessment module in working out the $SECOND\_INDEX_{id}$ and using it to find the right level in the abstraction hierarchy that is comparable with the new case. Therefore this module searches for similar cases which have similar types of surface features. The similarity between two cases is measured by comparing the main facts and events in each case. If two cases have a long sequence of common facts or events, the cases are recognised as similar.
- The third step is to identify the most similar three or four cases with respect to the new case. Here, the system assesses similarity by comparing and examining the details under $THIRD\_INDEX_{id}$ of the selected cases. It tries to bring out similarity hidden under the surface description of the selected cases, using knowledge stored in the case-base.

In summary, the process of refinement starts initially when the user makes a choice (in the sense given in section 4.1) and the system uses this to retrieve the cases that have some common salient feature(s). The second step is a further selection, this time comparing the new case with the related cases on the similarity measure $SECOND\_INDEX_{id}$. The final discrimination of cases takes place in the third step where the remaining cases are compared with the new case using a finer measure of similarity, i.e. $THIRD\_INDEX_{id}$. The schematic representation of stepwise similarity assessment is shown in Figure 4.

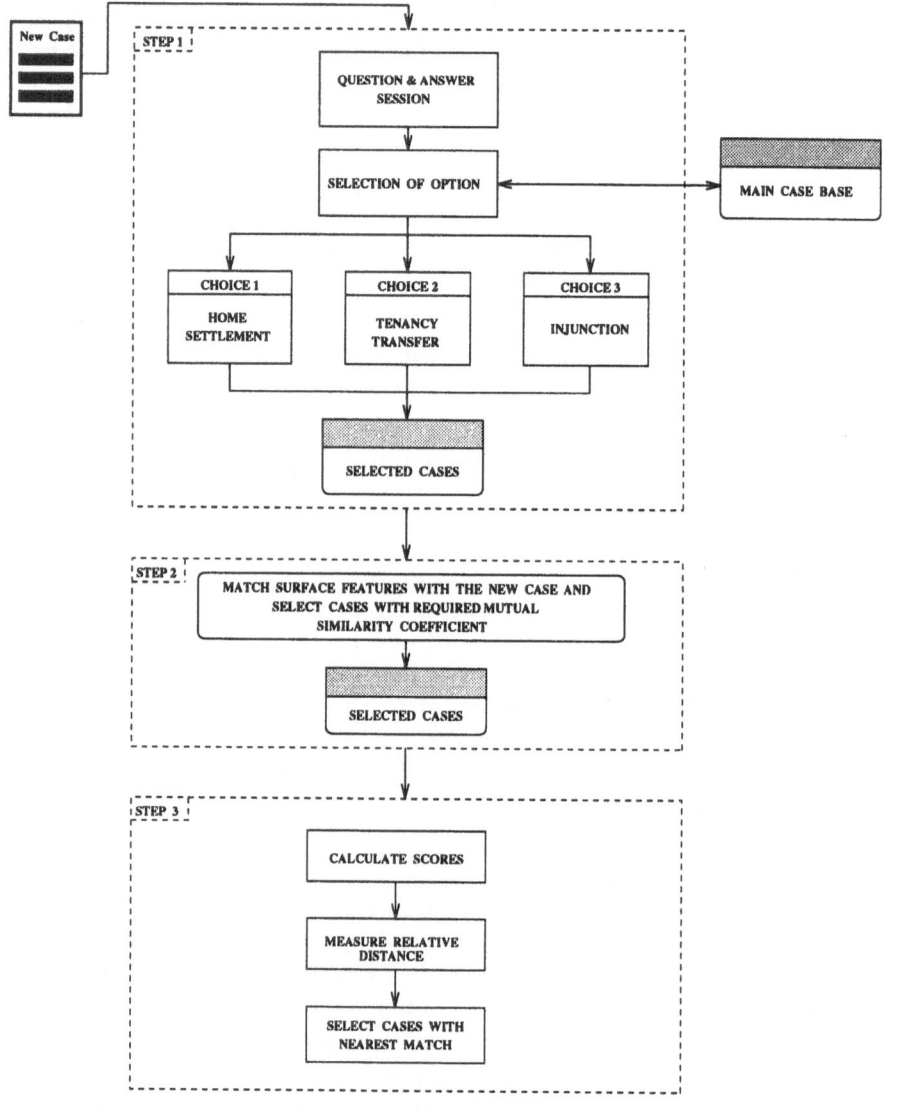

Fig. 4. Representation of steps in the similarity assessment

4 Example : The Injunction to Exclude One of the Spouses from the Matrimonial Home

In order to illustrate by an example, we consider the legal problem of the injunction to exclude one of the spouses from the matrimonial home. The following cases are given unique identifications for use in the case-base :-

case01	Silverstone v Silverstone [1953] 1 All ER 556
case02	Montgomery v Montgomery [1964] 2 All ER 22
case03	Gurasz v Gurasz [1969] 3 WLR 482
case04	Jones v Jones [1971] 1 WLR 396
case05	Hall v Hall [1971] 1 WLR 404
case06	Brent v Brent [1974] 2 All ER 1211
case07	Walker v Walker [1978] 3 All ER 141
case08	Rennick v Rennick [1978] 1 All ER 817
case09	Mayers v Mayers [1982] 1 All ER 776
case10	Samson v Samson [1982] 1 All ER 780

4.1 First Step of Similarity Assessment

In the first step the user will select the generalised feature 'injunction' option from a choice of settlement, tenancy transfer, and injunction. The system will retrieve all the above cases because they relate to injunction. However, even at this stage it is difficult to decide which of the cases represents the closest match. Therefore, the next action is to perform the similarity assessment as described in the second step.

4.2 Second Step of Similarity Assessment

In this step, the model of similarity is based on a binary relationship between the $SECOND\_INDEX_{id}$ hypernodes used. From the above example, we have selected two cases to assess the similarity or the association between them. Let SECOND_INDEX01, SECOND_INDEX02 for this example be the two second-index hypernodes for CASE01 and CASE02 respectively.

The *second_indexes* attribute of CASE01 refers to the main surface features. For example, in *Silverstone v Silverstone* (i.e. CASE01), the attribute *$second_indexes* refers to the surface features *'owned home'*, *'wife is the appellant'*, *'allegation of bad behaviour'*, *'adultery'*, *'appeal for divorce'*, *'divorce proceedings pending'*, *'appeal for exclusion order'*, *'respondent is the owner of the home'*, *'respondent cohabiting in a different home'*, *'exclusion order granted'*, *'counter appeal to defy exclusion'*, and *'counter appeal dismiss'*.

Similarly, in *Montgomery v Montgomery* (i.e CASE02), the attribute *$second_indexes* refers to the surface features *'rented home'*, *'wife is the appellant'*, *'allegation of bad behaviour'*, *'appeal for divorce'*, *'divorce'*, *'wife is the custodian of the young children'*, *'respondent is the legal tenant'*, *'couple living separately in the same home'*, *'appeal for exclusion order'*, and *'exclusion order dismiss'*.

The simplest of all association measures is SECOND_INDEX01 ∩ SECOND_INDEX02, which produces 4 shared index elements. In order to take an account of the size difference of the second-index hypernodes, the simple matching coefficient is normalised. Failure to normalise may led to counter-intuitive results. Because of this, we have taken the normalised association from both index hypernodes.

	CASE01	CASE02	CASE03	CASE04	CASE05	CASE06	CASE07	CASE08	CASE09	CASE10
CASE01	0.00	0.42	0.22	0.30	0.04	0.33	0.35	0.40	0.34	0.44
CASE02	0.42	0.00	0.20	0.12	0.46	0.09	0.07	0.02	0.76	0.86
CASE03	0.22	0.20	0.00	0.08	0.26	0.11	0.13	0.18	0.56	0.66
CASE04	0.30	0.12	0.08	0.00	0.34	0.03	0.05	0.10	0.64	0.74
CASE05	0.04	0.46	0.26	0.34	0.00	0.37	0.39	0.44	0.30	0.40
CASE06	0.33	0.09	0.11	0.03	0.37	0.00	0.02	0.07	0.67	0.77
CASE07	0.35	0.07	0.13	0.05	0.39	0.05	0.00	0.05	0.69	0.79
CASE08	0.40	0.02	0.18	0.10	0.44	0.02	0.05	0.00	0.74	0.84
CASE09	0.34	0.76	0.56	0.64	0.30	0.67	0.69	0.74	0.00	0.10
CASE10	0.44	0.86	0.66	0.74	0.40	0.77	0.79	0.84	0.10	0.00

Fig. 5. The similarity distances

The association of the $SECOND\_INDEX01$ with respect to SECOND_INDEX02 is defined as Sim(SECOND_INDE X01, SECOND_INDEX02) and the similarity coefficient of $SECOND\_INDEX02$ with respect to $SECOND\_INDEX01$ is $Sim(SECOND\_INDEX02, SECOND\_INDEX01)$. Then mutual similarity coefficient, $\mu_{sim}(SECOND\_INDEX01, SECOND\_INDEX02)$, is the mean of $Sim(SECOND\_INDEX01, SECOND\_INDEX02)$ and $Sim(SECOND\_INDEX02, SECOND\_INDEX01)$ and can be defined as:

$$\mu_{sim}(SECOND\_INDEX01, SECOND\_INDEX02) = \tfrac{1}{2}[S_{lr} + S_{rl}]$$

where $S_{lr} = Sim(SECOND\_INDEX01, SECOND\_INDEX02)$
and $S_{rl} = Sim(SECOND\_INDEX02, SECOND\_INDEX01)$

From the above discussion, we can conclude (here and in general) that:

1. if $\mu_{sim}(SECOND\_INDEX01, SECOND\_INDEX02) = 1$, then the two indexes $SECOND\_INDEX01$, $SECOND\_INDEX02$ are exactly similar.
2. if $\mu_{sim}(SECOND\_INDEX01, SECOND\_INDEX02) = 0$, then the two indexes $SECOND\_INDEX01$, $SECONF\_INDEX02$ are completely dissimilar.
3. As the value of $\mu_{sim}(SECOND\_INDEX01, SECOND\_INDEX02)$ approaches 1, the two indexes $SECOND\_INDEX01$, $SECOND\_INDEX02$ become more similar.
4. As the value of $\mu_{sim}(SECOND\_INDEX01, SECOND\_INDEX02)$ approaches 0, the two indexes $SECOND\_INDEX01$, $SECOND\_INDEX02$ are less similar.

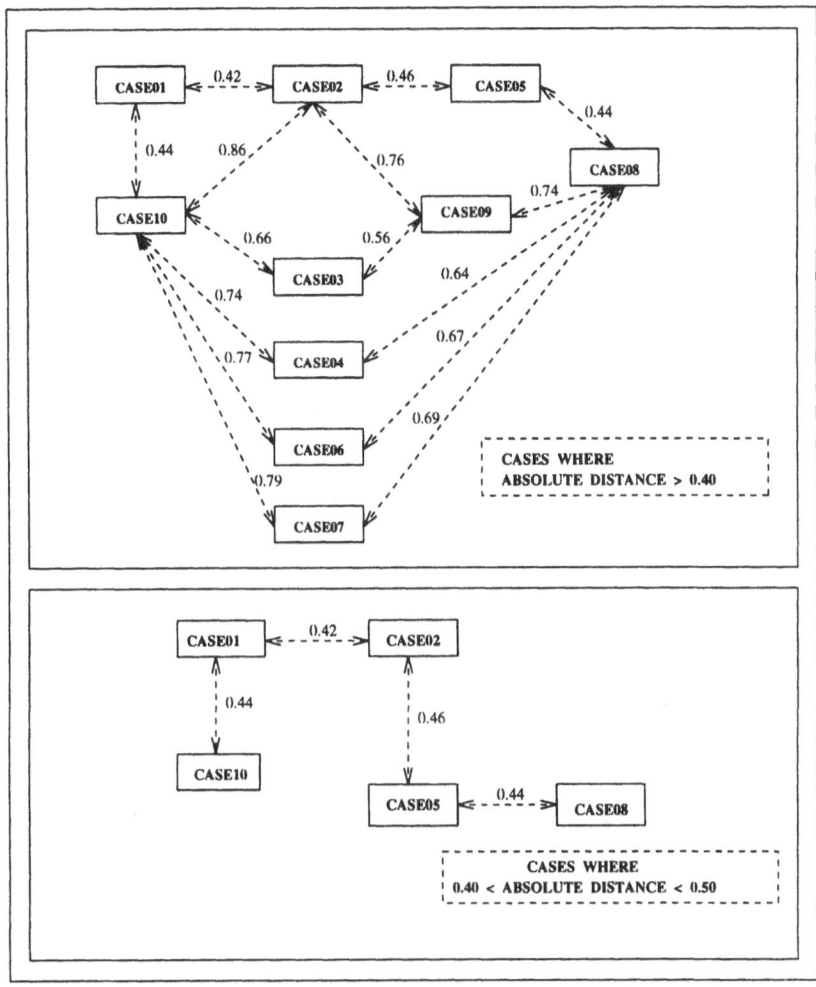

Fig. 6. Digrammatic representation of the relative distances between cases

4.3 Third Step of Similarity Assesment

The final step of similarity measurement is the assessesment of $THIRD\_INDEX_{id}$ for a selected number of cases from the second step. The $THIRD\_INDEX_{id}$ refers to the most distinctive characteristic(s) associated with the case. In this project, we have chosen six attributes which identify the final similarity measure for all selected cases. These attributes are $number\_of\_dependent\_children$, $length\_of\_stay\_in\_the\_matrimonial\_home$, $number\_of\_step\_children$, $number\_of\_divorce\_off\_spring$, $length\_of\_marriage$ and $couple\_social\_status$.

4.4   Measuring Similarity Distances

Once the $THIRD\_INDEX_{id}$ of the selected cases are calculated, we calculate the distance between the cases by using a metric on the values of features that characterise them. The absolute distances that we compute for the data in section 4 are shown in a tabular form in Figure 5 and the diagrammatic representation (the relative distances are not to scale) is shown in Figure 6. This is to demonstrate informally that the above graphical case representation captures the real-world legal knowledge. If the set of encoded cases is considered as a graph, then given a minimum distance 'd', we can find a subgraph consisting of a node N, all nodes distant d or less from N, and the edges from the original graph that join pairs of the nodes thus identified. These subgraphs allow us to identify similar cases. Splitting the resulting subgraph in a similar way produces progressively finer categorisations.

5   Concluding Remarks

The approach introduced in this paper provides a part of the foundation for integrating case-based and rule-based background knowledge to solve realistic problems. To demonstrate the effectiveness of our approach, we have implemented a system in which rule-based and case-based (legal) items of knowledge coexist, and in which convincing access and explanation behaviour is observed when either of the representational subsystems (for rules or for cases) is addressed. For either subsystem, the items retrieved as being similar to a given new divorce-settlement situation have an associated computed measure of similarity. The approach to computation differs in details between rules and cases; we have not discussed the method for rules in this paper. From a legal user's point of view, the system should be capable of finding automatically which of the subsystems retrieves the better answers for a given new problem, and of producing its result and explanations accordingly. This is basically a matter of normalisation of the rule-based and case-based similarity measures with respect to each other. We are now involved in the work of experimenting and testing that is needed to obtain the best normalisation.

Acknowledgements

We would like to thank Dr Mark Levene for helpful discussions.

References:

1. Ashley, K. D., Toward an Intelligent Case-Based Tutorial Program for Teaching Students to Argue with Cases. Working Notes, AAAI Spring Symposium Series: Argument and Belief, Stanford University, Palo Alto, CA (1991).
2. Ashley, K. D., Modelling Legal Argument: Reasoning with Cases and Hypotheticals. MIT Press, Cambridge, MA (1990).

3. Branting, L. K., Integrating Rules and Precedents for Classification and Explanation: Automating Legal Analysis, Ph.D. Thesis, available as Technical Report AI90-146, Artificial Intelligence Laboratory, University of Texas, Austin, TX (1991).

4. Cretney, S.M., Elements of Family Law : Sweet and Maxwell, London, (1992).

5. Goldman, S., and Dyer, M., and Margot, F., Representating Contractual Situations. In Charles Walter, editor, Computer Power and Language, chapter 10, page 99-118, Quorum Books, New York, (1988).

6. Kolodner, J., L., Judging Which is the Best Case for a Case-base Reasoner, In Proceedings : Case-Based Reasoning Workshop, Pensacola, (1989).

7. Levene, M. and Loizou, G., A Graph-Based Data Model and its Ramifications, IEEE Transaction on Knowledge and Data Engineering (to appear in October 1995).

8. Levi, E.H., An Introduction to Legal Reasoning, Chicago, University of Chicago Press.

9. Montazari, M., and Adam, A.E., Applications of Case Base Reasoning to the Law: the Problems of Multiple Case Reasoning and Indexing, First European Workshop on Case-based Reasoning, Otzenhausen, Germany, (1993)

10. Nitta, K., Haraguchi, M., and Sakurai, S., Representation of Legal Knowledge, Journal of Information Processing, vol. 15, No.3, (1992).

11. Pritchard, J., The Penguin Guide to the Law, Guild Publishing, (1985).

12. Rissland, E. L., Artificial Intelligence and Law: Stepping Stones to a Model of Legal Reasoning. Yale Law Journal, 99(8), 1957-1982.

Application of Case-Based Reasoning (CBR)
to Software Reuse

P. Maguire*, R. Szegfue**, V. Shankararaman* and L. Morss*

e-mail : venky@uk.ac.napier.dcs or les@uk.ac.napier.dcs

* Department of Computer Studies, Napier University, Edinburgh EH14 1DJ
** Fachhochschule Darmstadt, Department of Computer Science, Germany

ABSTRACT

In this paper we present a prototype CBR system CAROL (Case Assisted Reuse of Object Library) to support reuse of class descriptions in Object-Oriented programming [Szeg95]. CAROL computes similarities between, and returns a list of, class descriptions which are most similar to a target class specification. The case base consists of a set of PROLOG data base facts representing classes, attributes and relationships. Current work is directed at increasing the functionality of CAROL by implementing the automatic adaptation of a candidate class specification to the required target class specification.

1. Introduction

A major problem in software development is the need for greater productivity and quality in the development process. This has been brought about by the gap between the demand for, and our ability to produce (using current techniques), large complex computer programs. Software reuse is seen by many researchers as an important factor in improving software productivity and quality. One of the greatest outstanding problems with reuse is how to find a particular software component that matches (or nearly matches) a given requirement, and then specialise it to meet that requirement. One solution to this problem is the development of new tools and techniques to automate the retrieval and specialisation of not only existing software components but also analyses, designs and documentation from previous software development projects.

Using the Object-Oriented (OO) paradigm in software development projects has a number of advantages over conventional methods [Coad91] [Rumb91]. One of them, the encapsulation of data together with the functions which operate on it, holds the promise of greater reuse. In this paper we describe a prototype CBR system CAROL to support reuse of class descriptions in Object-Oriented programming.

The paper is organised as follows. In Section 2 we have a short discussion on reuse, and in Section 3 a conceptual model of CBR applied to reuse is discussed. In Sections 4 and 5 we present and discuss our prototype CAROL. In Section 6 we detail the work presently underway, and then conclude with Section 7.

2. Software Reuse

Software reuse is often thought of as the process of creating new software systems from existing software (as opposed to building from 'scratch'). However, reuse has failed to become a standard software engineering practice since it was first proposed as a means to overcome the so-called 'software crisis' at the 1968 NATO Software Engineering Conference. The greatest scope for reuse is at the highest level of abstraction at which it is possible to identify and construct reusable components. It is therefore linked to raising the level of abstraction at which software is constructed - in short, the reuse of components at abstraction levels higher than code (e.g. design structures, specifications, documentation, etc.) clearly promises more progress in overcoming the software crisis than code reuse alone. This has proved a very difficult task. Arguably the only significant progress over the last twenty-seven years has been the development of the OO paradigm. This may be a pointer to the reason for the 'failure' of reuse.

Design, analysis and specification may be considered as higher level abstractions above actual code. ROME is an interactive object modelling environment which supports design, documentation and C++ code generation. It was developed at Napier University and is used as a teaching tool [MacM94]. LOOM (Language for Object-Oriented Modelling), an Object-Oriented design language, defines an abstraction above the code/class level [MacM94]. Indeed it can be argued that this abstraction is at the design level because it is also a logical representation of a ROME class diagram. Therefore, using LOOM to define reuse components should increase the degree of reuse in any given development, whether by reuse of code (classes), or of parts of ROME designs.

At present, reuse in OO development is accomplished mostly by manually browsing through class libraries containing many class specifications. Clearly, as more and more class libraries become available, or are constructed in-house, browsing will become untenable. Therefore, there is a need to find more efficient methods to support reuse of these, as well as other, software components.

3. CBR Approach - Conceptual Model.

The conceptual model of a case-based reasoning approach to reuse in specification, analysis, design and programming stages of OO software development has been proposed [Szeg95]. All phases in a software development life-cycle can be used and structured to build a case base covering information such as specification, analyses, design and implementation about a certain project. The advantages are clear: at any phase during the development of a new application information about results of previous projects would be readily available. In OO terms, a class specification, its domain analysis, its design and implementation could be captured in some sort of formal description in order to represent and index it for a case-based reasoning reuse system. Once a representation for the various phases is obtained, each object and its corresponding reference to each phase can be stored as a case in the case base. The reuse can be effected by providing the CBR reuse system with the current problem definition specified at any level (e.g. specification, analysis, design, etc.). The case retrieval algorithm can then provide the user with the most similar past cases at the specified level.

4. Description of Prototype

The prototype system CAROL has been implemented in LPA-PROLOG running on a 486 PC. The system design diagram is shown in Fig. 1. The four main modules are *Case-Base Creation, Retrieval, Case Specification,* and *Evaluation/Adaptation.*

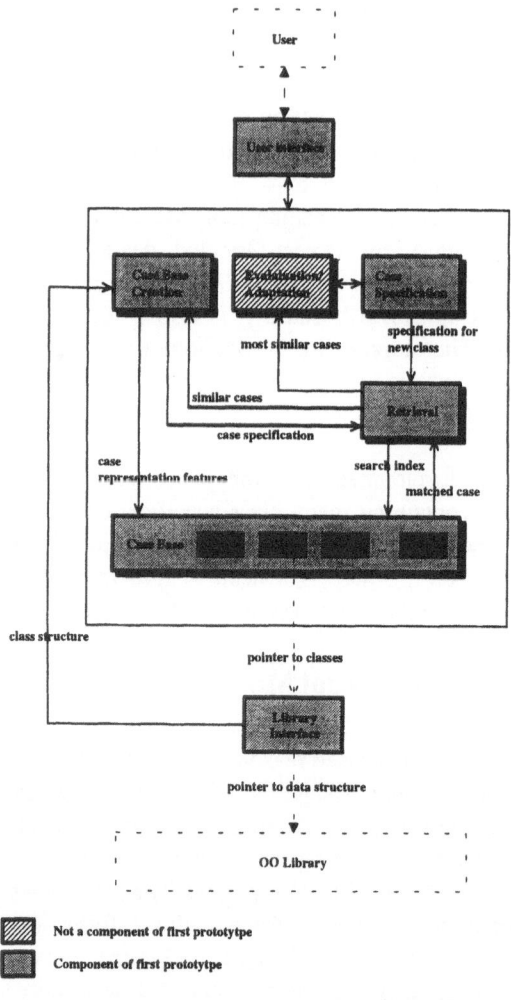

Fig. 1. CAROL System Design Diagram.

Case-Base Creation implements all features necessary for building cases from the information stored in LOOM library files. This process is divided into sub modules. These modules enable the system to parse through the LOOM library files, extract all class information and translate it into the case representation. Values of class features like class name, class type, instance variables and others are automatically stored in their corresponding case attributes. Class methods are classified by attaching labels to methods, describing their functionality in terms of their behaviour towards instance variables (e.g. modify_inst_var, check_inst_var, return_inst_var).

A very important function of *Case-Base Creation* is the categorisation of classes (cases). Cases are grouped into categories which represent similar concepts. The category of a new class can be defined either by users who add a new case to the system or by the systems own retrieval and matching modules. The later compares the new case with existing cases in the case-base and decides, whether it is similar enough to be grouped into an existing category or if it is necessary to ask users for a new category. Fig. 2. shows the LOOM script for the class company in the LOOM library and the corresponding case created from this class.

Retrieval implements three major functions:

1. Search indexing
2. Case matching
3. Attribute weighting

Indexing cases for searching the case-base enables building a search tree according to some user defined (or system-defined) restrictions in order to narrow or broaden the search space, depending on whether a quick search (requiring some user knowledge about the desired class's domain) is wanted or if users want the system to find as many semantic relations between cases as possible.

Case matching provides the system with different methods of pattern matching and a scoring system that defines similarity between two cases. The matching process is 'attribute oriented' meaning each attribute is matched in a way which represents its character and meaning as accurately as possible. Class names for example are matched by searching for synonyms or computing the largest common substring, whereas the superclass - subclass similarity between two classes is defined by a distance measure representing their positions in the inheritance hierarchy.

A facility for attaching weights to attributes in order to express their importance for users is the third function of the retrieval module. The prototypes weighting system provides the user with a means to experiment with the importance of attributes. The weighting is between 0 and 1 - the closer to 1, the more important. If a weight is set to 0, the attribute is NOT matched.

LOOM Script	Corresponding Case

CLASS Company
WITH
  OPERATIONS
   hasEmployee? (aName : String) :
Boolean
  PROPERTIES
   theName : String
  ASSOCIATIONS
   theEmployees : Collection[
Employee LINK]
   owns : Collection[Owner LINK]
   manages : Collection[Manager
LINK]
  AGGREGATES
  DEFINITIONS
 	
   METHOD hasEmployee? (aName :
String) : Boolean
   AS
    FOREACH emp : Employee
LINK IN theEmployees DO
     INSTANCE empName :
String(SEND emp THE MESSAGE
name?)
     IF empName == aName THEN
      RETURN TRUE
     ENDIF
    ENDFOREACH
    RETURN FALSE
   ENDMETHOD hasEmployee?
ENDCLASS Company
	% Case definition of case company
	
	instance(company,institution).
	current_value(name,company,
	company).
	current_value(class_type,company,
	concrete).
	current_value(lib_file,company,'C:
	\PRO386W\DIPLOM\EXAMPLES\
	COMPANY.OOM').
	inst_vars(company,theName,string).
	parents(company,object,full_parent,
	prototype).
	links(company,is_part_of,manager,
	to_one).
	links(company,is_part_of,owner,
	to_one).
	links(company,is_part_of,employee,
	to_one).
	methods(company,'hasEmployee?',[],
	[message_to_link,loop_over_link,
	use_temp_var]).
	parameter(company,'hasEmployee?',
	aName,string).
	parameter(company,'hasEmployee?',
	output_parameter,boolean).
	institution(company).
	
	% End of case definition

Fig. 2. Example of a LOOM Script and the corresponding parsed case

Case Specification provides users of the system with an input template for specifying a new case. They can define values for all attributes in order to find a similar existing class with only little knowledge about the actual implementation (which would be needed in a class-browsing-only system). The input template is basically an interface between users and the case representation structure and can be exchanged with a front end interface to the current library system. In Fig. 3. part of the case specification template, for the target studentEmployee, is shown.

Evaluation/Adaptation provides the user with the ability to adapt a retrieved candidate case, to form the target case. This module is currently being implemented and further discussions are presented in Section 6.

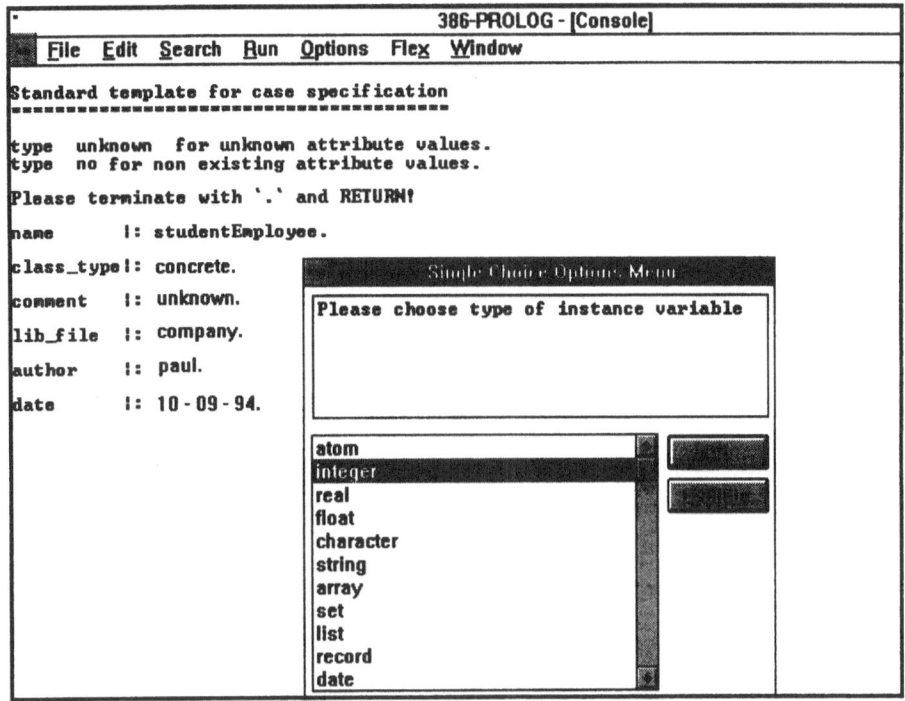

Fig. 3. Sample screen showing case specification.

5. Discussion of Prototype

The advantages of using CBR in a reuse system may best be explained by reference to [Maid93] in which a number of 'human' problems in using a reuse system are explored. Solutions to many of these problems are provide by CBR/CAROL. Fig. 4. summarises these problems and their solutions.

The prototype was not intended to have a perfect human-computer interface and it was not meant to be complete in the sense that all design ideas were implemented. It does show that it is possible to represent object oriented classes as cases in a case-base system and that these cases can be matched against a user specified new case in order to retrieve the most similar ones for reuse. The adaptation of the best candidate to generate the target was not implemented.

LOOM was used to build the source libraries and therefore it was necessary to build an interface to LOOM in order to implement a very high level of automation during the case-base creation process. LOOM was chosen because of its high level language characteristics and its mapping to C++. It should be possible to modify the system for reusing C++ libraries as well as LOOM files.

PROBLEM	SOLUTION
Support for describing new problems using terms which permit retrieval of reusable components	Provided by ability to use output of ROME as input for either insertion or retrieval, and a thesaurus associated with every category (facet).
Assimilation and understanding of retrieved components	Provided by the explanation facility of CBR systems (not yet implemented in CAROL)
Selection of the best component from several candidates	Provided by the weighting mechanisms built into CAROL
Adaptation of the selected component to fit the new problem	A design feature of CBR systems, and the focus of current work (see Section 6)
Adding extra functionality to the component while ensuring the validity of existing features	Realisable by the use of the LOOM compiler, post adaptation, and/or by the CBR repair function (not yet implemented in CAROL)

Fig. 4. Reuse Problems - CBR Solutions

There are two intended groups of users for this system, although it should be possible to have users which fit into both categories. The first group of users are the 'expert users', who build the categories of certain problem domains. This includes the definition of a category Thesaurus in order to provide the system with synonyms for that domain, similarity values to express similarities between the synonyms and the controlling of the categorisation process during case-base creation. The second group of users are the actual software developers who use the system for specifying classes in order to retrieve similar ones for reuse and adaptation.

6. Work in Progress

Two adaptation techniques were investigated. The first relies on standard CBR substitution methods [Kolo93] and is discussed in detail below. The second will not be discussed here but is, in fact, a form of model guided repair [Kolo93], which relies on a definition of the subtype relation in terms of the behaviour of types, as described by their specification.

The first technique is a variation on the local search and case-based substitution methods. Local search is the process of searching in an abstraction hierarchy in the environs of a concept for some close relative that could be substituted for it. Case based substitution is the process of looking for a substitute by finding a case that can suggest an alternative. This is being implemented utilising the existing systems Search Indexing. This enables the searching of the cases in the same category as the candidate case for a class definition which has the properties and operations not present in the candidate class definition, but required by the target.

For example, consider the following two (simplified) LOOM specifications already in the case base under a 'people' category (see Fig. 5.). This example is shown only to highlight the adaptation technique proposed. In practice StudentEmployee would inherit from both Employee and Student.

```
CLASS Employee WITH              CLASS Student WITH
OPERATIONS                       OPERATIONS
        name? : String                  name? : String
        salary? : Integer               matriculationNo? : Integer
        jobTitle? : String
PROPERTIES                       PROPERTIES
        theName : String                 theName : String
        theSalary : Integer              theMatriculationNo : Integer
        theJobTitle : String
METHODS                          METHODS
METHOD name? : String AS         METHOD name? : String AS
        RETURN (theName)                 RETURN (theName)
ENDMETHOD name?                  ENDMETHOD name?
//More...                        //More....
ENDCLASS Employee                ENDCLASS Student


We specify a target as follows:

        CLASS StudentEmployee WITH
        OPERATIONS
                name? : String
                salary? : Integer
                jobTitle? : String
                matriculationNo? : Integer
        PROPERTIES
                theName : String
                theSalary : Integer
                theJobTitle : String
                theMatriculationNo : Integer
        ENDCLASS StudentEmployee
```

Fig. 5. Simplified LOOM specifications

In the present implementation the Employee class is retrieved as a candidate for the target StudentEmployee and the *adaptation* module retrieves the Student class and extracts the Matriculation PROPERTY, OPERATION and METHOD and adds them to the candidate, thereby creating the target class.

An explanation facility is seen as an important aspect of a CBR system. Current work is directed towards adding such a facility in CAROL. It is envisaged that the explanation will consist of information supporting the adaptation process.

7. Conclusion

Case-based reasoning has clear application to reuse in the software development process. CAROL has shown that this technique is feasible. It supports reuse of class descriptions in Object-Oriented programming. Current work is directed towards enhancing the adaptation module and incorporating an explanation facility. Such tools and associated techniques will undoubtedly significantly affect the process of developing new software applications, allowing the profession to provide more and higher quality software to clients.

8. References

[Coad91]   Coad, P. and Yourdon, E., *Object-oriented design*, Prentice-Hall, 1991.
[Kolo93]   Kolodner, J., *Case-based reasoning*, Morgan Kaufman, 1993.
[MacM94]   MacMahon, R., *Richards Object-Oriented Modelling Environment*, unpublished project, Department of Computer Studies, Napier University Edinburgh. 1994
[Maid93]   Maiden, N.A.M., Sutcliffe, A.G., *People-oriented Software Reuse: the Very Thought*, Proc Advances in Software Reuse. Selected Papers from the Second International Workshop on Software Reusability, 1993
[Rumb91]   Rumbaugh, J., *Object-oriented modeling and design*, Prentice-Hall, 1991.
[Szeg95]   Szegfue, R., Morss, L. and Shankararaman, V., *A Case-Based Reasoning approach to Reuse in Object-Oriented Implementation* In: *Object Technology 95.* March 27-29, Oxford, England. Presented at the poster session.

Case-Based Reasoning Applied to Fault Diagnosis on Steam Turbines

E Georgin, F Bordin, S Lœsel and J R McDonald
Centre for Electrical Power Engineering
University of Strathclyde
Glasgow, Scotland

Abstract : Heuristic based expert systems have difficulty in providing comprehensive solutions to their end users. At the rule level, the knowledge is implicit and therefore can be difficult to justify. Such systems are accurate and efficient, but do not always provide comprehensive solutions. The use of case studies was therefore investigated alongside fault models, both of which are capable of providing solutions acceptable to end users. The research then lead to the design of a second generation expert system, where different knowledge sources (i.e. heuristics, models and cases) can support each others, or can be combined to produce a diagnosis which will still be accurate, but will gain in performance and comprehension. This paper discusses such ideas where case based reasoning can be at the core of the system.

1 Introduction

Expert systems have been developed in the last decade for the fault diagnosis of turbine generators and have shown to have an important role in the condition monitoring of the plant (see for example [3][5][8]). These systems provide quick and accurate solutions. Nevertheless, they face a major problem: they rely on heuristic associations in which their end users i.e. plant operators are seldom specialists. These heuristics represent the way a turbine expert analyses vibrations. Plant operators are not necessarily trained in vibration neither do they require to understand the reasoning paths of the expert system but they still have to accept the proposal/solution. The only explanations they can provide to their users are based upon their reasoning trace, whereas a human turbine expert could explain the same situation in different manners. Therefore, there is a need to improve expert system explanations in order to fulfil their role as experts. Acknowledging that knowledge which is contained in rules originates from different sources (e.g. human experts, engineering models, cases studies, common sense, etc.) and is "compiled", the explanation of this knowledge is possible with the provision and use of explicit knowledge representation, the application of various reasoning techniques or with its form. Combining artificial intelligence (AI) techniques is one issue to be addressed providing a better evaluation of each technique as well as a better understanding of human reasoning.

This paper discusses the above ideas, present the benefits and shortcomings of different paradigms which provide an overall diagnostic explanation of what was going wrong in a turbine generator set. In particular, case based reasoning techniques can provide significant advantages such as pruning the search space and explaining similar events. This paper also reviews an Electricité de France (EDF)'s expert system for fault diagnosis on turbines called DIVA [3]. This heuristic based system is operational in a French power station. DIVA is used in this project as a test bed to validate our results.

2 Solutions to the Problem

In order to develop complex AI systems which provide *comprehensive , accurate and rapid* solutions, we propose two different ways to achieve this:

- the system can be produced around a paradigm, which should produce fast and accurate solutions (e.g. heuristic or case based reasoning). Such solutions can be justified with explanations concocted by other means (i.e. model based reasoning).
- a system is built around a blackboard type architecture and uses different agents to solve a problem together or individually.

When analysing human expert behaviour, experts always try to match the level of understanding of the person they talk to. When confronting a problem, firstly they think about similar problems, i.e. they use their brain to retrieve similar cases, and then think about it in a more methodical manner.

As the first generation expert systems began to show its limitations in term of brittleness, flexibility, taking into account different types of knowledge, etc., the idea of Second Generation Expert Systems (SGES) emerged in the end of the 1980s [2]. These systems are designed to be:

- flexible: several functions will be achieved (e.g. diagnosis, maintenance, design. etc.)
- modular
- robust and reliable
- reusable: both reasoning agents (e.g. rule, case and model-based reasoning) or domain (cases, models, data) knowledge should be reusable.
- responsive to user needs with respect to their available amount of knowledge

An architecture for implementing such an SGES is represented by the conceptual framework (Fig. 1) of a second generation expert systems where there will be a control layer (meta knowledge), a medium for exchanging information (called here a blackboard), some generic reasoning agents, an explanation module and interfaces to the user, data and knowledge bases and monitoring systems [6].

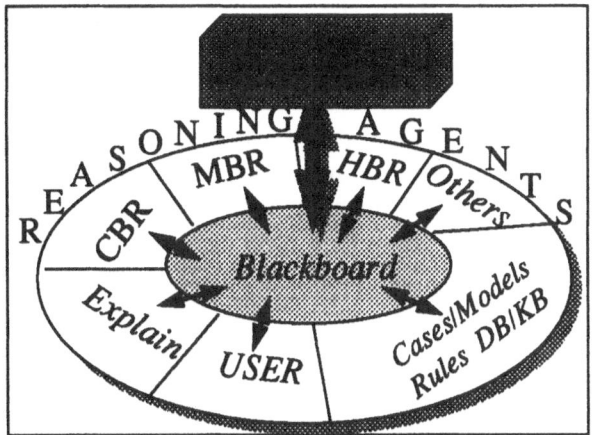

Fig. 1. High Level Conceptual Framework

The reported work was developed with these ideas in mind.

The *Control* module controls data exchanges and sends commands through the blackboard. Its role is also to resolve conflicting situations with meta-knowledge. It knows how agents should behave, and is the organiser to fulfil a required task.

The *Reasoning Agents* are generic paradigms. At the present time, three agents have been developed which can on their own, give reasonably comprehensive solutions. These include an Establish/Refine paradigm using prototypes/rules, an Abductive Reasoning paradigm using fault models and a Case Based Module. A functional (General Diagnostic Engine type [4]) module is under examination. They all share their inferred knowledge through the blackboard (BB). Each agent is also required to be able to explain what it did. The reasoning agents can send messages, through the BB, to the data bases (DB) and knowledge bases (KB) in order to retrieve cases, models, rules, etc., to archive cases, to access data from acquisition systems and from the user.

The user can make requests (interactive diagnosis, on-line diagnosis, explanations), examine the BB trace and access data and answers.

Explain builds up an explanation of the reasoning when requested by the user or the control, and can also send messages to each individual agent to get their contribution to an explanation, alternative explanation, etc.

Messages which can be sent between agents, DB/KB and user, are exchanged within the BB in a queuing process, the control layer checking the messages and acting if necessary. Another function of the blackboard is to record the stream of messages.

DB/KB contain the domain data/knowledge required to achieve particular sub tasks. There are case studies, rules, prototypes, structural, functional and fault models.

Such knowledge is accessed via the blackboard and can be reused for other purposes (such as monitoring, planning and design purposes). The DB also contains stored data from acquisition systems.

At present, this is not a true *non deterministic* system: different strategies are set up as explained in Section 7 i.e. case based reasoning pruning the search space and producing solutions which are then validated by the heuristic and model based modules.

3 DIVA

DIVA is the Electricité de France (EDF)'s expert system for fault diagnosis of turbine generators [3]. DIVA is a heuristic-based system and its reasoning is based on the recognition/rejection of prototypes i.e. typical fault situations organised in a hierarchical classification. Its reasoning is based on vibration analysis since decades of experience exist in the field. Its main advantages are the separation of its explicit knowledge representations for both domain and reasoning purposes. Its "Establish/Refine" strategy, which principally uses the knowledge which is expressed in terms of rules within prototypes, is composed of three high level tasks:

- a **Matching** task (request to data bases, acquisition systems and/or users) to accept or reject the prototype.
- an **Establish** task which establishes the recognition of a prototype above a given threshold.
- a **Refine** task to refine the diagnosis and examine sub prototypes.

DIVA's reasoning is explicit due to its high level of knowledge abstraction. For explanation purposes, explanations of "why" and "how" types (e.g. "why are you asking this information?" "how did you establish the recognition of this situation?") are a reflection of the system's reasoning and an explanation of how the knowledge expressed at different knowledge levels (task, inference, domain) was used [3].

Such a system heavily relies on heuristic associations which experts make between faults and symptoms. Therefore, it is difficult to take into account nuances brought by their experience. To this end, DIVA uses weights and certainty factors but their meaning and their interpretation to justify conclusions of the system are questionable.

4 Case Based Reasoning

4.1 Case Modelling

The case base contains some 55 case studies. These cases were previously used to validate EDF's DIVA system. The knowledge acquisition was therefore greatly reduced. Nevertheless, finding a way of how of representing a case is a difficult task study. The result of the case modelling is represented by Fig. 2.

```
Identification
    reference
                name of fault = LP-Blade-Loss
                details = "text file"
    location = rotor
Context
    turbine type = CP2
    etc.
Description
    when
                speed regime = steady state
    how
                type of signal = 1A
                dominant frequency = ω
                vibration signal
                        evolution
                                duration = instantaneous
                        magnitude
                                exces-amp-th-criticals = yes
                                HP-Front
                                        ω/2 = 0
                                        ω = 10
                                        2ω = 0
                                        3ω = 0
                                        4ω = 0
                                LP1-Front
                                        ω= 30
                                        etc.
                        etc.
                steps
                        isolated step = yes
        etc.
```

4.2 Induction or Nearest Neighbour?

Both induction and nearest neighbour techniques were tested in this project. The tool that was used to implement our case based module was KATE™ from AcknoSoft [7]. The flexibility of KATE and the end user interface development packages KATE is based on i.e. Toolbook™, allowed us to built a system the way we wanted (as explained in Section 7), the case based module was well integrated in the whole SGES.

The nearest neighbour techniques provided good results: these results were tested against DIVA and were consistent. In addition, this technique provides multiple solutions to a given problem. The precision of the diagnosis has still to be improved due to the fact that the cases are "complete", but have not yet been validated by turbine experts. The performances should even be improved in the future with more and better case studies. Table 1 shows the kind of diagnosis that is produced with this method.

Table 1 Diagnosis produced with the Nearest Neighbour Technique

Current Case	1st Retrieved Case = Case No 7	2nd Retrieved Case = No 8
fault name = ?	**fault name = LP-Blade-Loss**	**fault name = LP-Blade-Loss**
dominant frequency = ω	dominant frequency = ω	dominant frequency = ω
turbine type = CP2	turbine type = CP2	turbine type = CP2
description = ?	description = (text)	description = (text)
signal shape = 1A	signal shape = 1A	signal shape = 1A
location = rotor	location = rotor	location = rotor
which part = LP	which part = LP	which part = LP
duration = ?	duration = instantaneous	duration = instantaneous
exces-amp-th-criticals = ?	exces-amp-th-criticals = true	exces-amp-th-criticals = true
other steps = ?	other steps = no	other steps = no
HP front $\omega/2 = 0$	HP front $\omega/2 = 0$	HP front $\omega/2 = 0$
HP front $\omega = 2$	HP front $\omega = 5$	HP front $\omega = 0$
HP front $2\omega = 0$	HP front $2\omega = 0$	HP front $2\omega = 0$
HP front $3\omega = ?$	HP front $3\omega = 0$	HP front $3\omega = 0$
HP front $4\omega = 0$	HP front $4\omega = 0$	HP front $4\omega = 0$
LP1 front $\omega/2 = 0$	LP1 front $\omega/2 = 0$	LP1 front $\omega/2 = 0$
LP1 front $\omega = 30$	LP1 front $\omega = 20$	LP1 front $\omega = 0$
etc.	etc.	etc.
LP2 front $\omega = 60$	LP2 front $\omega = 60$	LP2 front $\omega = 30$
etc.	etc.	etc.
MATCHING	0.49	0.48

The second method used for retrieving cases was based on induction. Although KATE offers good inductive functions i.e. its dynamic induction [7], the results produced were not those we were looking for and are not always the way experts discriminate cases: the benefits of inductive techniques in explanation are therefore lowered. Another fact was the limited size of the case base: after a few questions, a case is retrieved whereas turbine experts would ask dozens of questions. Fig. 3 represents a part of the produced decision tree.

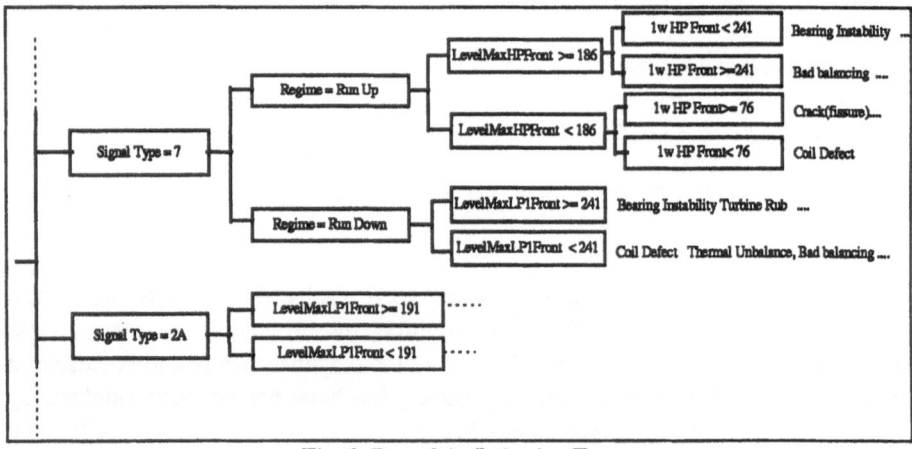

Fig. 3. Part of the Induction Tree

5 Model Based Reasoning

The use of fault models was investigated because causal networks explain how faults propagate inside a turbine: this is the type of explanation that plant operators are looking for. The method used to reason on these models is abductive and is taken from [1]. This has produced encouraging results.

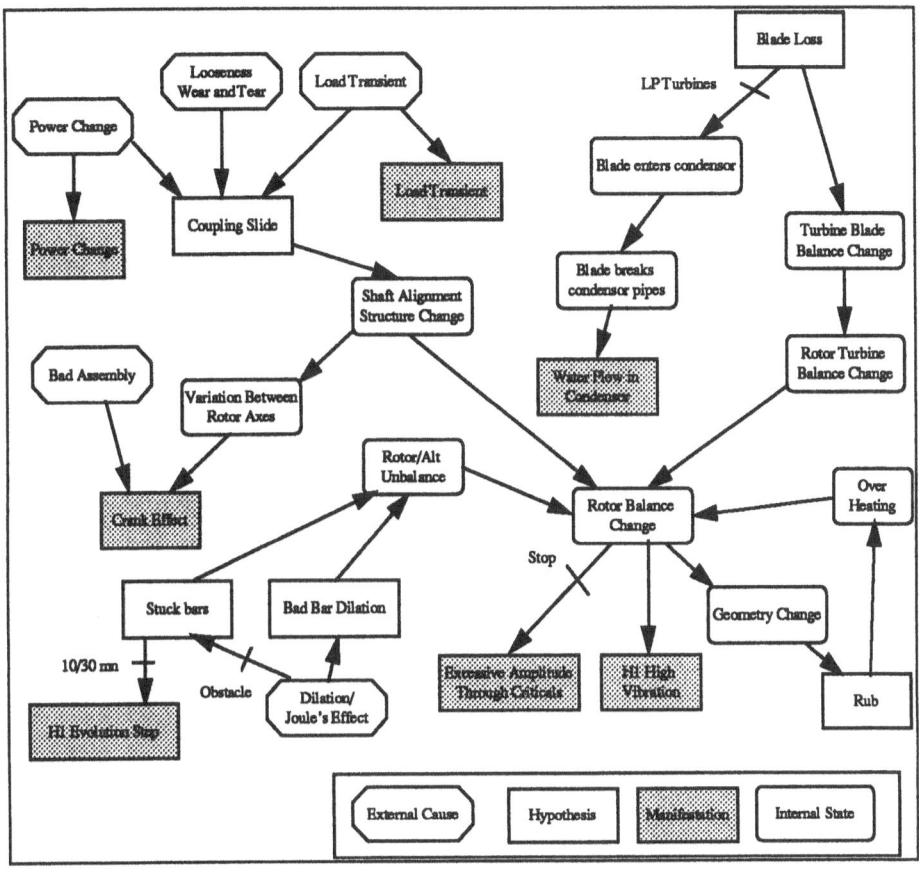

Fig. 4. Part of the Behavioural Model

From our experience, the use of fault models has the following advantages:

- it explains how faults propagate inside the turbine
- models can be described at different qualitative levels to match different user profiles
- models can be used to produce predictive diagnoses
- end users understand such explanations, etc.,

It has also some shortcomings:

- an abduction technique supposes that the symptoms created by a fault, are all known and present.
- models are very difficult to built and then to use. This is certainly due to the fact that different faults can produce similar symptoms, and are consequently "linked" by internal states
- special abductive techniques have to be used to prune the search space and avoid combinatorial explosions., etc.

The models used are of the same type of the one described in Fig. 4 where four distinct nodes are used: external causes, hypotheses or faults, internal causes and symptoms. Arcs link different nodes, conditions may be attached to a node.

6 The Use of Case and Models in Justifications

Case studies and fault models can easily justify a heuristic based system solutions: for example, we can say (after DIVA has found a diagnosis):

" you have a Low Pressure blade loss problem, here is some similar problems which have happened in the past. If you look at them, you will discover similar symptoms
　　In addition, for each event, you would know what the plant operator did to restore the machine"

　　or

"The blade loss propagates the following effects within the turbine:
It can enter the condenser and break some condenser pipes: you should see a water entry in the condenser
It can also create a unbalance of the rotor: you should see high vibration of the first harmonics and excessive amplitude through the criticals in case of a stop
It can also create a geometry change which can create a rub

7 The quick CBR Solver

The system which is currently under development aims to be a *non deterministic* system which can evaluate the performance of a given agent (CBR, MBR, etc.) at a given time. This meta knowledge which is difficult to acquire, is not really present. Instead, testing different combinations will allow us to decide upon which strategies to follow.

At the present time, CBR techniques have intensively been used in our SGES. The system offers both an on line and an interactive mode to the user. For both approaches, after describing a few symptoms, the CBR proposes accurate solutions like shown previously. The first solutions are then validated by heuristic and model based approaches. The combination of these techniques shows that there are consistent and also that each brings something to the final diagnosis. They can be more or less accurate, comprehensive, they can remember the case, etc. They all contribute to a certain extend, the CBR having the major role.

8 Conclusion and Future Work

Building a system can involve many sources from experts and specialists through the use of archives and literature. Each knowledge source has a number of positive features and some shortcomings which are either specific to the application or modelling, or to the technique. Listed here are some advantages and shortcomings of some paradigms which base their reasoning on heuristics, case studies or engineering models.

- **Heuristic-based reasoning** systems perform well in specific domain of expertise. They do not identify new fault types and do not cover "neighbouring faults". They do not learn from experience and therefore the diagnosis of similar faults is carried out at the same cost every time. Nuances in expert reasoning are usually represented by confidence factors or similar artefacts, which are difficult to justify.
- **Case-based reasoning** (CBR) does not always propose the optimal solution: cases which are very close are not always initially retrieved. This is certainly due to the fact that more knowledge needs to be embodied within a case e.g. knowledge to differentiate cases or originating from additional tests. However, this is a learning technique and can still propose "approximate" matches.
- **Model-based reasoning** (MBR) is susceptible to the level of detail modelled, and has also been proven computationally expensive. Models may be too simple and may not cover every aspect such as qualitative, quantitative and temporal modelling. Abductive methods can explain what has gone wrong, whereas this is more difficult to achieve with component- or function-based approaches. Nevertheless, MBR has the potential to integrate fully qualitative, temporal and quantitative aspects which should more effectively match different user profiles and discover new faults.

With those ideas in mind, the paper reported the work carried out in developing a second generation expert system for fault diagnosis on turbine generators. In this system, case based reasoning plays a major role:

- CBR prunes the search space very easily
- It provides accurate solution
- It is a learning system
- Its solutions are comprehensive, etc.

Our future direction in CBR is to search for more robust nearest neighbour algorithms: for example, in fault diagnosis, weights would be assigned differently depending on which fault the system is looking for. Such problems have also to be taken into account.

9 Acknowledgements

The authors would like to thank Electricite de France, Research and Development Division, in Chatou, France, for their financial and technical support.

10 References

[1] L Console, L Portinale and D T Dupre, "Focusing Abductive Diagnosis", *AICOM* Vol. 4 (2/3) 1991, pp. 88-97.

[2] J-M David, J-P Krivine and R Simmons, *Second Generation Expert Systems,* Springer Verlag, 1993.

[3] J-M David, J-P Krivine, and B Ricard, "Building and Maintaining a Large Knowledge-Based System from a 'Knowledge Level' Perspective: The DIVA Experiment", in *Second Generation Expert Systems*, J M David, J P Krivine, R Simmons eds., Springer Verlag, 1993.

[4] J de Kleer and B C Williams, "Diagnosing Multiple Faults", in *Artificial Intelligence*, **32**(1), 1987, pp. 97-130.

[5] S M Divakaruni and R Scheibel, "Development and Testing of Turbine and Generator Expert Monitoring Systems", in *Industrial Applications of Knowledge-Based Diagnosis* G Guida and A Stefanini eds., 1992, Elseviers Science Publishers. pp. 51-76.

[6] E Georgin, F Bordin and J R McDonald, "Using Prototypes in Case-Based Reasoning for Steam Turbines", in Proceedings of *IEE Colloquium on Case-Based Reasoning: Prospects for Applications*, London, UK, 7 March 1995.

[7] M Manago, "Using KATE for Case Based Reasoning in Maintenance", in Proceedings of *IEE Colloquium on Case-Based Reasoning: Prospects for Applications*, London, UK, 3 March 1994.

[8] M A Moradian, M P Chow, R L Osborne and M A Jenkins, "TurbinAID: Turbine Artificial Intelligence Diagnostics", in Proceedings of the *1st annual ISA/EPRI Joint Controls and Automation Conference*, St. Petersburgh Beach, FL, USA, 3-5 June 1991.

Nirmani : An Integrated Case-Based System For Strategic Design And Estimating

Srinath Perera

Department of Building Economics, University of Moratuwa, Moratuwa, Sri Lanka.

Ian Watson

Department of Surveying, University of Salford, Salford, M5 4WT, U.K..

Abstract

An integrated Case-Based Design and Estimating system (NIRMANI) is proposed in this paper as a means of integrating the fragmented construction industry. This paper evaluates the Case-Based Design and Case-Based Estimating processes and suggests a combined approach for design and estimating in construction. It briefly explains the system conceptual model, case retrieval and adaptation strategy. Case presentation aspects are improved with the use of multimedia. The system helps in developing the design brief effectively and improves the understanding of design. The system is implemented in the domain of warehouse design and produces a schematic design and its cost plan.

Keywords :   Case-Based Design, Case-Based Estimating, Computer Aided Design, Integrated Design & Estimating, Multimedia.

1. Introduction

The use of IT in the construction industry has mostly resulted in the creation of isolated automated systems (Brandon et.al., 1988 ; Kartam, 1994 a & b). This has encouraged fragmentation of the construction industry (Hillebrandt, 1984 & 1985; Raftery, 1992).

Unlike in industries such as manufacturing the design, estimating and construction processes are separated resulting in ill co-ordinated and sub-optimum designs (Alshawi & Underwood, 1994), poor budgetary control and unsatisfied building client (Brandon, 1987). These necessitate the integration of these distinct processes. Since, 80% of cost effective design decisions are made during the early stage of design (Turner, 1993) it is more important that such integration be achieved from a very early stage of design.

This paper, therefore, describes a Case-Base methodology for the integration of design, estimating and construction using previous designs, estimates and construction experiences. The NIRMANI (meaning creator or designer in "Sinhalese") system develops a schematic design and the respective Cost Plan with the use of similar previous designs and Elemental Cost Analyses while using construction experience during the adaptation process.

The high level aims and the objectives of the research reviewed can be summarised as follows ;

1. Develop a case representation suitable for building design and estimation,
2. Determine the most appropriate case indexing method for this problem,
3. Develop an efficient multimedia case storage and retrieval structure,
4. Develop a method for adapting (architectural, structural, services and cost) retrieved cases,
5. Develop a method of generalising cases from new cases thereby letting the system learn in a controlled and efficient way,
6. Implementing a robust documented prototype that demonstrates 1 to 5 above,
7. Demonstrate to the construction industry, through CBD & Estimating project, how CBR can apply to their sector   and
8. Create a CBD & Estimating system that generates a schematic design and cost plan that forms the source for an intelligent CAD/VR based system for further design development and construction planning.

This paper briefly analyses the concepts of Case-Based Design and Case-Based Estimating, presents the conceptual model of NIRMANI and briefly describes the case retrieval and adaptation strategies.

2. Case-Based Design & Case-Based Estimating

2.1 Case-Based Design (CBD)

Design is an ill-structured problem where an explicit model does not exist or is not yet adequately understood (Simon, 1973). Thus, there could be many solutions to any given design problem. Sometimes, all constraints cannot be considered in isolation.

During the design process architects do reason using previous architectural designs (parts of designs or the whole design). (Akin, 1988 ; Schmitt, 1993 a ; Bartsch - Sporl, 1995) with CBR, the designer is offered previous solutions to a similar problem (Schmitt, 1993 a). It indicates how a previous set of constraint combination was handled (Kolodner, 1993). The technique of using previous designs for creating new designs is known as Case Based Design (CBD) (Schmitt 1993 a & b). This uses the Artificial Intelligence (AI) technique of Case Based Reasoning (CBR) (Kolodner, 1993 ; Watson & Marir, 1994) which organises previous design solutions as design cases in a library.

Hence, CBD can be defined as ;

> *"the process of creating a new design solution by combining and/or adapting previous design solution(s)."*

It provides the designer at least a starting point, if not a complete or comprehensive solution.

The first CBR workshop (Kolodner, 1988) was held in 1988 which saw the presentation of the earliest CBD systems : JULIA (Hinrichs, 1988) a meal planning system and CYCLOPS (Navinchandra, 1988) a landscape architectural layout design system. This was soon followed by many other CBD systems such as, ARCHIE (Goel et.al., 1991), KRITIK (Goel, 1989), CADSYN (Maher, 1991), CAB-Assembly (Pu, 1991) etc.

Domeshek & Kolodner (1993) identifies the emergence of two approaches in the use of CBR for design subsequent to 2nd International Conference on AI in Design, held in 1992 at Carnegie Mellon University. Viz.:

1. Systems that aid human designers
2. Systems that aim at automating design fully or partially with human interaction

Most systems developed fall in to the first category.

2.2 Case-Based Estimating (CBE)

Cost estimating in general is the prediction of cost of an artefact or project using experience and/or a methodology. In the construction industry, there are numerous methods of estimating developed over time. To name a few unit method, storey enclosure method, elemental estimating etc. Most of these methods are highly depended on the experience of the estimator and cost data derived from previous construction projects.

Cost planning primarily uses the elemental estimating method for cost estimation (Nisbet, 1970). This method uses similar cost analysis of projects Elemental Cost Analysis (ECA) as the basis for estimation. The elemental rates are adjusted or adapted in terms of quantity, quality and price (tender, market conditions, location etc.) (Cartlidge & Mehrtens, 1982; Ferry & Brandon, 1991). Thus, in other words, uses a previous case on the basis of new estimate. Hence, is a prime example where CBR is used for estimation. But this process exists only as a manual process and the previous case selection mostly depends on the experience of the estimator.

Surprisingly, there are very few examples of where CBR is used for estimating in other domains. FACE - Finding Analogies for Cost Estimation (Bisio & Malabocchia, 1995) is a system for estimating cost of software projects. It uses a case-base of previous estimates, a general global database for adaptation. Nearest - neighbour algorithm which enables the user to weigh the retrieval criteria is used for appropriate case retrieval. The retrieved case is adapted using an analogy based algorithm to provide the new estimate. The system is implemented using CBR-Express™ & ART IM™.

Estor (Mukhopadhyay et.al., 1992 ; Eliot, 1993) is another system used for software effort estimation and Stottler (1992) explains another system for bid preparation in manufacturing.

3. The Conceptual Model

A conceptual framework for a CBD system which achieves both the concepts of *design to cost* and *design to construct* was developed. The system named NIRMANI (meaning creator or designer in Sinhalese) (Perera, 1994) thereby integrates the numerous design disciplines and the design and construction processes. The CBD process of the NIRMANI system is semantically described in Fig. 1. In addition, a structured analysis using Data Flow Diagrams (DFD) was carried out to improve the understanding of the processes involved and also to structure the system.

The NIRMANI system aims at generating a schematic design for warehouse buildings by retrieving a previous designs that matches the problem specification from a case library. The retrieved design shall be adapted if required, architecturally, structurally, for services requirements ultimately providing a cost plan for the building to form as the budgetary guide for further design development. The entire CBD process is interactive giving the designer sufficient authority to guide the design process and achieve creativity as much as possible.

Once a case is selected, all information is mapped to create a new case. The user is allowed to develop the design brief by changing the features of the new case as required. This establishes design constraints by comparing with the original case. A problem decomposition and constraint satisfaction approach is then used for the design adaptation.

The design problem is decomposed into the four main design perspectives identified previously. The system will then indicate the non-satisfied constraints that need to be satisfied under each perspective. The Propose-Critique-Modify (PCM) design methodology (Chandrasekeran, 1990) will be used for adaptation and design development using case specific adaptation knowledge and domain specific adaptation knowledge interactively (for the most part), with greater user participation and guidance. The system, uses the interactive adaptation process to satisfy design constraints and revise the design using knowledge obtained from the knowledge base in the form of methods and rules. Once constraints are satisfied (to a level acceptable to the user) and the user accepts the new design, it is stored in the case library as a new experience to the system, thus completing the CBD cycle and learning from the new experience, i.e. the system conforms to the *dynamic memory model* (Schank & Abelson, 1977).

The system architecture at a high level consists of a KBS as the core using CBR technique for experience based reasoning, CAD and Multimedia facilities for visualisation. Fig. 2 depicts the provisional system architecture.

The CBD systems developed for the Construction industry and found in literature can be classified as :

| 1. | Design Aid Systems | ARCHIE, FABEL, MEMORABILIA |
| 2. | Design Generative Systems | CADSYN, ACABAS, CADRE |

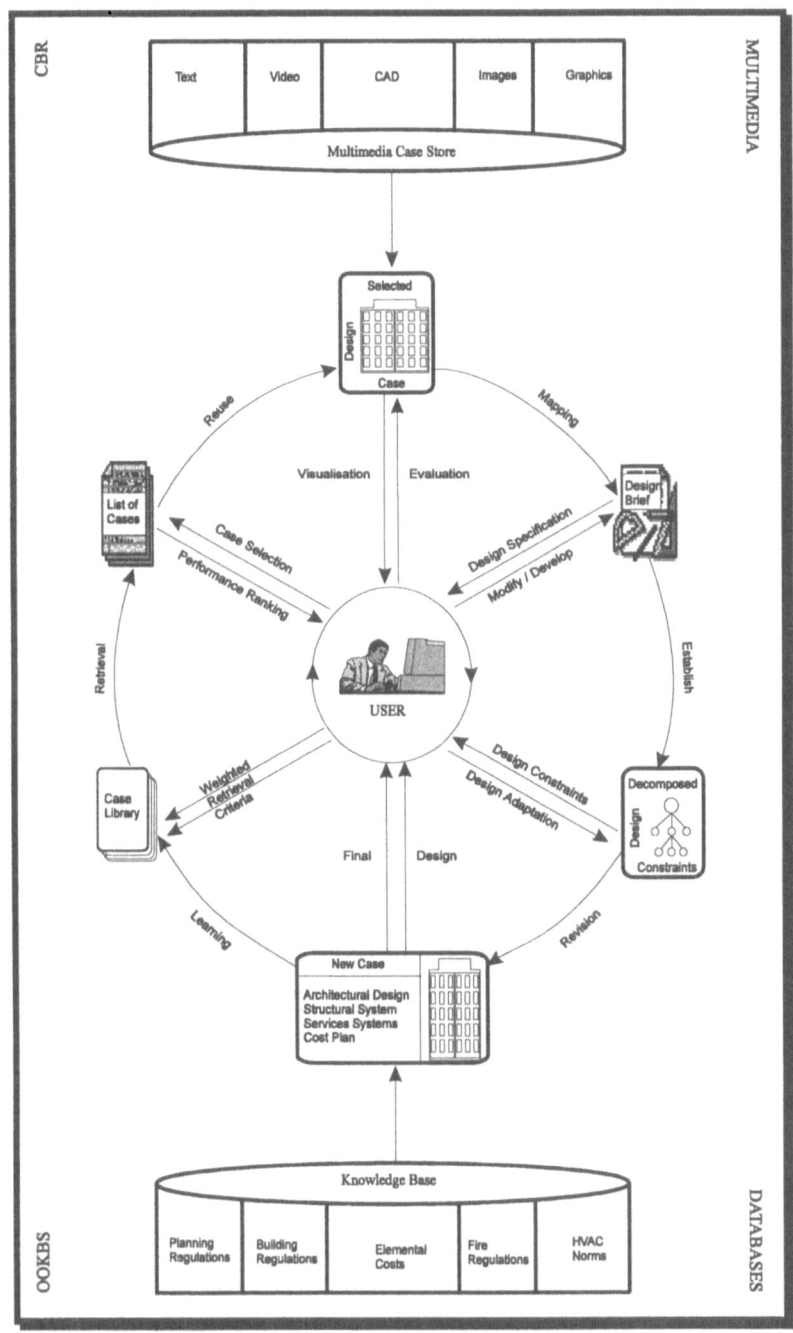

Fig. 1 CBD & Estimating Process : An Overview

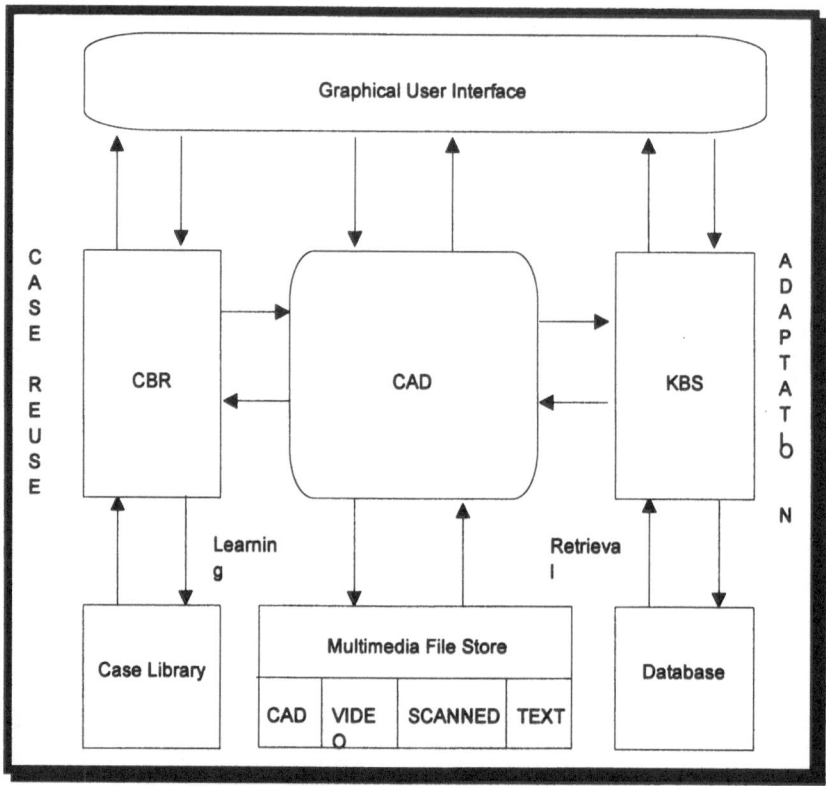

Fig. 2   Overview of System Architecture

The system proposed, mostly falls into the second category with a component of design aiding while adaptation.

Most of these systems deal with either architectural design or structural design. Only ACABAS & CADRE approaches both structural and architectural design. The system proposed deals with architectural schematic design, structural grid optimisation, services system selection and cost planning.   Thus, attempts at giving a comprehensive design.

In terms of design re-use, CADRE (Hua et.al. 1993) and ACABAS (Schmitt, 1993 a & b) use a manual case selection procedure whereas ARCHIE (Goel et.al. 1991) & MEMORABILIA (Oxman, 1993 a & b) selects matching cases to provide guidance to the designer but not for direct re-use. Whereas, FABEL (Reports 13 & 24, 1994; Bakhtari & Barth-Spoerl, 1994; Voβ et. al., 1994) stores design segments as cases provides a "*smart cut & paste*" facility encouraging re-use of design. Only SEED (Flemming et.al. 1994 a & b), a system at conceptual stage, proposes a complete re-use of design for design generation. But it is more of a design generative system using first principles of design with a component of case-based reasoning to assist the design generation task.   On the other hand, the proposed system which stores the full schematic design as cases provides automatic retrieval of the most appropriate case directly for adaptation and/or re-use.

Unlike most CBD systems developed, it is envisaged to learn by itself, acquiring new cases it generate thereby maturing with experience along with the user or the architectural firm, using the system. This puts the system in line with SEED & FABEL but clearly distinguishing from other approaches that rely on considerable efforts to build a memory of cases (Rosenman et.al. 1991 ; Domeshek et.al. 1992 ; Hua et.al. 1992 a & b; Schmitt 1993 a & b, 1994). SEED uses a combination of rule-based space generation expert systems for the generation of cases while FABEL uses the DANCER (A4 prototype) in cojunction with the ARMILLA & MIDI (Haller, 1974, 1988) design methodologies to generate cases. With NIRMANI cases are generated within the system while case indexing will be hidden from the user thus providing greater enhancement in usability.

It is intended that case adaptation to be semi-automatic allowing a certain degree of user interaction. The adaptation process will prompt the user with alternatives and suggestions from which the user can select or confirm. This is, therefore, partially in line with CADRE & FABEL but more similar to that proposed by SEED.

In terms of implementation, the proposed system would be an integration of CBR development shell with Object Oriented Knowledge Base facilities with CAD and Database system in MS Window environment, thus PC based. However, most systems found in literature, differs from this being developed in an UNIX and/or XWindows environment.

4. Case Retrieval and Adaptation

4.1 Case Memory Organisation and Retrieval

The NIRMANI system uses the state of the art technology of multimedia to store previous design cases (Maher & Balachandran, 1994) in the form of objects (attribute value pairs), textual descriptions, 2D and 3D CAD images, video and photographic (still) images. The multimedia case store enables the client and the design team to view previous design cases selected according to a set of basic requirements.

Case information is structured in a design perspective based hierarchical object oriented structure consisting of four main design perspectives : architectural, structural, services and estimating (Fig. 3). This itself forms a useful natural indexing schema for case retrieval. Each perspective is then further classified so as to provide information to the each of the professions in the form they require.

However this representation may encourage redundancy. But, this could be effectively reduced with the use of multiple inheritance characteristics attributable to object orientation. The hierarchical representation of a case also provides a natural indexing schema for the retrieval of case information.

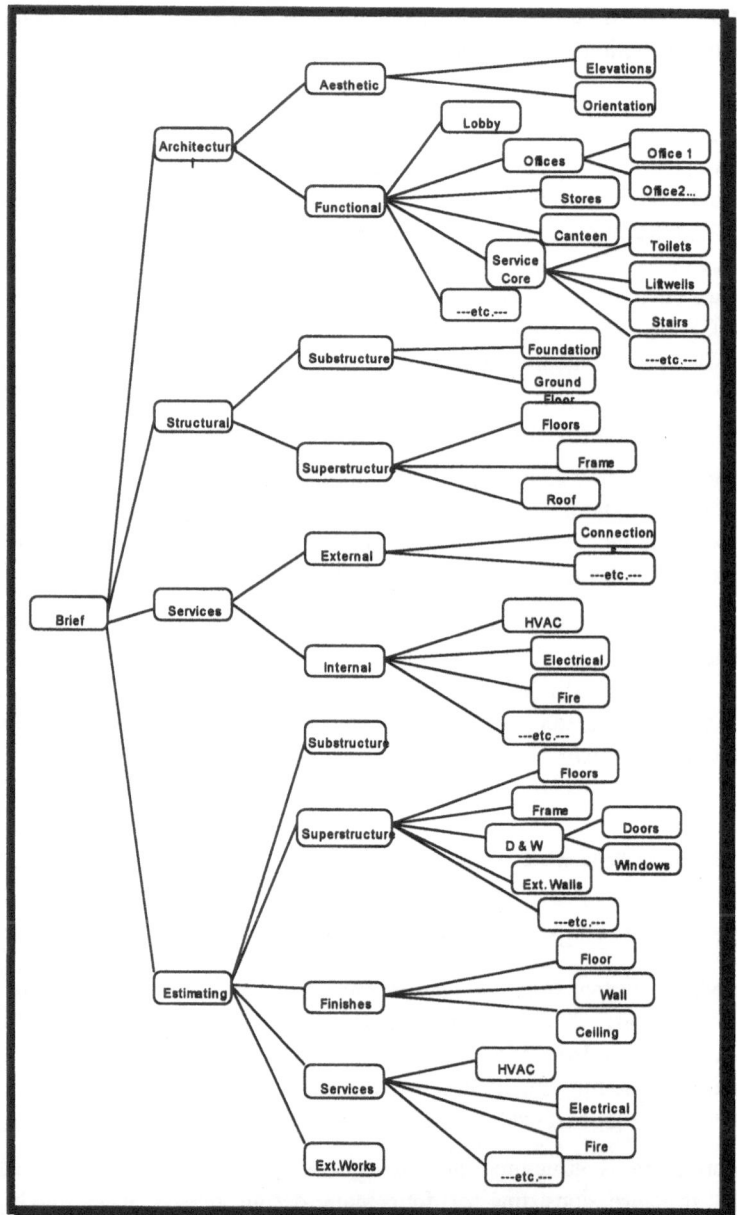

Fig. 3 Perspective-Based Hierarchical Case Structure

The user is provided with 3 main modes of case retrieval. i.e. *Use of Design Brief, Clues, User Information.* The first mode provides the primary form of retrieval while the latter two enables more specific form of case retrieval where the user vaguely knows the specific case he/she wants. When using the design brief mode the user is required to enter the requirements of the building he/she needs. It is done in two levels : *Primary Retrieval* and *Secondary Retrieval*. Primary Retrieval criteria (e.g. Total Cost, Gross Floor Area, Occupancy, Shape, etc.) represents high level information whereas Secondary Retrieval criteria (e.g. Functional requirements in detail, Elemental costs, Elemental specifications, etc.) represents more detailed and specific low level features of the expected building. Each of these retrieval criteria can be relatively prioritised by attaching a weighting to each criterion. The NIRMANI system provides a list of cases along with an indication of the extent of match from which the user is allowed to select a case upon visualising the cases with the use of multimedia.

4.2 Case Adaptation

Knowledge in the system can primarily be categorised as :

i. Automatically Upgradable Knowledge :-
    This constitutes cases stored in the case library and the associated Multimedia storage of information. This type of knowledge is automatically upgraded as a learning process.

ii. Relatively Static Knowledge :-
    This constitutes the domain specific knowledge represented as rule and objects. These are upgradable only by the case-base administration or the system administrator.

The latter type mainly represents the domain specific adaptation knowledge.

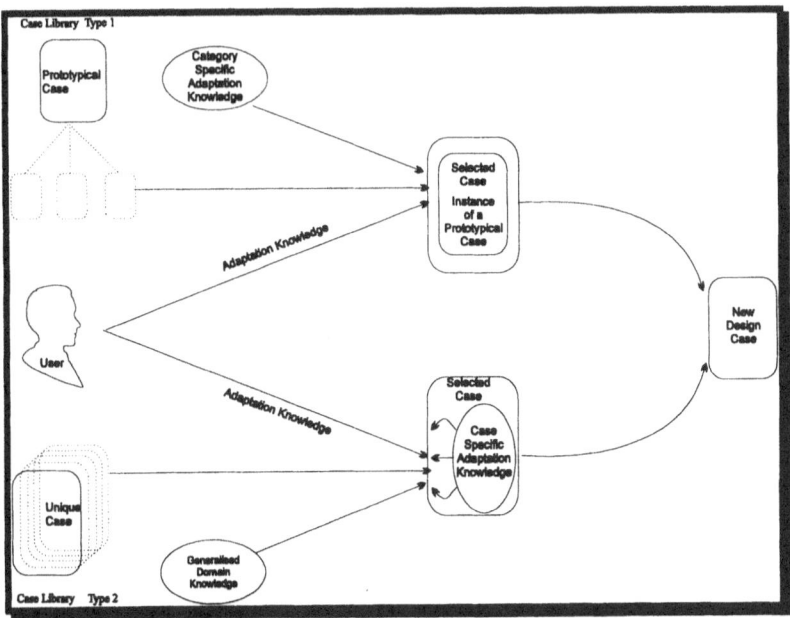

Fig. 4   Methods of Organising Adaptation Knowledge

Hua & Faltings (1993), identifies two main approaches to organise adaptation knowledge (Fig. 4 above).

i. By categorising the case as instances of prototypical designs which can simply be reinstantiated. Adaptation knowledge can then be stored as *case category specific knowledge*. However, this raises the question of why cases are required at all, as prototypes could fulfil the same function (to a great extent).

ii. By providing specific adaptation knowledge which modifies aspects of cases instead of regenerating or reinstantiating them.

The use of specific adaptation knowledge is proposed as the method of formulating adaptation knowledge as opposed to adaptation of prototypical cases. This is because the use of prototypical case may negate the context sensitivity of design and cost elements. Hence, the use of such would result in inaccurate design or estimates. In the NIRMANI system, specific adaptation knowledge is stored with individual cases as well in a generalised adaptation knowledge base. This has the advantage of being efficient in terms of knowledge representation as all the adaptation knowledge required is not stored with the case, but only the one that needs to be case specific. For example, the context dependent features of a case could then be stored with the case so that any adaptation and subsequent modification will indicate any violations of the contextual features of the case. Adaptation knowledge that can be generalised shall be stored separately in domain specific perspective based knowledge bases. These could be database or object oriented knowledge bases that reside on the central KBS hidden from the user.

Adaptation of designs (as detailed in Fig. 5) will be carried out as an iterative process with greater user interaction. Once a case is selected all its features, characteristics design and context based knowledge are mapped directly to create a new case, exactly the same as the previous case. The new case would then be updated with the information provided for the retrieval. The mapping process enables the *design brief* to be developed on the guidelines of the original case (selected case). On this phase of developing the *design brief* the user is offered the opportunity of changing the characteristic, feature, design or context based knowledge. By doing so. the user would be creating a unique specification for the new design.

On completion of the *design brief* development, the system shall identify the differences between the original case and the new case, thus establishing design constraints. The system then uses a constraint satisfaction approach for all subsequent adaptations.

Problem decomposition is used to decompose the design problem into sub problems, viz. Architectural, Structural Services and Estimating and each sub problem is further decomposed into another layer.

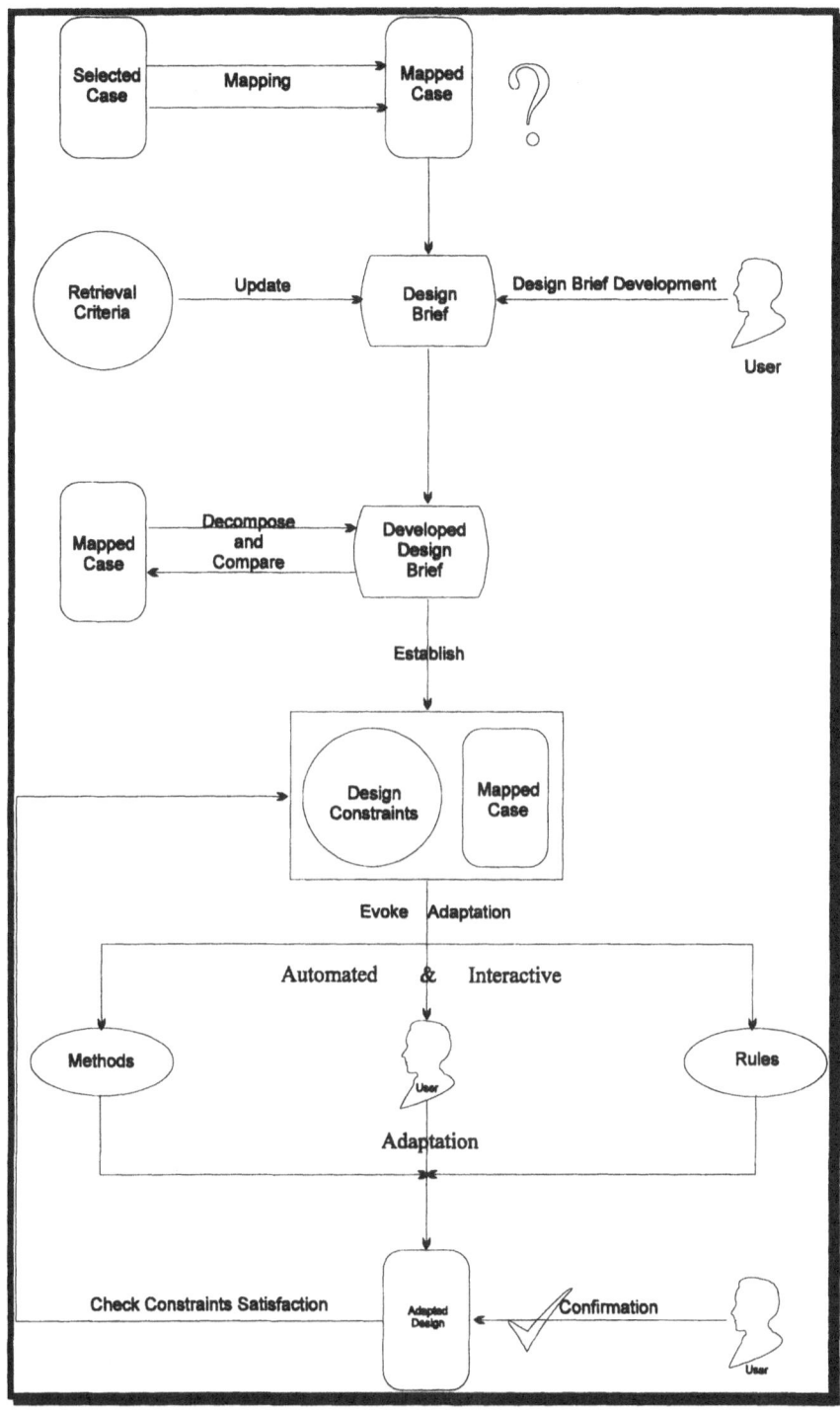

Fig. 5 Overview of the Adaptation Process

Architectural adaptation first achieves the gross floor area required and fits the building to the new site. Internal layout of the building will then be adapted interactively with user being guided by the system. Structural adaptation process optimises the grid layout with the use of an Expert System to optimise bay design (Alshawi & Underwood, 1994). Services adaptation process enables the user to select a different type of HVAC or Fire system. Once design features are adapted the Cost adaptation process generates a Cost Plan for the new building based on the original building's Cost Analysis, thus integrating design and estimating.

5. Conclusions

It is envisaged that once fully implemented the NIRMANI system will enhance the design process in many ways. It is expected that the design brief development could be fairly effectively be achieved with greater understanding of the end product by the client and the client requirements by the design team. The schematic design development time could be effectively reduced and the cost plan generated will form the basis for further design development.

The hierarchical perspective based case memory organisation forms an effective method for representing many views of the design team, thus facilitating effective retrieval of information. The multimedia case presentation enhances the design visualisation and understanding capabilities of the system which will reduce subsequent client oriented design variations. The interactive adaptation process provides sufficient authority to the designer to induce creativity during the adaptation process. The use of previous designs, estimates and construction experience enables the user to achieve "*best practice*" in design, avoiding repetition of previous mistakes. Moreover, the system grows with the experience of the organisation providing a corporate experience bank of designs and their cost structures for the design organisation.

References

Aamodt, A.,and Plaza Enric, (1994), Case-based reasoning: Foundational issues, methodological variations and system approaches, *The European Journal on Aritificial Inteliigence, AICOM Vol. 7 No.1*, pp. 39-59.

Akin, O. (1988), *"Expertise of the Architect"*, Expert Systems for Engineering Design, Edited: Rychener, M., pp 173-196. Academic Press. London.

Akin, O.,(1986), *Psychology of architectural design*, Pion, London.

Alshawi, M.,and Underwood, J., (1994), Information analysis approach for integrating design and construction, Dept. of Surveying, University of Salford.

Aouad, G.,Cooper, G., Brandon, P.S., Brown F., Child, T., Ford, S., Kirkham, J., Oxman, R., and Young, B., (1993), Integrated databases for design and construction.

Bakhtari, S. and, Bartsch-Sporl, B. (1994), *"Bridging the Gap between AI Technology and Design Requirements"*, Artificial Intelligence in Design 94', Edited: Gero, J.S.;, and Sudweeks, F., pp 753-768. Kluwer. Dordrecht.

Bartsch-Sporl (1995), *"Towards the Integration of Case-Based, Schema-Baesd and Model-Based Reasoning for Supporting Complex Design Tasks"*, Proceedings of the ICCBR 95, Portugal.

Bisio, R. and, Malabocchia, F. (1995), *"Cost Estimation of Software Projects through Case-Based Reasoning"*, to be published in the Proceedings of ICCBR-95, Portugal.

Brandon, P.S.,(1984), Cost vs. quality : A zero sum game ? In : Powell, J.A., et. al. (ed.) Designing for building utilisation, E & FN SPON, London, pp. 108-123, 1984.

Brandon, P.S. (1987), Building cost modelling and computers, Edited: Brandon, P.S., E & FN SPON.

Brandon, P.S.,Basden, A., Hamilton, I., Stockley, J., (1988), Expert systems, The strategic planning of construction projects, RICS.

Cartlidge, D.P. and, Mehrtens, I.N. (1982), *"Practical Cost Planning"*, Hutchinsons. London.

Chandrasekeran,B.,(1990), Design problem solving: A task analysis, In *AAAI, AI Magazine*, pp. 59-71, Winter.

Coyne, R.F., and Flemming, U., (1990), Planning in design synthesis: Abstraction-based LOOS in: J.Gero (ed.), *Artificial Intelligence in Engineering* V, Volume 1: Design, Springer, New York, pp. 91-111.

Cutkosky, M.R., and Tenenbaum, J.M., (1990), A methodology and conceptual framework for concurrent product and process design, mechanism and machine theory, 25(3), pp.365-381.

Domeshek, E.,and Kolodner, J., (1992), A case-based design aid for architecture. In *Artificial Intelligence in Design,* edited J.Gero. Boston: Kluwer.

Domeshek, E., and, Kolodner, J., (1993), *"Using the points of large cases"*, AI EDAM, Vol.7, No.2, pp 87-96.

Eliot, L.B. (1993), *"Case-Based Reasoning in Estimation"*, AI Expert, Vol.8, No.5, Miller Freeman.

FABEL (1993), *"Report No.13"*, Similarity Concepts and Retrieval Methods, Edited: Angi Voβ.

FABEL (1994), *"Report No.24"*, Evaluation of Retrieval Methods in Case-Based Design, Carl-Helmut Coulon, Friedrich Cebhardt.

Ferry, D.J., and, Brandon, P.S. (1991), *"Cost planning of buildings"*, 6th edition, BSP.

Flemming, U.,(1989), More on the representation and generation of loosely packed arrangements of rectangles, In *Environment Planning, Building, Planing and Design,* 16, pp. 327-359.

Flemming, U.,(1994 a), Case-based design in the SEED system, *Automation in construcion 3,* pp. 123-133.

Flemming, U.,Coyne, R., and Snyder, J., (1994 b), Case-based design in the SEED system, ASCE, pp. 446-453.

Goel, A., (1989), *"Integration of Case-Based Reasoning and Model-Based Reasoning for Adaptive Design Problem Solving"*, PhD Thesis, Department of Computer & Informaiton Science. The Ohio State University, USA.

Goel, A.,Kolodner, J. L.; Pearce, M.; Billington, R.; and Zimring, C. (1991), Towards a case-based tool for aiding conceptual design problem solving. In E.R.Bareiss, edited *Proceedings : Workshop on case-based reasoning (DARPA)*, Washington, D.C. San Mateo, CA: Morgan Kaufmann.

Haller, F. (1974), *"MIDI - ein offenes system fur mehrgeschossige bauten mit integrierter medieninstallation"*, USM baaaaaausysteme haller, Munsingen.

Haller, F. (1988), *"bauen und forschen"*, Fritz Haller Solothurn, Ausstellung des Knustvereins Solothurn.

Heisserman, J.,and Woodbury, R., (1993), Generating languages of solid models, Proc. *Second ACM / IEEE Conference on Solid Modelling and Applications*, Montreal, Canada.

Hillebrandt, P.M., (1984), Analysis of the British Construction Industry, Macmillan.

Hillebrandt, P.M., (1985), Economic Theory and the Construction Industry, Macmillan.

Hinrichs, T.R, (1988), *"Towards an architecture for open world problem solving. In "*, Proceedings of Workshop on CBR (DARPA), Edited: Kolodner, J.L, Morgan Kaufmann. New York:.

Hua, K.,Schmitt, G., and Faltings, B., (1992a), What can case-based design do? In: (ed.) Pu, P., *Unpublished proceedings of the AID '92, workshop on case-based design systems*, pp. 44-53.

Hua, K.,Faltings, B., Smith, I., Schmitt, G., and Shih, S.G., (1992b), Adaptation of spacial design cases, In: *2nd International conference on AI in dsign*, CMU, Pittsburgh, pp. 559-575.

Hua, K.,and Faltings, B., (1993),), *"Exploring case-based building design-Cadre"*, In: *AI EDAM, Vol. 7, No.2*, pp. 135-143, Academic Press Limited.

Kartam, N.A.,(1994a), A knowledge-intensive database system for making effective use of construction lessons learned, ASCE.

Kartam, N.A.,(1994b), ISICAD: Interactive system for integrating CAD and computer-based construction systems, In: *Microcomputers in civil engineering, Vol. 9*, pp. 41-51.

Kolodner, J.L.,(1983), Maintaining organization in a dynamic long-term memory. *Cognitive Science* 7(4).

Kolodner, J.L. (1988), *"Proceedings of the 1st case-based reasoning workshop"*, Morgan Kaufmann. New York.

Kolodner, J.L.,(1993), Case-Based Reasoning, Morgan Kaufmann Publishers, Inc..

Maher, M.L.,and Zhang, D.M., (1991), CADSYN: Using case and decomposition knowledge for design synthesis, In: *Artificial intelligence in Design*, Gero, J., (ed.).

Maher, M.L.,and Zhang, D.M., (1993), CADSYN: A case-based design process model, In: *AI EDAM, Vol. 7, No. 2*, pp. 97-110.

Maher, M,L.,(1994), Representation of case memory for structural design, pp. 2030-2037.

Maher, M.L.,and Balachandran, B., (1994), Multimedia approach to case-based structural design, In: *The journal of computing in civil enginnering, Vol. 8, No. 3,* pp. 359-376, July.

Marir, F.,and, Watson, I.D., (1994), A categorised bibliography, in "The Knowledge Engineering Review, Vol 9, No 4.

Mukhopadhyay, T., Vicinanza, S.S. and, and Prietula, M.J. (1992), *"Examining the Feasibility of a Case-Based Reasoning Model for Software effort estimation (Technical)"*, MIS Quarterly, Vol.16, No.2.

Navinchandra, D. (1988), *"Case-based reasoning in CYCLOPS, a design problem solver"*, Proceedings: Workshop on case-based reasoning (DARPA), pp 286-301. Morgan Kaufmann. Ckearwater, Florida. San Mateo, CA.

Nisbet, J. (1970), *"It's Elemental My Dear Bill Said the QS to the Builder"*, London.

Oxman, R.,(1994 a), Precedents in design: A computational model for the organisation of case knowledge, ASCE, pp. 438-445.

Oxman, R.,and Oxman, R., (1993 a), PRECEDENTS: Memory structure in design case libraries, In: *CAAD Futures '93,* Flemming, U., and Wyk, S.V., (ed.), pp. 273-287.

Oxman, R.E.,(1993 b), INDEX: C case-based reasoning approach of content-based indexing for design, In: *The 8th international conference on appliation of aritificial intelligence, Vol. 1,* pp. 203-218.

Pearce, M.,Goel, A.; Kolodner, J. L; Zimring, C.; Sentosa, L.; and Billington, R. (1992), Case-Based design support: A case stody in architectural design. *IEEE Expert* 7(5), pp 14 -20.

Perera, R.S. (1994), *"A Case-Based Design Approach for the Integration of Design & Estimating"*, MSc Dissertation, Department of Surveying. University of Salford,Salford, UK.

Perera, R.S., Watson, I.D and Alshawi, M., (1995), Case-Based Design Approach For The Integration Of Design And Estimating, to be published in the proceedings of the AI-Civil Comp 95 conference, Cambridge.

Porter, B.W.,and Bareiss, E.R., (1986), PROTOS: An experiment in knowledge aquisition for heuristic classification tasks. In: *Proceedings of the First International Meeting on Advances in Learning (IMAL),* France, pp. 159-174.

Pu, P., and, and Reschberger, M. (1991), *"Assembly sequence planning using case-based reasoning technique"*, Artificial intelligence in design '91, Butterworth Heinemann. London.

Raftery, J. (1991), *"Principles of Building Economics "*, An Introduction, BSP Professionals.

Riesbeck, C.K.,and Schank, R.S., (1989), Inside case-based reasoning. *Northvale, NJ: Erlbaum.*

Rosenman, A.,Gero, J.S., and Oxman, R.E., (1991), What's in a case : The use of case bases, knowledge bases and databases in design, In : Schmitt, G.N., (ed.) *CAAD Futures '91,* pp. 285-300, Germany.

Rutherford, J.H.,and Maver, T.W., (1994), Knowledge-based design support, In: *Automtion in construction 3,* pp. 187-202.

Schank, R.,and Abelson, R., (1975), Scripts, plans, and knowledge. In *Proceedings of the fourth international joint conference on Aritificial Intelligence,* pp. 151-157, Menlo Park, Calif.: International joint conferences on Artificial Intelligence.

Schank, R.C.,and Abelson, R.P., (1977), *Scripts, plans, goals and understanding.* Erlbaum, Hillsdale, New Jersey, US.

Schank, R.C.,(1982), *Dynamic memory: A theory of learning in computers and people.* NY:Cambridge Univ. Press.

Schmitt, G.,(1993 a), Case-based design and creativity, In: *Automation in construction, Vol. 2,* pp. 11-19.

Schmitt, G.N.,(1993 b), Case-based reasoning in an integrated design and construciton system, In: *The International Journal of Construction Information Technology, Vol. 1, No. 3,* pp. 39-51.

Schmitt, G.,Bailey, S.F., and Smith, I.F.C., (1994), Advances and challenges in case-based design, ASCE, pp. 301-309.

Simon, H.A., (1973), The structure of the ill structured problems, *Artificial Intelligence 4,* pp. 181-201.

Slade, S.,(1991), Case-based reasoning: A research paradigm, AI magazine, pp. 42-55.

Stottler, R.H. (1992), *"Case-Based Reasoning for Bid Preparation",* AI Expert, Vol.7, No.3, Miller Freeman.

Turner, J.A.,and Tsou, J.Y., (1993), "Using an object oriented system and a conceptual building model to represent architectural information during early design phases", *Proceeding of the 5th international conference (V-ICCCBE),* Computing in civil and building engineering, Anaheim, Cal, U.S.A., pp. 1175.

Voβ, A.,, Coulon, C.H.,, Grather, W.,, Linowski, B.,, Schaaf, J.,, Bartsch-Sprol, B.,, Borner, K.,, Tammer, E.C.,, Durschke, E., and, Knauff, M. (1994), *"Retrieval of Similar Layouts - About a Very Hybrid Approach in FABEL",* Artificial Intelligence in Design '94, Edited: J.S.Gero and , and F.Sudweeks, pp 625-640. Kluwer Academic Publishers. Netherlands.

Watson, I.D., and Marir, F., (1994), Case-based reasoning: A review, in "The Knowledge Engineering Review, Vol 9, No 4.

Case-based Task Management
for Computer-aided Learning

Tariq Khan
Yau Jim Yip
Information Technology Institute, University of Salford, Salford M5 4WT

Abstract

Recently computer-supported planning has benefited from Case-based reasoning techniques for reuse of plans, and proposals are presented here for a case-based planning component to be used for selection and sequencing of learning experiences in a case-based teaching environment. We present a Task Manager that uses retrieval and adaptation methods to generate a tailored set of learning experiences in response to a user's specification. We also discuss Instructional Design Theory and Goal-Based Scenario, which are used to specify the classification system, including similarity and functional knowledge, on which the task manager operates.

Introduction

Planning is a major area of interest in both case-based reasoning and intelligent tutoring. Until recently most planners had to regenerate plans for situations they had planned for previously when faced with the same problem again. When planning instruction there are certain similarities between situations a planner must deal with, e.g., instructional objectives that must be taught. In these cases it would be beneficial to be able to reapply an old plan in the new context, and this is exactly what Case-based Reasoning enables. CHEF (Hammond 1989) demonstrates the worth of case-based reasoning for sequencing subgoals to obtain a global goal. The same capabilities are needed for sequencing individual lessons to make a curriculum for tutoring. In order to be effective a curriculum plan must not be static, i.e, it should adapt to any goal failures and feedback from students during the teaching session. This feature requires a powerful plan creation and management method that can handle the dynamic requirements of individual students. Irrespective of the planning technique used, however, there is a common dependence on classification. A classification of goals that reflects the learning objectives the course seeks to fulfil is needed. Without a reliable classification scheme, selection and sequencing of learning objectives becomes, at best, ad hoc with little or no pedagogical relevance, and at worst, yields a learning sequence that can confuse and 'damage' a student's existing understanding. This paper considers application of case-based planning and learning theory to the management of tasks in a learning environment.

Our long term objective is to incorporate the planner in a *case-based teaching* (Schank *et al* 1993) environment. Planners are not widely used in case-based teaching because their introduction poses problems for student modelling since the content of a lesson is usually a video story that is not readily reasoned about by the system (Khan *et al* 1995a). A favoured and necessary assumption taken with case-based teaching is to infer students' goals to be 'learning information required to enable them to traverse an impasse.' Although this assumption imparts some guidance for pedagogical decision making, it is certainly insufficient to reliably model a student's intentions. Notwithstanding the problems of automated student modelling with case-based teaching systems we describe here a planning component that interacts with a student record to support the student in a case-based teaching environment (the student model has to be updated by a human instructor).

Case-based Planning

Hammond (1989) defines three basic processes a case-based planner must posses: (i) a plan retriever that finds the best previous plan from memory to match requirements of the new situation; (ii) a plan modifier that can change the retrieved plan to meet all requirements of the new situation; and (iii) a plan storer to place in memory the complete plan under the goals it satisfies and the circumstances under which it applies.

One advantage of case-based planning over conventional planners is plan reuse. A case-based planner recalls and modifies past plans instead of regenerating plans for situations already planned for. The central processes involved are *recall* of previously used plans and *modification* of near-miss plans when an exact match cannot be found. Recall is a matter of maintaining an indexing scheme so an optimal selection of relevant plans presents itself when called. Modification requires identification of features in the problem description that differ with the problem-features of the saved plan, and then compensating for those failures to meet the goals of the new situation.

Several different adaptation techniques are available to modify a retrieved plan to make it fit better with the requirements of the new situation (e.g., Riesbeck and Schank 1989). These include: Null Adaptation, Parameterized Solutions, Critic-based Adaptation, and derivational analogy. However, the *Abstraction and Respecialization* adaptation method we feel is the best suited to curriculum planning. The abstraction and respecialization technique operates thus: when a step in the solution does not apply, a replacement is sought by abstracting up a hierarchy to a more general version of the solution and then specializing down a different branch to an alternate solution at the original abstraction level. The Abstraction and Respecialization approach is better for curriculum planning because it can take advantage of the hierarchical nature of the domain. Success of this technique depends on a reliable classification scheme of knowledge needed in planning; in this case, a hierarchy of instructional objectives. Such a hierarchy can provide the similarity and functional knowledge needed to guide the adaptation process.

Learning/Instructional Design Theory

To provide the classification hierarchy for similarity and functional knowledge we utilize research on learning theory and instructional design.

We are interested in facilitating learning in the domain of *Stock Market Analysis*, which requires learning the concepts, procedures, and considerations involved in deciding an investment strategy and selecting an investment product. The work of Schank *et al* (1993) on *Goal-Based Scenario (GBS)* is blended with that of Gagné *et al* (1992) on *Learning Hierarchy* to define the classification structure on which the *Task Manager* operates. The structure consists of a top level goal-based scenario that defines the purpose of the learning system. It is defined in terms of skills that will be learned and exercised. This is reduced to 12 subGBS' at the second level that define the subskills and procedures to be demonstrated. The subGBS' are reduced into approximately 10-15 decisions or operations for each subGBS. Each decision/operation is further specified by between 1-5 performance objectives that need to be demonstrated.

Goal-based scenarios are designed to allow students to learn skills, however, there is no specified method of identifying the skills to include. We have applied the framework developed by Gagné *et al* (1992) for designing instructional systems based on an analysis of skills. The framework was used to create the classification hierarchy of subGBS', and importantly for specifying the low level performance objectives that allow a student's performance to be evaluated.

We describe this framework briefly as it stands and then discuss its bearing on automated curriculum planning.

Step 1 sets the scope of what is to be taught in terms of general *instructional goals* (or Mission Context in GBS); Step 2 considers resources needed to deliver these goals; and Step 3 relates instructional goals in terms of more specific *performance objectives* (mission focus/scenario operations), which are capable of measurement on yearly basis. Step 4: organization of goals into *units of instruction* consisting of *target objectives* (artifacts), which indicate that to be achieved by the end of a course; Step 5: detailed analysis of target objectives to identify *enabling objectives*, which are prerequisite subgoals of achievement of target objectives; and to provide information for further definition of performance objectives. Step 6: identification and definition of performance objectives (scenario operations), i.e., measurable actions that indicate whether or not an instructional goal is achieved; Step 7: selection and sequencing of activities to achieve each performance objective; Step 8: selection of materials to present; Step 9: diagnostic tests are chosen to determine whether or not a learner has achieved stated goals in terms of performance objectives. Step 10 teacher preparation, Steps 11, 12, 13 evaluation and testing, and Step 14 installation are not immediately relevant to the present discussion so they will not be expanded any further.

The design model was described with a human planner in mind but when considering an automated task manager not all these steps are achievable. The first phase, steps 1-3, is inappropriate for an automated curriculum planner because a great deal of 'world knowledge' is needed to prioritize social needs, or to appraise alternate delivery systems. And it is not expected that any practical ITS will attempt to encode a whole year's curriculum. Step 4 is the responsibility of the task manager. It should select appropriate target objectives in response to a learner's current needs. Step 5 requires the system designer to analyze target objectives and associate with them all necessary enabling objectives. However, since much of the process of selecting enabling objectives is dependent on a learner's current knowledge, the actual selection among alternate enabling objectives must be done by the task manger in response to the student model. At this point, a hierarchical goal/subgoal structure is formed. The mission context is the top node, and subsequent branches lead to nodes of subGBS' and decisions/operations.

Step 6 must be performed by the system designer who should develop suitable performance objectives and associate them with levels in the goal hierarchy. There will be a further level in this second *performance* hierarchy containing suitable activities that can realise performance objectives. From this level the task manager will select and sequence activities to meet the performance objectives currently active - Step 7. Classified under each activity will be relevant examples and exercises from which the task manager will choose the most appropriate examples (for advice) - Step 8. It is important that these examples are classified according to objectives they serve and not in terms of content.

Task Analysis

The domain we are interested in is Securities Analysis - the evaluation and selection of stocks available on the London Stock Exchange. We have conducted a preliminary *task analysis* that includes a *concept map*, which relates the concepts of interest in to a taxonomy; a *procedural analysis*, and the construction of a *learning hierarchy*.

Fig. 1. Procedural Analysis for task of selecting Derivatives

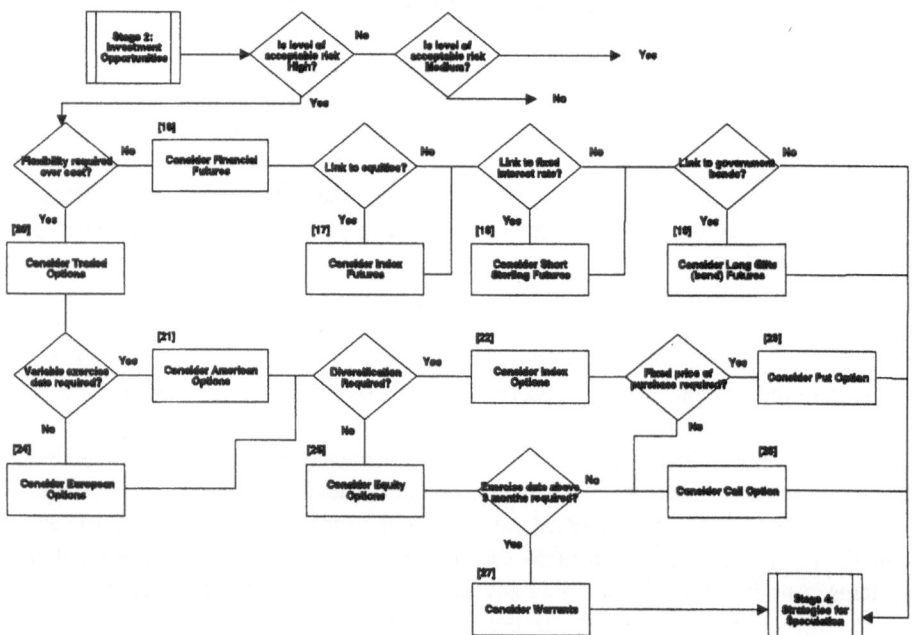

205

Figure 1 shows, at a high level, a procedural analysis of the task of selecting derivatives. The symbols have their usual meaning. Figure 2 shows the corresponding learning hierarchy. The rectangular boxes represent skills to be learned and correspond

to the stages in the procedural analysis, and the rounded rectangles represent performance objectives for the demonstration of skill attainment. A path through the procedural flow chart (Figure 1) therefore, represents a curriculum plan to meet a particular skill. For example, the path STAGE 2-20-24 is the necessary plan to teach the skill Consider-European-Options. For the student to acquire this skill he/she must 'learn' to answer the questions *Is level of acceptable risk high? Is flexibility required over cost? Is variable exercise date required?* Additionally the skill Consider-Traded-Options must be mastered. The learning hierarchy (Figure 2) shows one of the performance objectives associated with this skill. At the level of instruction aimed for in this curriculum the student is required to be able to classify the concept by definition to demonstrate understanding.

Fig. 2. Learning Hierarchy for Procedural Analysis of Fig. 1

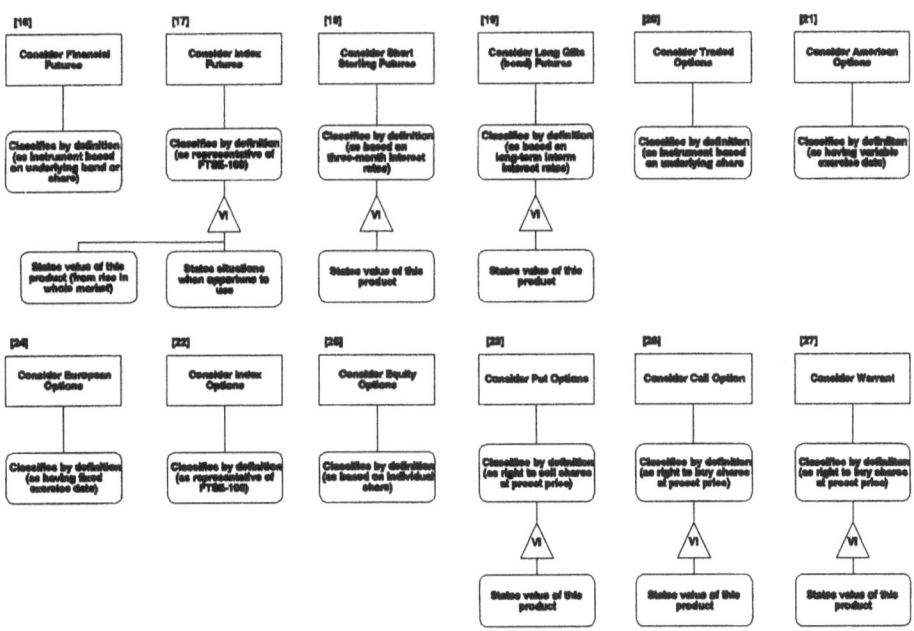

The procedural analysis illustrates the prerequisite order for the *performance* of a skill but the learning hierarchy imposes additional constraints on the prerequisite order for *learning* a skill. Therefore, when selecting tasks the task manager must take both into consideration since best learning will occur when task performance and learning coincide.

Case-based Task Management

Three distinct case libraries are used in the task manager: (i) a *Student Record* library; (ii) a *Plan* library; and (iii) a *Mapping* library (Figure 3).

Fig. 3. Architecture of Task Manager - three case-libraries

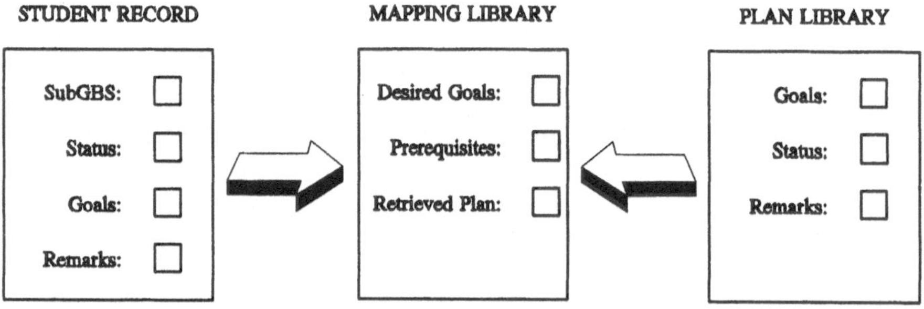

Student Record

The Student Record contains records of every student. It is represented as a case and contains fields for every subGBS and their subskills. Values for the fields indicate the student's level of mastery. The goal-based scenario is reduced into 12 subGBS' and each of these has a separate subcase. In this subcase numerical data about the student's performance in the performance objectives associated with every decision/operation are entered. These will be used as retrieval indexes to retrieve a stored subcase for the same subGBS. The retrieved case will have as an *Outcome* field a performance level, i.e., Mastery, Novice, Beginner, etc. This value will be entered into the outcome field of the subcase for the present student. In this way the entire set of decisions/operations of a subGBS can have their performance levels evaluated in *Qualitative* terms using case-based methods. In addition to an evaluation other qualitative information about the student can be determined by the same methods. The student model is described more elsewhere (Khan *et al* 1995b).

A hierarchical case structure is maintained on two levels: (i) SubGBS Library - a case library for every subGBS, i.e., 12 libraries. Each case is represented by the subGBS and its 10-15 decisions/operations as fields, their status, and other qualitative information; (ii) GBS Library - a case library for the entire goal-based scenario. Each student record is represented by the 12 subGBS' and their qualitative status. The records of different students with similar histories are compared in order to use the status of one student's record to suggest an outcome status for the current student.

The qualitative information used in evaluating the student has to be provided by the user (an instructor). A self-evaluation by the student and an evaluation by the instructor are included, as well as any affective factors that might have effected the student's performance, e.g., tiredness, distractions. This information is also used to suggest advice to present to the student and in the selection of tasks.

Plan Library

The Plan library contains plans for presenting a specific subGBS under certain conditions. A plan contains a description of the subGBS (based on the principles of Schank *et al* 1993), a normative model of the procedure for completing the subGBS (based on the procedural analysis), and an enumeration of the subskills that need to be learned by the student (based on the learning hierarchy of Gagné *et al* 1992). Each plan is maintained as a case with fields representing the description outlined above, a description of the *type* of student that it applies to, i.e., a profile of the student provided by the student record, and an evaluation of the plan in its previous use, i.e., whether or not it was successful during execution. A plan is retrieved as a result of being chosen by a mapping case.

Mapping Library

The Mapping Library contains a case representation that *maps* the input from the student record and any new data about the student's goals, with a plan from the plan library that satisfies those goals. A special *Outcome Field* in the hypothetical Map case will receive the case identification (ID) for the plan that meets its needs. The user (student or instructor) enters his or her goals in the hypothetical case. These are the decision/operations that the student wants to encounter during a session with the learning environment, or the ones the instructor decides the student should encounter. Based on these desired goals, relevant information is retrieved from the student record, e.g., the status of these goals, their prerequisites and status. *Essential* prerequisites are specified as well as any non-essential *Supportive* prerequisite decisions/operations the student might wish to learn. These form the retrieval indexes for when a search is made of the mapping library to identify a plan that contains as many of the essential prerequisite concepts and the desired goals. The supportive concepts are less important in deciding which cases to retrieve. The similarity information provided by the concept map enables substitutions that are in keeping with the *type* of skill desired. The status of each prerequisite determines if it should be included in the new plan, and at what level of performance objective.

The hypothetical case is used to retrieve a previously completed mapping case. A retrieved case will be a case that has similar goals denoted and has a similar performance record. Its Outcome field will contain an identification of a plan in the plan library that was used to satisfy it. The pointed to plan will then be retrieved and possibly adapted. The adapted plan will be saved under a new ID, and this ID will be placed in the Outcome field of the hypothetical case, which in turn will be stored in the mapping library. The new plan is then available for application. The output is a partially ordered plan that allows the student to move about within the constraints of the plan as he or she wants, i.e., partially self-directed learning.

Plan Adaptation

With the present implementation adaptation is restricted to replacement, deletion, and addition of decisions/operations. The retrieved plan is compared to the set of desired goals specified by the user and the prerequisites retrieved from the student record. Goals present in the plan and not specified as desired goals are either deleted if the

208

student record shows the student is ill equipped to deal with them, or retained if the student record shows that the student has not obtained a specified level. A trade off is necessary between maintaining all extra goals that could be desirable and maintaining focus on the specified desired goals. Each decision/operation is given an importance weighting, which is referenced during retrieval to decide which can be contained in the new plan and which can be deleted. These weightings are initially provided by hand and reflect the relative difficulty of adapting plans to cater for a particular decision/operation. That is, if a decision/operation is identified as possibly being satisfied now, which otherwise would require considerable adaptation if it were not already included in a plan then it will have a better chance of being retained. Goals specified as desired but not included in the retrieved plan are added along with their prerequisites. Sequencing of goals is not crucial since the learning environment is assumed to be a self-directed one (although restricted by the plan). The plan essentially places constraints on the directions available to the student during browsing in a case-based teaching environment.

Plan Evaluation
After a plan is created and executed it will be evaluated in its effectiveness to provide for the student's goals. The feedback received is the test performance of a student and any qualitative evaluations provided by the instructor or the student. This information is used to assess if the plan has been successful. A successful plan will be indicated as such and will be available for future use; a failed plan will not be available again. It is useful to determine why the plan failed and use this information to design better plans in future, but because student diagnosis is beyond the current capabilities of case-based teaching systems a failure memory cannot be maintained in any useful way.

Diagnosis requires the 'cause' of failure to be found, from which appropriate repair strategies can be invoked. A plan failure is usually attributed to an expectation failure where a goal has not been achieved, or a combination of goals has resulted in an unanticipated and undesirable outcome. In systems where evaluation is conducted internal to the system, e.g., simulation in CHEF, the scope of possible causes is confined to, and identifiable by, domain knowledge embedded in simulation rules and general heuristics. With tutoring systems an additional factor is introduced that must be considered as a possible 'cause' of failure, namely the student. Our future work intends to research the application of case-based diagnosis to the problem of identifying the cause of plan failure in instructional design.

Conclusion
Case-based task management uses instructional design theory to maintain a classification of the concepts in a domain. Information from the student model identifies students' weak points and, therefore, their 'learner's needs'. This information is used in a retrieval schema to retrieve and modify a prior case to produce a plan that targets each student's specific needs. Presently we are completing the implementation of the case-based task manager and further work includes incorporating more informative output in the case-based student model, e.g., tailored advice and feedback,

and importantly, how to pinpoint cause of plan failure when the cause lies within the student.

References

Gagné, R M; Briggs, L J; Wager, W W (1992) *Principles of Instructional Design*, (4th edition) Harcourt Brace Jovanovich College Publishers.

Hammond, K J (1989) *Case-Based Planning - viewing planning as a memory task*, Academic Press.

Khan, T; Yip, Y J (1995a) "CBT II - Case-based Computer-aided Instruction: Survey of Principles, Applications, and Issues" to appear in *Knowledge Engineering Review*, 10:3 September 1995.

Khan, T; Yip, Y J (1995b) "Case-based Evaluation with Fuzzy Indexes in User Modelling" Submitted to *Expert System '95 - 15th Annual Conference of the British Computer Society Specialist Group on Expert Systems*
Cambridge, UK: 11-13 December 1995.

Riesbeck, C K; Schank, R C (1989) *Inside Case-Based Reasoning*, Lawrence Erlbaum.

Schank, R C; Fano, A; Bell, B; Jona, M (1993) The Design of Goal-Based Scenarios, *The Journal of the Learning Sciences*, 3(4) pp:305-345

Springer-Verlag
and the Environment

We at Springer-Verlag firmly believe that an international science publisher has a special obligation to the environment, and our corporate policies consistently reflect this conviction.

We also expect our business partners – paper mills, printers, packaging manufacturers, etc. – to commit themselves to using environmentally friendly materials and production processes.

The paper in this book is made from low- or no-chlorine pulp and is acid free, in conformance with international standards for paper permanency.

Lecture Notes in Artificial Intelligence (LNAI)

Vol. 835: W. M. Tepfenhart, J. P. Dick, J. F. Sowa (Eds.), Conceptual Structures: Current Practices. Proceedings, 1994. VIII, 331 pages. 1994.

Vol. 837: S. Wess, K.-D. Althoff, M. M. Richter (Eds.), Topics in Case-Based Reasoning. Proceedings, 1993. IX, 471 pages. 1994.

Vol. 838: C. MacNish, D. Pearce, L. M. Pereira (Eds.), Logics in Artificial Intelligence. Proceedings, 1994. IX, 413 pages. 1994.

Vol. 847: A. Ralescu (Ed.) Fuzzy Logic in Artificial Intelligence. Proceedings, 1993. VII, 128 pages. 1994.

Vol: 861: B. Nebel, L. Dreschler-Fischer (Eds.), KI-94: Advances in Artificial Intelligence. Proceedings, 1994. IX, 401 pages. 1994.

Vol. 862: R. C. Carrasco, J. Oncina (Eds.), Grammatical Inference and Applications. Proceedings, 1994. VIII, 290 pages. 1994.

Vol 867: L. Steels, G. Schreiber, W. Van de Velde (Eds.), A Future for Knowledge Acquisition. Proceedings, 1994. XII, 414 pages. 1994.

Vol. 869: Z. W. Raś, M. Zemankova (Eds.), Methodologies for Intelligent Systems. Proceedings, 1994. X, 613 pages. 1994.

Vol. 872: S Arikawa, K. P. Jantke (Eds.), Algorithmic Learning Theory. Proceedings, 1994. XIV, 575 pages. 1994.

Vol. 878: T. Ishida, Parallel, Distributed and Multiagent Production Systems. XVII, 166 pages. 1994.

Vol. 886: M. M. Veloso, Planning and Learning by Analogical Reasoning. XIII, 181 pages. 1994.

Vol. 890: M. J. Wooldridge, N. R. Jennings (Eds.), Intelligent Agents. Proceedings, 1994. VIII, 407 pages. 1995.

Vol. 897: M. Fisher, R. Owens (Eds.), Executable Modal and Temporal Logics. Proceedings, 1993. VII, 180 pages. 1995.

Vol. 898: P. Steffens (Ed.), Machine Translation and the Lexicon. Proceedings, 1993. X, 251 pages. 1995.

Vol. 904: P. Vitányi (Ed.), Computational Learning Theory. EuroCOLT'95. Proceedings, 1995. XVII, 415 pages. 1995.

Vol. 912: N. Lavrač, S. Wrobel (Eds.), Machine Learning: ECML – 95. Proceedings, 1995. XI, 370 pages. 1995.

Vol. 918: P. Baumgartner, R. Hähnle, J. Posegga (Eds.), Theorem Proving with Analytic Tableaux and Related Methods. Proceedings, 1995. X, 352 pages. 1995.

Vol. 927: J. Dix, L. Moniz Pereira, T.C. Przymusinski (Eds.), Non-Monotonic Extensions of Logic Programming. Proceedings, 1994. IX, 229 pages. 1995.

Vol. 928: V.W. Marek, A. Nerode, M. Truszczynski (Eds.), Logic Programming and Nonmonotonic Reasoning. Proceedings, 1995. VIII, 417 pages. 1995.

Vol. 929: F. Morán, A. Moreno, J.J. Merelo, P.Chacón (Eds.), Advances in Artificial Life. Proceedings, 1995. XIII, 960 pages. 1995.

Vol. 934: P. Barahona, M. Stefanelli, J. Wyatt (Eds.), Artificial Intelligence in Medicine. Proceedings, 1995. XI, 449 pages. 1995.

Vol. 941: M. Cadoli, Tractable Reasoning in Artificial Intelligence. XVII, 247 pages. 1995.

Vol. 946: C. Froidevaux, J. Kohlas (Eds.), Symbolic Quantitative and Approaches to Reasoning under Uncertainty. Proceedings, 1995. X, 430 pages. 1995.

Vol. 954: G. Ellis, R. Levinson, W. Rich. J.F. Sowa (Eds.), Conceptual Structures: Applications, Implementation and Theory. Proceedings, 1995. IX, 353 pages. 1995.

Vol. 956: X. Yao (Ed.), Progress in Evolutionary Computation. Proceedings, 1993, 1994. VIII, 314 pages. 1995.

Vol. 957: C. Castelfranchi, J.-P. Müller (Eds.), From Reaction to Cognition. Proceedings, 1993. VI, 252 pages. 1995.

Vol. 961: K.P. Jantke. S. Lange (Eds.), Algorithmic Learning for Knowledge-Based Systems. X, 511 pages. 1995.

Vol. 981: I. Wachsmuth, C.-R. Rollinger, W. Brauer (Eds.), KI-95: Advances in Artificial Intelligence. Proceedings, 1995. XII, 269 pages. 1995.

Vol. 984: J.-M. Haton, M. Keane, M. Manago (Eds.), Advances in Case-Based Reasoning. Proceedings, 1994. VIII, 307 pages. 1995.

Vol. 990: C. Pinto-Ferreira, N.J. Mamede (Eds.), Progress in Artificial Intelligence. Proceedings, 1995. XIV, 487 pages. 1995.

Vol. 991: J. Wainer, A. Carvalho (Eds.), Advances in Artificial Intelligence. Proceedings, 1995. XII, 342 pages. 1995.

Vol. 992: M. Gori, G. Soda (Eds.), Topics in Artificial Intelligence. Proceedings, 1995. XII, 451 pages. 1995.

Vol. 997: K. P. Jantke, T. Shinohara, T. Zeugmann (Eds.), Algorithmic Learning Theory. Proceedings, 1995. XV, 319 pages. 1995.

Vol. 1010: M. Veloso, A. Aamodt (Eds.), Case-Based Reasoning Research and Development. Proceedings, 1995. X, 576 pages. 1995.

Vol. 1011: T. Furuhashi (Ed.), Advances in Fuzzy Logic, Neural Networks and Genetic Algorithms. Proceedings, 1994. VIII, 223 pages. 1995.

Vol. 1020: I. D. Watson (Ed.), Progress in Case-Based Reasoning. Proceedings, 1995. VIII, 209 pages. 1995.

Lecture Notes in Computer Science